New Frontiers in Real Estate Finance

This book introduces three innovative concepts and associated financial instruments with the potential to revolutionise real estate finance.

The factorisation of commercial real estate with factor-based real estate derivatives is the first concept analysed in this book. Methodological issues pertaining to factors in real estate risk analysis are covered in detail with in-depth academic reference. The book then analyses the digitalisation of commercial real estate. The environment in which buildings operate is changing fast. Cities which used to be made up of inanimate architectural structures are growing digital skins and becoming smarter. Smart technologies applied to the built environment are fundamentally changing buildings' role in cities and their interactions with their occupants. The book introduces the concept of smart space and analyses the emergence of 'digital rights' or property rights for smart buildings in smart environments. It proposes concepts and methods for identifying, pricing, and trading these new property rights which will dominate commercial real estate in the future. Finally, the tokenisation of commercial real estate is explored. Sometimes described as an alternative to securitisation, tokenisation is a new tool in financial engineering applied to real assets. The book suggests two innovative applications of tokenisation: private commercial real estate index tokenisation and data tokens for smart buildings.

With factorisation, digitalisation, and tokenisation, commercial real estate is at the forefront of innovations. Real estate's unique characteristics, stemming from its physicality, trigger new ways of thinking which might have a profound impact on other asset classes by paving the way for micro markets. Factor-based property derivatives, digital rights, and tokens embody how commercial real estate can push the boundaries of modern capitalism and, in doing so, move at the centre of tomorrow's smart economies. This book is essential reading for all real estate, finance, and smart technology researchers and interested professionals.

Patrick Lecomte is professor in real estate at the Université du Québec à Montréal (ESG-UQAM), Quebec, Canada.

Routledge Studies in International Real Estate

The Routledge Studies in International Real Estate series presents a forum for the presentation of academic research into international real estate issues. Books in the series are broad in their conceptual scope and reflect an inter-disciplinary approach to Real Estate as an academic discipline.

For more information about this series, please visit: https://www.routledge.com/Routledge-Studies-in-International-Real-Estate/book-series/RSIRE

New Frontiers in Real Estate Finance

The Rise of Micro Markets

Patrick Lecomte

Routledge
Taylor & Francis Group

LONDON AND NEW YORK

First published 2021
by Routledge
2 Park Square, Milton Park, Abingdon, Oxon OX14 4RN

and by Routledge
605 Third Avenue, New York, NY 10158

Routledge is an imprint of the Taylor & Francis Group, an informa business

© 2021 Patrick Lecomte

British Library Cataloguing-in-Publication Data
A catalogue record for this book is available from the British Library

Library of Congress Cataloging-in-Publication Data
Names: Lecomte, Patrick (Professor in real estate), author.
Title: New frontiers in real estate finance : the rise of micro markets /
Patrick Lecomte.
Description: 1 Edition. | New York : Routledge, 2021. |
Series: Routledge studies in international real estate | Includes
bibliographical references and index.
Subjects: LCSH: Real property—Finance. | Financial instruments.
Classification: LCC HD1375 .L43 2021 (print) | LCC HD1375 (ebook) |
DDC 332.63/24—dc23
LC record available at https://lccn.loc.gov/2020054821
LC ebook record available at https://lccn.loc.gov/2020054822

ISBN: 978-0-367-36143-3 (hbk)
ISBN: 978-1-032-00966-7 (pbk)
ISBN: 978-0-429-34414-5 (ebk)

Typeset in Goudy
by codeMantra

To Isabelle (in memoriam),
To my parents.

Contents

Boxes

Figures

Appendices

Appendices

Acknowledgements

In writing this book, I made the deliberate choice to refer to many important thinkers from a variety of fields. Numerous relevant quotes are therefore mentioned in the text. Nobel Prize laureate physicist Richard Feynman once said that what is needed in scientific pursuits is "imagination in a straitjacket". Letting one's imagination run wild is not scientific research. Limiting oneself due to past discoveries set in stone is not scientific research either. My objective is to combine broad thinking with rigour. I don't claim to present the truth; instead, I present a vision, my vision, of what could be. This is my out-of-the-box thinking; others might see other boxes that one should get out of.

References to past authors are also a way to pay tribute to their contributions while building solid foundations to ideas which might seem a little shaky otherwise. Everything in this book is carefully constructed on what others before me have discovered. Innovations presented here are crafted from current knowledge in real estate finance. I am grateful to all those who, along my journey on the paths of academia, have helped me develop my understanding of commercial real estate pioneer thinkers such as Arthur Weimer, Homer Hoyt, James A. Graaskamp, Nobel Prize Laureate Robert Shiller, and many others.

I would like to express my gratitude to Dr Rainer Schultz (Aberdeen University), Pr. Bryan MacGregor (Aberdeen University), Pr. Michel Baroni (ESSEC Business School), and Pr. Teck Yong Eng (University of Reading) as well the American Real Estate Society's members and leaderships who, in my early years as a researcher, were never afraid to award prizes to and publish my "out-of-the-box" research papers. I would also like to express my thanks to the team at Routledge who made this book possible, Ed Needle and Patrick Hetherington, in particular. I hope that ideas presented in this book will serve as catalysts for others to innovate and cross-fertilise for more sustainable innovations in the years to come.

Introduction

Real estate is a big sector of the economy, and it's a very interesting operations research problem. It is not exactly like the portfolio selection problem. You really have to start from scratch, use whatever methodology the problem calls for... What I am saying is you folks ought to develop your own real estate theory which addresses itself very much to the illiquidities of the problem, and you want a theory that is practical.

Nobel Prize Laureate Harry Markowitz (1993)

This book is about an old story: that of real estate and financial markets, and their oftentimes awkward union. Although the story is not new, the plot of this book is significantly different. This book is about redefining the "box" which has so far constrained attempts to combine real estate and financial markets in sustainable ways.

In the perfect world of finance, there would be no real estate. Real estate is heterogeneous, lumpy, and illiquid, traded on inefficient markets dominated by asymmetric information. Real estate is heresy to the financial orthodoxy.

However, there is no denying that humans are physical creatures. They dwell in space. They leverage on space to meet their human needs. In his "Rational Approach to Feasibility Analysis", James A. Graaskamp (1972) jokingly linked the existence of real estate to a Neanderthal developer:

> A Neanderthal developer once rolled a rock to the entrance of hive and created real estate, providing the natural void with some additional attribute not found in nature, such as warmth, security and exclusiveness. He had successfully interlaced land (a finite natural resource) with an artefact (the rock- the first solid-core door) to serve an unmet need of a space consumer (a market).

In a capitalist economy, the interlacing of land, a finite resource, with a building, a manufactured product, to serve humans' need for space opens up another realm for real estate: that of economics and finance, where real estate's institutional time dimension translates into monetary flows. Ideally, finance should provide the conceptual framework to make sense of real estate's dual nature, as defined by Graaskamp (1970), i.e. its intrinsic physicality in the space x time realm and its ability to generate cash flows in the money x time realm. Any innovation in real estate finance should act as a bridge between real estate's two realms. Finding the right formula to faithfully encapsulate and connect both realms has proven to be key to the sustainability and success of both real estate and financial markets.

This book is about commercial real estate. Despite its massive importance for the world's economy, residential real estate has struggled to become a driver for radical financial innovations. On the other hand, finance applied to commercial real estate has a long-standing tradition of innovative thinking: the construction of private real estate indices, the securitisation of property portfolios in tax efficient vehicles with the Real Estate Investment Trust (REIT) regime now adopted almost globally, or the collateralisation of mortgages into commercial mortgage-backed securities (CMBS).

Long before there were REITs or CMBS, Scottish financier John Law (1671–1729) advocated the implementation of land-backed securities as a way to contain what he saw as silver-based, money-induced inflation. Among the early innovators in real estate finance were also the French revolutionaries who, facing imminent bankruptcy soon after they seized power, used the value of land and properties confiscated from the Catholic Church as collaterals to a paper money known as 'Assignat' (1790–1796).

Closer to us, American financier Simon W. Strauss set the foundations of what would become modern-day mortgage-backed securities. In 1909, he issued the first real estate bonds recorded in history. The bonds, which offered a guaranteed annual return, were marketed as safe investment. They were all the rage for two decades. In 1924, the New York Evening Post noted (Brine and Poovey, 2017):

> Real estate bonds have been sold perhaps more widely than any other type of bonds; they have been placed with the small investors so well in cases that may have come to regard them as the personification of safe investing. Real estate mortgage bonds have probably done more to increase the investor class in this country [the USA] than any other influences since the government war bonds selling campaigns.

The real estate mortgage bonds boom came to an abrupt end in 1926 when it was revealed that some of Strauss's competitors had resorted to a Ponzi scheme to pay guaranteed returns (Brine and Poovey, 2017). Irrespective of their infamous demise, early attempts to securitise commercial real estate debts are worthy pioneers of real estate finance insofar as they exemplify how, due to its sheer importance for the economy, commercial real estate makes any financial innovation potentially ground-breaking for the financial system.

There is another noteworthy point about Strauss's real estate bonds: they were commonly used to finance the construction of very large commercial buildings through the securitisation of mortgages linked to a single building in fast-growing metropolis such as New York and Chicago. Interestingly, these pioneering single property bonds did not comply with one of the fundamental tenets of financial innovation since the advent of Modern Portfolio Theory: pooling.

Aggregate thinking in real estate finance

Pooling is sacrosanct in modern finance. It is the central foundation of risk management (Shiller, 2004a). Indeed, structured finance relies on three key processes whose outcome is the synthetic standardisation of risk: pooling of assets, tranching of liabilities backed by an asset pool, and delinking of the credit risk of the collateral asset pool. Through pooling, there is a reengineering of the assets' risk profiles and the transformation of "a pool of assets into one or more securities that are referred to as asset-backed securities" (Fender and Mitchell, 2005).

Conceptually, pooling is convenient inasmuch as it enables us to shift the attention away from single assets' idiosyncrasies, which are objectively not very well understood in the case of commercial real estate. Indeed, pooling is not only a financial technique but also an implied, subconscious, way of thinking, or rather not thinking, about individual assets. The securitisation process might seem like a disappearing act in which individual buildings' specific risks vanish in the overall return distribution. Securitisation creates the illusion that a proper understanding of individual assets' risks is not required, in total rupture with the very origins of real estate as an academic discipline. In their assessment of Graaskamp's legacy, Miles, Eppli and Kummerow (1998) point out that

> Conduit and REIT investors properly view real estate from a portfolio risk perspective. The risks inherent in any one property can be reduced via diversification through the pooling of assets. We think that Graaskamp would take a different view; emphasizing micromarket analysis […] and would suggest that the pool of assets is in the end only as good as the cash flows from individual properties.

The focus on aggregates underlying most innovations in real estate finance since the 1980s, be they mortgage-backed securities (pooling) or derivative securities on private real estate indices (standardisation), is a powerful tool which has enabled commercial real estate to compete with financial assets for a spot in institutional investors' portfolios. However, it is also a roadblock which might have prevented the academic community from thinking out-of-the-box, asking what-if questions, and conducting thorough research into the unchartered complexity of individual assets' risk factors. A granular approach to real estate assets' risks and returns, which is rare in real estate academic literature, would be at the opposite end of spectrum from orthodox real estate finance.

There are undoubtedly strong forces pulling researchers in the direction of aggregate thinking. To some extent, real estate researchers are only following finance researchers' lead in this matter. MacKenzie (2006) notes that finance academics' shift of attention from corporation to market was a factor of success for the Modern Portfolio Theory as it allows the "application of orthodox microeconomic ways of thinking". Aggregate thinking is indeed a legacy of neo-classical economics. Neo-classical finance applied to commercial real estate looks for 'normalities'.

American economist Thorstein Veblen (1857–1929), who identified neo-classical economists' tendency to engage in 'taxonomic' projects, opposed this quest for normalities to evolutionary thinking, which only assumes "a cumulative causal sequence" rather than "normal cases" preferred by the neo-classicals (Brine and Poovey, 2017). Unsurprisingly, aggregate thinking dominating real estate finance results in normalities, even though property heterogeneity overrides theoretical normalities, even if derived from the most solid methodological tools.

Another crucial dimension affecting the ability to innovate in real estate finance stems from the notion that financial innovation ought to improve real estate markets' completeness. Yet real estate's extreme heterogeneity at the granular level has proven to be a major hurdle in the necessary standardisation required to create a liquid market for real estate derivatives (Fabozzi, Shiller and Tunaru, 2010). The fact is that real estate is resistant to abstraction, which ultimately tends to foster aggregate thinking even more.

Hence, Shiller (2004a) questions the practical relevance of Arrow securities as guidelines to radical financial innovation and labels the 'abstract ideal' developed by Kenneth Arrow as an obstacle to overcome when designing risk management instruments. Indeed, what role should completeness play in the context of heterogeneous assets such as commercial real estate? Can debundling a building's intrinsic components into tradable pure securities help solve this conundrum? If so, what should be the optimal level of granularity selected for the analysis (e.g. individual property or factor)? The more granular the analysis, the more choices have to be made, for instance, when selecting factors in a model. Last but not least, what "apparatus, financial and information and marketing structure" (Shiller, 2004a) should be put in place to turn these innovations into functioning markets?

In this context, where pooling and standardisation dominate real estate finance, the hedonic regression model developed by Lancaster (1966) and Rosen (1974) appears as an exception. It relies on a totally different concept, i.e. factorisation, and considers properties at a low granular level. An hedonic model is a "distinct, homogeneous, marketable tied bundle of characteristics [...] restricted to those who pertain to the good itself" (Edmonds, 1984). Although factor analysis of real estate assets might not have been part of Lancaster's research objectives when formulating his new approach to consumer theory, it is a consequence of the model implementation which has unfortunately failed to bear fruit. Markedly, hedonic regression modelling is mostly used in real estate finance to standardise individual properties' characteristics while accounting for quality changes in the construction of hedonic and repeat-sales indices, such as housing price indices (Halifax in the UK). That's a paradox, and another indication, if needed, of the dominance of aggregate thinking in real estate finance.

One fundamental reason for the limited impact of hedonic pricing theory in commercial real estate arises from the

> arbitrary or judgmental decisions one must inevitably make in constructing hedonic indices. Not only is there the decision of which quality variables

to include, but there are also decisions to make about allowing non-linear effects of each and interaction effects.

(Shiller, 1993)

Hence, the hedonic regression model suffers from the absence of a well-defined and widely accepted model of real estate assets: a "map of the cat", as Richard Feynman once said (1985). It is as if the hedonic pricing theory has never been fully translated into a workable paradigm for commercial real estate. To be fair to real estate researchers, Lancaster himself was quite evasive in his seminal paper (1966), only mentioning "the properties or characteristics of the goods from which utility is derived".

So, what has happened with real estate's academic paradigm that has led researchers to think in terms of aggregates? The focus on heterogeneity and especially the land/site location as a driver of buildings' uniqueness was at the core of urban land economics' holistic analysis of real estate property (Miles, Eppli and Kummerow, 1998; Clapp and Myers, 2000). Urban land economist Richard Ratcliff (1949) insisted on real estate's heterogeneity stemming from immobile and indestructible land:

The geometric division of the earth's surface into areal units of ownership has imparted each unit an individuality [...]. No two buildings' lots are oriented identically with respect to any other lot or to all lots, nor with respect to the wind and the sun.

Conversely, urban economics, which has come to dominate real estate's academic paradigm (Clapp and Myers, 2000), focuses on "relatively few causal factors [...] within a general theory that lends itself to mathematical and statistical analysis". The dominant academic paradigm is "to test a set of hypothesized relationships among variables with a sufficiently large and homogeneous data set to allow the application of statistical techniques" (Miles, Eppli and Kummerow, 1998). The consequence is a reductionist approach, making it impossible to fully describe a phenomenon influencing an economic system. How can we model the great complexity of "living systems and highly diversified individuals and behaviours" (Clapp and Myers, 2000) underpinning property heterogeneity under such a paradigm?

Hence, it might be necessary to move away from aggregate thinking and revisit urban land economics' legacy for interdisciplinarity and holism in order to make progresses in today's real estate finance. Dealing with real estate in all its complexity without artificially erasing its heterogeneous dimension is a necessary condition to establishing sustainable markets in real estate finance. The bottom line is clear: whenever one tries to override real estate's idiosyncrasies, they come back with a vengeance, and the associated innovations are doomed to fail and/or massively disrupt global financial and real estate markets sooner or later (e.g. Residential Mortgage Backed Securities during the 2007 Global Financial Crisis).

The emergence of micro-markets in real estate finance

Shiller (2006) emphasises the role of technology in financial innovations and foresees the impact that "the revolution in electronic computing and communication" will have on financial institutions. Thanks to information technology, complex financial contracts and instruments will be made available and exchanged in user friendly ways (Shiller, 2004b). This is precisely where we are at today with the rapid emergence of smart technologies in finance and real estate. Building on these technological innovations, this book introduces three new instruments which have the potential to profoundly revolutionise commercial real estate markets.

Factor-based real estate derivatives

In the early 2000s, attempts were made to launch property derivatives in the UK, continental Europe, and the USA, i.e. total return swaps, futures contracts, and options using direct commercial real estate indices as underlyings. The success has been limited. Research shows that there is potentially a different and more appropriate approach to design and trade derivatives on commercial real estate: factor hedges (Lecomte, 2007). The market for factor-based real estate derivatives is the first market analysed in this book (Chapter 1). Methodological issues related to factor identification, pricing, and the trading of factor-based derivatives are covered in detail, as is the role that technology can play in enabling such a market.

Digital rights

The environment in which buildings operate is changing fast. Cities which were made up of inanimate architectural structures are growing digital skins and becoming smarter. Smart technologies applied to the built environment are fundamentally changing the role of commercial real estate in cities. The result is the emergence of a new type of space, called smart space, as a hybrid of physical space where buildings are located, and digital space (Lecomte, 2019a, 2020). This is a unique space, which, by turning buildings into platforms to digital space, questions the very meaning of property ownership. As a result, new types of property rights are emerging in smart buildings. Chapter 2 introduces the concept of smart space and analyses the emergence of 'smart property rights' for smart buildings in smart urban environments. It proposes concepts and methods for identifying, pricing, and trading these new property rights known as digital rights, which will dominate cities in the future.

Real estate tokens

Powered by blockchain, a cutting-edge technology applied in cryptocurrency, tokenisation enables the establishment of decentralised markets for property units or tokens. Sometimes described as the new securitisation, tokenisation is hailed by its proponents as revolutionary. Tokens would make it possible to unlock value in real assets and democratise access to commercial real estate markets for small investors globally. Noticeably, many claims related to real estate tokens have not been tested in practice, nor have they been analysed in view of established concepts and findings in real estate finance. Chapter 3 provides an in-depth study of real estate tokenisation, with a special focus on single asset tokens, and assesses tokens' true potential to become a radical financial innovation in real estate finance.

This book describes two financial engineering processes which can be applied to innovate in real estate finance: factorisation underpinning a new type of real estate derivatives and associated derivatives market (Chapter 1) and tokenisation embodied in property tokens (Chapter 3). Chapter 2 does not introduce a new process per se but instead defines new property rights with the potential to open up many avenues for allocating real estate resources and exchanging value in smart buildings in smart cities.

This book fits into a line of research on real estate financial innovation developed by academics. Nobel Prize Laureate Robert Shiller, who initiated the tradition with *Macro Markets* (1993), proposed the creation of a range of new innovative markets to insure against major income risks affecting households' standard of living. These markets include a market for real estate risk, especially as far as it relates to housing. Although they can involve "different levels of aggregation from the nation to the individual", macro markets do not require an in-depth analysis of real estate risk at the granular level by focusing on index-based derivatives.

By contrast, the three innovations introduced in this book resolutely adopt a bottom-up approach to real estate finance. To varying degrees, they focus on buildings' unique characteristics at the property level. These innovative instruments pave the way for the rise of micro markets. Micro markets are markets organised around the usually overlooked idiosyncratic dimensions of commercial real estate. Real estate finance does not need more patches borrowed from neo-classical finance to make commercial real estate fit within modern portfolio theory. Instead, it needs the freedom to explore new ways of thinking, or at least the freedom to discuss the 'what-if' out of any references to an orthodoxy that does not define the actual world.

Contrary to instruments introduced by financial institutions, there is no certainty that innovative ideas, no matter how relevant they might be in theory, will one day materialise into actual financial products available to all for investing, hedging, and trading direct real estate on sustainable markets. This is the main limitation of financial innovation coming from the Ivory Tower. It might actually stay there.

With the three frontier markets analysed in this book, commercial real estate is at the forefront of financial innovation. Interestingly, real estate's unique characteristics, derived from its physicality, can trigger new ways of thinking about optimal risk sharing. Factor-based derivatives, smart property rights, and real estate tokens might have a profound impact on other asset classes. They redefine what can be traded and how markets can be organised. In that sense, micro markets epitomise commercial real estate's potential to push the boundaries of modern capitalism and, in doing so, move at the centre of tomorrow's smart economies.

References

Brine K., and Poovey M. (2017) *Finance in America: An Unfinished Story*, Chicago: University of Chicago Press.

Clapp J., and Myers D. (2000) Graaskamp and the definition of rigorous research, in *Essays in Honor of James Graaskamp: Ten Years Later* (DeLisle J. and Worzala E., eds), Boston: Kluwer Academic Publishers, pp. 341–364.

Edmonds R.C. (1984) A theoretical basis for hedonic regression: A research primer, *AREUEA Journal*, 12:1, pp. 72–85.

Fabozzi F., Shiller R., and Tunaru R. (2010) Property derivatives for managing European real estate risk, *European Financial Management*, 16:1, pp. 8–26.

Fender I., and Mitchell J. (2005) Structured finance: Complexity, risk and the use of ratings, *BIS Quarterly Review*, June, pp. 67–79.

Feynman R. (1985) *Surely, You are Joking, Mr. Feynman: Adventures of a Curious Character*, New York: W.W. Norton & Company.

Graaskamp J.A. (1970) The role of investment real estate in portfolio management, in *Graaskamp on Real Estate*, Urban Land Institute (Jarchow S., ed), 1991, pp. 310–363.

Graaskamp J.A (1972) A rational approach to feasibility analysis, *Appraisal Journal* (October), pp. 513–521.

Lancaster K.J. (1966) A new approach to consumer theory, *The Journal of Political Economy*, 74:2, pp. 132–157.

Lecomte P. (2007) Beyond index-based hedging: Can real estate trigger a new breed of derivatives market? *Journal of Real Estate Portfolio Management*, 13:4, pp. 345–378.

Lecomte P. (2019a) New boundaries: Conceptual framework for the analysis of commercial real estate in smart cities, *The Journal of Property Investment and Finance*, 37:1, pp. 118–135.

Lecomte P. (2020) iSpace: Principles for a phenomenology of space user in smart real estate, *The Journal of Property Investment and Finance*, 38:4, pp. 271–290.

MacKenzie D. (2006) *An Engine Not a Camera*, Boston: The MIT Press.

Miles M., Eppli M., and Kummerow M. (1998) The Graaskamp legacy, *Real Estate Finance*, 15:1, pp. 84–91.

Ratcliff R.U. (1949) *Urban Land Economics*, New York: McGraw-Hill Book Company.

Rosen S. (1974) Hedonic prices and implicit markets: Product differentiation in pure competition, *The Journal of Political Economy*, 82:1, pp. 34–55.

Shiller R. (1993) *Macro Markets: Creating Institutions for Managing Society's Largest Economic Risks*, Oxford: Oxford University Press.

Shiller R. (2004a) Radical financial innovation, *Cowles Foundation Discussion Papers 1461*, Yale University.

Shiller R. (2004b) *The New Financial Order: Risk in the 21st Century*, Princeton: Princeton University Press.

Shiller R. (2006) Tools for financial innovation, *The Financial Review*, 41, pp. 1–8.

1 The factorisation of commercial real estate

Factor-based real estate derivatives

Introduction: a brief history of real estate derivatives

As far back as recorded history goes, there is no evidence of the use of property derivatives until very recently. In fact, property derivatives did not exist. Mesopotamians could hedge the price of grain, barley, or red garlic, but they had no way to hedge the price of their houses (Swan, 2000).

In modern times, property derivatives were first introduced on the London Futures and Options Exchange (FOX) in London in May 1991 (Patel, 1994). Trading in the four index-based contracts only lasted for a few months until the contracts plagued with illiquidity were withdrawn amid allegations of false trading.

A few years later, Barclays Capital started to issue Property Income Certificates (PICs) akin to structured notes linked to Investment Property Databank (IPD) indices (all property income return and all property capital return). Almost GBP 800 million of PICs were issued in the 1990s. McNamara (2010) reports that from 1996 to 1998, Barclays Capital also issued Property Index Forwards (PIFs) designed after contracts for differences with returns linked to the IPD UK All Property Index.

In the early 2000s, after the Financial Services Authority and the Inland Revenue in the UK clarified their stances on property derivatives, interest for property derivatives was rekindled. By 2004, 21 investment banks acquired licences to commercialise IPD index-based property derivatives (Baum, 2015). IPD Total Return Swaps grew rapidly, reaching 265 contracts (GBP 3.5 billion notional) written in Q1 2008 when they fell victim to the subprime crisis (Torous, 2017).

Whilst the UK has been at the centre of property derivatives innovation (due to the serendipity of a well-organised property sector and innovative financial markets), the USA swiftly jumped on the bandwagon with the first NCREIF Property Index (NPI)-based swap agreement organised by Credit Suisse First Boston in January 2006 for US$10 million over two years (Fisher, 2005; Syz, 2008).

By October 2007, the Chicago Mercantile Exchange (CME) launched trading in futures and options on the S&P/Global Real Analytics Commercial Real Estate indices (Syz, 2008). Jud and Winkler (2009) note that the plan was to trade cash-settled commercial real estate futures in office, warehouse, apartment, and retail property sectors for all US regions with electronic trading out 20 quarters. This attempt to list direct real estate derivatives on standardised markets abruptly ended in December 2008 when the underlying index was no longer produced (Torous, 2017).

Meanwhile, in continental Europe, the largest European futures and options market, EUREX, listed IPD index-based futures. These cash-settled annual contracts were based on the total returns of MSCI-IPD UK quarterly indices. Starting with the UK All Property Index listed in February 2009, Eurex enlarged its listing in 2013 and 2015, by offering quarterly index futures on granular IPD UK indices (All property type x Region). Nine standardised futures contracts were open for trade until June 2020 when the market was shut down (Eurex circular 042/2020).

Despite the ebullient 30 years since the FOX Futures contracts were introduced, Tunaru and Fabozzi (2017) sound quite disillusioned with the actual success of property derivatives. They write:

> Commercial real estate is directly linked to the real economy; by total size, it represents a significant spot market. However, it is still quite difficult for investors to hedge the risk exposure arising from investing in this important asset class [...]. Almost 25 years [after Shiller's Marco Markets (1993)], we are still waiting for standard derivatives such as such futures and options to be established as main contract with healthy liquidity.

As a matter of fact, in spite of the Global Financial Crisis, the real estate derivatives market is still in its infancy and has failed to develop beyond "an embryonic stage" (Tunaru, 2017). Lecomte (2007) argues that the main shortcoming of past attempts to launch property derivatives lies in these instruments' poor hedging effectiveness for direct real estate assets. Tunaru (2017) notes that "overall the pace of financial innovation is very slow in this area [of real estate derivatives]". Past research have focused on underlyings by looking at ways to improve the reliability of private real estate indices (e.g. Geltner, 1989). The problem with property derivatives stems not only from their reliance on direct commercial real estate indices, which do not capture the full range of idiosyncrasies in real estate risk at the granular level, but also and perhaps more importantly from their use of an index-based format.

Indeed, irrespective of the forms they have materialised into (e.g. Total Return Swaps, contracts for differences, listed futures contracts and options, structured notes), real estate derivatives have systematically been structured as index-based instruments using private commercial real estate indices (such as IPD indices in the UK or NCREIF Property Index in the USA) as underlyings. That is, they imply that private property indices are the optimal choice of underlying for a property derivative. The application of the index-based format of derivatives to commercial real estate supposes that whatever parameters led to the creation of index-based derivatives for equity portfolios also apply to commercial real estate. But, is it so? This chapter addresses this question and proposes two alternatives to the index-based format of derivatives in real estate finance: combinative derivatives and factor-based derivatives.

These two models of real estate derivatives epitomise what Shiller (1993) calls "a different approach to identifying potential new markets". As this chapter explains, combinative derivatives have already been applied to other asset classes. Furthermore, factor-based real estate derivatives have been mentioned by Shiller (1993) in his analysis of macro markets applied to real estate:

> One could imagine some factor analytic modelling to discover factors underlying variation in prices of claims on incomes, to enable contracts to cash settle on the basis of these factors.

This chapter reviews the notion of factors in classical finance and real estate finance. It describes the two new factor-based models of real estate derivatives proposed by Lecomte (2007) in line with Shiller's early intuition. It then proposes solutions to overcome the difficulties inherent to the use of factor models. It concludes by reviewing the concept of stochastic process in real estate finance and devising a novel way to model commercial real estate's price dynamics.

1 Factors versus indices

1.1 Models of derivatives and real estate risk

1.1.1 The perfect world of CAPM

The year 1982 was crucial in the history of modern finance with the introduction of index-based derivatives on US markets. The negotiation leading to this outcome was long and arduous with the first attempt to launch Dow Jones Futures dating back to the late 1960s (Brine and Poovey, 2017).[1] Against all odds, Leo Melamed, chairman of the Chicago Mercantile Exchange, managed to convince regulators that index-based futures contracts were not akin to gambling, but instead that they met a real need from investors and hedgers.

Index-based derivatives' innovativeness results from two unique features: cash settlement and the use of a broad financial index as underlying. Both conceptually and historically, index-based derivatives are linked to the Capital Asset Pricing Model (Neiderhoffer and Zeckhauser, 1980). Bernstein (1995) notes that Capital Asset Pricing Model (CAPM)'s dominance in the financial industry following the 1973 oil price crisis provided some badly needed relief to investors unsettled by market turbulences.

Indeed, index-based derivatives were designed for the perfect world of CAPM's normalities. They take care of systematic risk while portfolio diversification is supposed to reduce idiosyncratic risk to a negligible entity. CAPM's reductionist approach to risk imposes on index-based derivatives a binary framework in terms of systematic risk/specific risk, which does not sit well with individual properties' heterogeneity. Young and Graff (1996) sum up the dilemma facing real estate finance when applying Modern Portfolio Theory and its antecedent the Efficient Market Hypothesis:

> MPT and EMH seem to have been introduced into real estate to justify the use of particular statistical techniques and portfolio strategies rather than as a consequence of empirical analysis of investment return and risk characteristics. In science, the situation is generally reversed: theories are developed to explain observations.

1.1.2 Real estate risk is different

As repeatedly mentioned in the academic literature (e.g. Weimer, 1966; Miles and Graaskamp, 1984), real estate has a number of idiosyncrasies which set it apart as an asset class from equities and fixed income: asymmetry of information, high transaction cost, illiquidity, importance of physical characteristics. Numerous evidence show that real estate fundamentally differs from CAPM's perfect world (Clapp, Goldberg and Myers, 1994).

Since the early 1980s, literature on portfolio diversification has abundantly explored real estate risk. These studies focus on diversified portfolio's risk, in particular as it relates to risk breakdown between systematic risk and specific risk. For instance, Miles and McCue (1984), Hartzell, Hekman and Miles (1986) indicate that systematic risk as defined in CAPM rarely exceeds 20% of total risk for a portfolio of buildings in the USA. Likewise, Brown and Matysiak (2000) who research the UK commercial real estate market identify that market risk accounts for less than 10% of the average fluctuation in a building's total returns, versus 30% on average for a listed stock.

Bruggemann, Chen and Thibodeau (1984), Titman and Warga (1986) confirm these findings, and conclude that CAPM is not adapted to capture the risk/return relationship of direct real estate assets. As a result, researchers have explored other models more suited to explain real estate returns (e.g. Hoag, 1980). Some of these models are based on hedonic price regression described by Clapp and Myers as one of real estate's fundamental paradigms. In terms of risk structure, the hedonic model is comparable to a multifactor model insofar as hedonic indices are made up of a range of hedonic variables whose individual contribution to the asset's total utility makes up the asset price.

Whilst CAPM supposes that there is only one source of non-diversifiable risk captured in the market portfolio, factorial models acknowledge that risk might stem from multiple sources. The CAPM explicitly validates a mono-causal approach to real estate risk, whereas multifactorial models take into account various causes and their varying degrees of influence. The consequence of the index-based derivatives model applied to heterogeneous assets whose risk structure is not compatible with the CAPM is basis risk (Figlewski, 1984). In contracts for difference, a model which has been used for real estate derivatives, cross-hedge basis risk stemming from intrinsic differences between the asset returns to be hedged and the index price changes can become an insurmountable problem for hedgers and an obstacle to the smooth working of any standardised derivative market.

One cannot help wondering why real estate derivatives are, or have been, designed after a CAPM framework (i.e. using a composite index as underlying). A possible explanation is that there are no derivatives market capable of dealing with the myriad of factors that an instrument designed to address multiple sources of risk would entail.

1.1.3 The two realms of commercial real estate

Given the conceptual deadlock that composite index-based derivatives represent for real estate assets, an alternative model of derivatives using a hedonic index as underlying has been mentioned as part of Shiller's macro markets (1993). Shiller's model puts the spotlight on the true nature of commercial real estate. In a nutshell, when designing a derivative, shall a building be considered as a physical entity or as a financial asset?

Grissom and Liu's analysis of the different paradigms in real estate sheds some light on this question (1993). Two models can be applied to commercial real estate:

- A space-time model best defined by James A. Graaskamp (1976) and urban land economists before him, such as Richard U. Ratcliff (1949), and
- A money-time model.

Any real estate investment aims to achieve the monetary cycle leading to the conversion of space-time into money-time, or more prosaically square feet into money. A real estate derivative instrument designed after commodity derivatives focuses on real estate's physical characteristics. It positions real estate risk in the space-time realm by emphasising real estate's physical characteristics over its financial dimension. Conversely, a real estate derivative designed according to equity index-based derivatives assumes that real estate assets are akin to financial assets. It overlooks real estate's physical dimension and reduces risk to the money-time realm. Grissom and Liu (1993) make clear that it is essential to capture both dimensions:

> The money-time component represented in the classical literature is only a portion of the total return equation. The space-time dimension must be fully comprehended to understand the nature of real estate products, markets and problems. In a financial context, the failure to grasp space-time component will result in inappropriate analysis of the risk dimension of real estate.

A hedonic index seems like an astute way to combine commercial real estate's two realms: a hedonic underlying encapsulates the spatial dimension through the selection of utility contributing variables while the derivative's index-based structure accounts for the financial dimension. Notwithstanding its great theoretical interest, is such model operational? As noted by Shiller (1993), hedonic index-based derivatives instruments would be very challenging to implement in practice. Widespread arguments over the choice of underlyings (i.e. factor selection and pricing) have traditionally been a major hurdle in the implementation of hedonic demand theory beyond the confines of academia.

As a matter of fact, there is no agreement on what a hedonic underlying should be for commercial real estate assets (Shiller, 1993). Hedonic indices are difficult to construct, in particular for buildings with limited transaction flows and/or significant alterations in-between transactions. In *Macro Markets*, Shiller proposes an alternative which would rely on a rental index to create a market for "perpetual futures". Noticeably, these perpetual futures are based on indices of revenue rather than price. Such model which would overlook the full space-time dimension of commercial real estate has not managed to take hold among promoters of property futures markets since it was introduced as a concept in the 1990s.

1.1.4 Narrow price index-based derivatives and other possible models of real estate derivatives

Fisher (2005) proposes a simpler alternative to Shiller's perpetual futures: derivatives on narrow price indices of direct properties. In any market for physical assets, the more granular the index, the narrower the definition of the market. A real estate index is more or less narrow according to the choice of property type(s) and location(s). A narrow index should theoretically allow for better hedging than a large index, by making it possible to closely replicate the returns to be hedged.

However, the more precisely defined the property type and sub-type as well as the location in the underlying, the larger the risk of manipulation of the real estate derivatives market using such narrow price index as underlying. Market authorities have traditionally been very suspicious of derivatives instruments based on narrow indices. There are good reasons for such distrust. Shiller (1993) underlines the risk of market manipulation as a major concern for commercial real estate derivatives, contrary to what the situation would be for residential real estate. Manipulation risk of derivatives based on narrow residential price indices seems fairly remote due to the intrinsically atomised nature of residential property markets. Whilst investments in commercial real estate involve a much smaller number of investors, residential real estate imply large numbers of owners, buyers, and sellers in most submarkets.

That's one of the paradoxes of real estate derivatives. Real estate derivatives ought to reflect as much as possible commercial real estate's space-time dimension. However, the more they do so, the less likely they are to make it into the world of finance. Finding the right balance between buildings' physical characteristics and the granularity of the index used as underlying is a challenge.

1.2 Factor hedges

The existing index-based model of derivatives is not well suited for commercial real estate. Its binary framework does not capture real estate risk, which is overwhelmingly unique. Lecomte (2007) proposes an alternative called "factor hedges". Factor hedges apply a biomedical analogy to define derivatives as a combination of a format (e.g.

index-based) and underlying (e.g. narrow index). Based on this analysis, two alternative models of derivatives are proposed: combination hedges and pure factor hedges.

1.2.1 Combination hedges for commercial real estate

With combination hedges, the idea is to deal with risk from different concomitant angles. The main shortcoming of this approach stems from the potential interactions between instruments used in the ad-hoc combination. Lecomte (2007) suggests that a combination hedge materialise as an index-based futures contracts with some granularity (e.g. property type x location) combined with add-on instruments, resulting in a hybrid customisable risk management tool. Figure 1.1 illustrates this format.

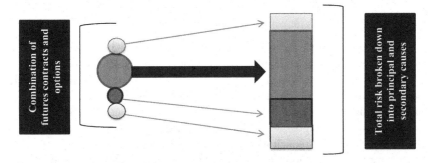

Figure 1.1 Model of combinative derivatives.

The combination hedge model implies a hierarchy of causes with the principal source of risk being encapsulated in a futures contract whilst additional causes serve as underlying to, for instance, options. Such a causal analysis of real estate risk is supported by past research's findings which show that property type is usually the most important criteria in terms of portfolio diversification (e.g. Miles and McCue, 1982 for the USA; Hamelink et al., 2000 for the UK), whereas geographic criteria are secondary.

In its simplest form, a combinative instrument could be made up of a futures contract tied to a property type sub-index and options linked to selected economic indicators. Lecomte (2007) suggests the design of options based on economic bases (after Mueller and Ziering, 1992; Mueller, 1993). Components of this aggregate hedge might even be individually tradable. Appendix 1.6 presents a model of combinative derivatives prioritising property type over the other factors in the combinative.

The idea of combining several standard derivatives instruments within one hedge is not new. It has been used in the context of yield curve risk management. Appendix 1.2 presents a detailed analysis of alternative hedging methods in interest rate risk management. By comparison, an index-based derivative follows a dual model (Figure 1.2). Risk analysis is minimal, which results in potentially significant basis. Basis risk is all the more important as the hedged asset does not comply with CAPM's hypotheses. The derivatives instrument hedges systematic risk whilst basis is left unhedged.

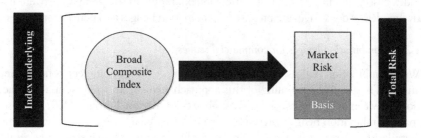

Figure 1.2 Model of index-based derivatives.

1.2.2 *Pure factor hedges for commercial real estate*

Real estate derivatives can also be designed as pure factor hedges, i.e. a combination of derivatives instruments using a single 'pure' risk factor as underlying. The atomisation of the hedged asset's risk structure is essential in this approach, as each factor should be theoretically exchangeable as stand-alone. Pure factor hedges are highly customised instruments. Besides, they have the ability to adapt to changes in the hedged asset's risk structure, thereby enabling very dynamic hedging strategies and reducing basis risk to a minimum.

Lecomte (2007) mentions that factors in real estate derivatives may come from two sources:

- Macro-factors resulting from the interaction of buildings and their environments. Akin to economic indicators, they would easily be exchangeable. The search for macro-factors explaining commercial real estate returns have been extensively covered in the academic literature (e.g. Kling and McCue, 1987; Chen, Hsieh and Jordan, 1997; Ling and Naranjo, 1997).
- Micro-factors stemming from a building's intrinsic characteristics. They are specific to each building, its property type, its location. Defining them, valuing them, and ultimately hedging them would be a challenge. Contrary to macro-factors which are standardisable and applicable to a wide range of assets classes other than commercial real estate, micro-factors are asset class specific.

This distinction between macro-factors or micro-factors is consistent with Hoag's analysis (1980) which is presented later in this chapter. Lecomte (2007) explains that the factor-based structure would be comparatively easier to implement than the process of identifying and pricing underlying micro-factors. Central to this issue are the number of factors to include in a factor hedge (Breitung and Eickmeier, 2005) as well as individual factors' contribution to a building's total risk and factor collinearity. These questions have traditionally plagued the implementation of factor models in finance (Shiller, 1993). Furthermore, they have also prevented the widespread use of multifactor models in real estate (Draper and Findlay, 1982).

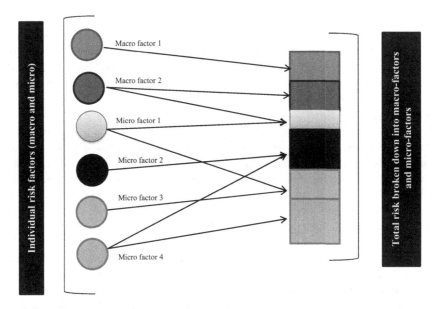

Figure 1.3 Model of factor-based derivatives.

Figure 1.3 illustrates a derivatives instrument with atomised underlyings. The model relies on six factors, which is within the usual range of factor models in real estate (e.g. Chen, Hsieh and Jordan, 1997 who select five factors). Each model of derivatives implies a specific way of conceptualising risk. From a binary structure in the index-based model, real estate risk becomes multifactorial in the factor-based model. The link between factors and risk components is achieved through customisation, whereby each factor impacts a specific part of total risk. One factor can affect one risk or several risk component(s), either alone or concomitantly with other factors.

By combining macro-factors with micro-factors specific to commercial real estate, the model produces sophisticated risk management tools for dynamic hedging strategies. Basis risk is reduced to a minimum. Nonetheless, the model comes with its fair share of problems. First, as previously mentioned, a factor can impact several risk components in the total risk structure. Collinearity issues are instrumental to the model implementation. This is all the more important as factors might be selected out of a clearly defined risk model, which explicitly sets the network of causal relations between factors and risk.

1.3 Pending issues with factor hedges

Based on the analysis presented in this chapter, it should make no doubt that the way one thinks about commercial real estate risk as well as tools available to deal with it are directly dependent on models applied to analyse that risk. In theory, derivatives should adapt to models which are themselves representative of empirical observations. With index-based derivatives, a financial economics model not applicable to commercial real estate is driving the choice of derivative format and underlying. Unless the application of CAPM ends up modifying empirical observations pertaining to commercial real estate risk and return, there is no way that index-based real estate derivatives can efficiently deliver what they are supposed to. MacKenzie (2006) notes that "financial models shape markets" inasmuch they are engines designed to power markets, and not cameras meant to perfectly reflect reality.

Hence, one can legitimately wonder whether efficient risk management tools can ever be designed for commercial real estate without a widely accepted risk model. Irrespective of the asset class, any derivative instrument designed without a solid underlying risk model, or at least the belief that it can provide a relevant framework to analyse risk is likely to be simplistic and reductionist in its approach. A poor understanding of risks involved in assets will sooner or later jeopardise such derivatives' hedging effectiveness, and overall ability to fulfil its role.

Factorisation is the key to more gradated approaches to commercial real estate risk management effectively addressing real estate's granular dimension. When it comes to derivatives, real estate should set free from the theoretical orthodoxy of financial economics in modern finance. Many exciting ideas can be explored beyond the restrained world of CAPM. For instance, Lecomte and McIntosh (2005) mention the concept of "standardised customisation" to describe a derivative model able to optimally capture commercial real estate's highly idiosyncratic risk while setting up liquid standardised markets for these real estate derivatives of a new kind. 'Standardised customisation' of derivatives instruments is made possible owing to factorisation.

Notwithstanding their attractiveness on paper, factor hedges would come with their fair share of unresolved practical issues if they were to be implemented:

- What factors should be selected and how?
- What risk model could underpin factor selection in factor hedging?
- Can a standardised market be set up to trade such instruments?
- What market structure would enable liquid and efficient trading of real estate factor-based derivatives and their components?

The rest of the chapter addresses these questions.

2 Factorisation: a nuclear approach in real estate finance

2.1 Factors in commercial real estate analysis: epistemological foundation of factorisation

2.1.1 The real estate paradigm and factors

Real estate as an academic discipline has known two paradigms: urban land economics and urban economics. As noted by Clapp and Myers (2000), the history of real estate post 1960s was marked by a very rapid shift from the older urban land economics paradigm to the newer urban economics paradigm. The choice of urban economics as the real estate paradigm has had a huge influence on the role played by factors in real estate analysis.

During the 1970s and 1980s, the evolving intellectual context for real estate academia led to fundamental changes in the nature of real estate analysis, from being "problem-oriented, inductive, and interdisciplinary" to becoming "deductive and oriented to quantitative hypothesis testing". The former school of thought, which finds its roots in the urban land economics tradition, includes real estate luminaries such as Richard U. Ratcliff, Homer Hoyt, Arthur Weimer, and James A. Graaskamp.

Whilst urban land economics is based on direct observation of all the facts, "urban economics focuses the researcher on relatively few causal factors [...] within a general theory that lends itself to mathematical and statistical analysis" (Clapp and Myers, 2000). Hence, urban economics does not encourage the search for multiple factors and their interactions in explaining real estate risk as a complex phenomenon at the macro-level, or a series of complex interacting phenomena at the micro-level.

However, the deductive paradigm in real estate is not without its detractors. Starting in the 1980s, the role of deduction and econometrics in social sciences has been questioned. Social sciences deal with 'living systems' characterised by great complexity. Complexity stems from the large number of variables involved in explaining phenomena, variables whose relative influences can change over time. As such, economic theory should keep changing and adapt to new realities. Noticeably, Bell (1980) argues that there are no "economic laws". Clapp and Myers underscore that this argument is particularly compelling for real estate.

Owing to its holistic perspective and descriptiveness, urban land economics has traditionally focused on direct and thorough observation of reality while ignoring narrow causation derived from statistical analysis. Inductive reasoning needs the full picture whereas deductive reasoning tends to be more parsimonious with factors as well as reductionist in its reliance on quantitative modelling. As a matter of fact, quantitative models can only accommodate so many factors before becoming meaningless. An inductive way of thinking about real estate lays the ground to a factor-based analysis of commercial real estate. It also has the ability to capture real estate at the micro-level in all its uniqueness and heterogeneity. This is great in theory, but it can only be applicable if there is a widely accepted risk model for commercial real estate in order to make sense of a myriad of factors and their interactions.

2.1.2 Ratcliff and Graaskamp's view of real estate analysis

Urban land economists provide some guidance about factor identification and selection in real estate analysis. Land is at the core of their perspective. For instance, Ratcliff (1949) identifies four characteristics of urban land: space, immobility, indestructibility, and heterogeneity. These four characteristics provide a framework to study different types of residential and non-residential space: (a) *space*: "both the space provided and the shape are physical characteristics of urban land [that] influence economic behaviour"; (b) *immobility*: "each unit lies in an immutable physical relationship with every unit. [...] It lies helplessly vulnerable to external social and economic forces which determine its use and influence its value"; (c) *indestructibility*: space cannot "be created or destroyed"; (d) *heterogeneity*: a unit of land's individuality arises from "its geological characteristics and from its special geometric relationship to every other unit and to the several elements of the physical world".

The above-mentioned characteristics of land have economic implications insofar as "the physical basis of the utility of raw land is the support and space that it provides for the activities of man, the structures he occupies, and the artefacts he employs". Ratcliff explains that when considering the urban land market, "it is appropriate [...] to view [the physical characteristics of land] as economic factors in the functioning of the market". Implied in Ratcliff's analysis is the idea that "complex but singular set of space relationships with the social and economic activities" define uniqueness in space to which "the market attaches a special evaluation".

By focusing on land as the core component of space, Ratcliff's analysis tells us that real estate value stems from interactions between physical characteristics and a range of external factors which define both the physical surroundings of the space and the socio-economic environment from which it derives its utility. Although anchored in land's immobility, this process is extremely dynamic.

In *Real Estate Analysis* (1961), Ratcliff details his views by defining real estate as "a complex commodity". Urban real estate is a "manufactured product" of which land is one of many, albeit crucial, components. Ratcliff posits that:

> many problems [in real estate analysis] relate to a unique characteristic of real estate, i.e. that it is valuable in large degree because it is the focus of complex set of space relationships popularly called *location*. And to complicate things further, these space relationships are constantly, if slowly, changing as the result of whole groups of economic, social, political, and technological factors.

The "locational services of land" must take into account "the probable future changes in all of the factors which influence the benefits of the site for the intended use".

In particular, Ratcliff emphasises the role that economic base plays in predicting real estate market changes. As "urbanism is essentially an economic phenomenon", cities' future growth is affected by economic factors. Primary and secondary economic bases define the rate of growth, its quality and stability at the city-level, all factors affecting real estate value. In addition to real estate's physical foundations (i.e. urban land), which contribute to value in "varying degree" as well as the dynamic factors of location, real estate's legal dimension, i.e. "the legal content of ownership", impacts its value.

James A. Graaskamp who was Ratcliff's doctoral student and successor at the University of Wisconsin (Seldin, 2000) was also a major sceptic of real estate's dominant academic paradigm, preferring to practise "an alternative research paradigm [...] that focused on less orderly site specific problem". Miles, Eppli and Kummerow (1998) explain:

> [Graaskamp] refused to accept generalizable macroeconomic models as answers to real estate questions, and instead recognized that most real estate problems are unique to a particular site. With that in mind he constructed micromarket decision systems to address specific problems. After all, the primary distinguishing characteristics of real estate is its fixed location, which makes each situation unique and gives rises to the interesting aspects of its situs.

Graaskamp's holistic perspective underpins his interdisciplinary approach to commercial real estate problems (DeLisle, 2000). The focus on site fosters a micro-level analysis of real estate decision making, which might involve a wide range of factors.

2.1.3 Role of factors in Weimer and Hoyt's real estate analysis

The term factor is omnipresent in Weimer and Hoyt's analysis of commercial real estate. In their seminal textbook *Real Estate*, (1966), Weimer and Hoyt insist on the role played by location in conditioning a property's income producing ability. Although it is fixed, location is a very dynamic concept:

> Each piece of real property may be a fixed point on the earth's surface, but this fixed point is a part of a highly dynamic framework. All manner of forces-economic, political, and social; international, national and local- are operating constantly to add to or to detract from the property's capacity to produce income at a given site.

Factors might be physical, legal or economic. Among the physical factors which "affect [a property's] income-producing ability, either directly or indirectly" are land (e.g. location, size, and shape of the lot, topography), and buildings (e.g. type of building in relation to land, quality and durability, style and attractiveness). Buildings are necessary "in order to earn income from urban land". They are "the means by which the earning power of urban land is released. [...] If the wrong type of building is constructed, the value of the land may be destroyed".

Two sources of factors are especially important: *market* factors and *location* factors. They explain:

> To a considerable degree, a property's income-producing potential is determined by location factors, conditioned of course, by market changes and by trends in the local, regional, and national economy.

Location factors refer to the "various sets of relationships [...] involving a property's immediate surroundings and its position relative to the local area and region".

Hence, a property's "dynamic economic (and social and political) framework [...] is made up of the property's immediate environment, its local economy and community, and the broader national and international environment".

2.1.4 Teachings from urban land economics: a blueprint for a risk model of commercial real estate

In many respects, urban land economists provide a blueprint for a factor-based risk model of commercial real estate. Their analysis pinpoints to a selection of factors and a non-quantitative description of the processes by which these factors affect real estate values.

Teaching #1: Land is instrumental in assessing a real estate property. Site location's economic function and value should be analysed in a broad, holistic manner (Clapp and Myers, 2000). Hence, the search for factors affecting a property's returns should start with the site. A site-specific analysis naturally leads to a bottom-up approach of real estate (i.e. from micro-level to macro-level).

Teaching #2: Factors affecting real estate value are not static, but dynamic as a result of complex spatial relationships between an immobile unit of land and socio-economic activities. These relationships are impacted by economic, social, political, and technological factors.

Teaching #3: Real estate value derives from the physical foundations of real estate (dominated by land), locational factors (spatial relationships between the site and other points on the urban landscape), and the legal dimension (titles and leases). Whilst physical foundations and locational factors belong to Graaskamp's space-time realm, the legal dimension projects real estate into the money-time realm.

Teaching #4: Buildings are only a means to earn income from the land.

Teaching #5: Effective real estate risk management requires the modelling and hedging of forces, which might disrupt a property' income-producing potential. These forces interacting with the fixed component of real estate are constantly changing.

2.2 Factors in finance: an etymological approach

The term factor is everywhere in finance, whether it is in asset pricing models (e.g. Asset Pricing Theory) or in the field of risk management, such as Value-at-Risk (VaR) model, among others. Finance researchers frequently use metaphors derived from physics to refer to factors. For instance, Jorion (2007) describes risk management as the 'theory of molecular finance'. Likewise, Sharpe (1995) pleads for the emergence of "nuclear financial economics". Depending on the origin of the metaphor used, the term factor might encompass different meanings: atoms for Sharpe, or particles for Jorion. The common points shared by these various meanings are:

- A fundamental active element which, once identified, becomes standardised due to its primary simple dimension, and

- The combination of fundamental elements leading to an outcome, be it material (solid or liquid) or immaterial (such as a complex phenomenon).

By focusing on factors, finance researchers are following the lead of great scientists over the centuries. To get as close as possible to a complex phenomenon's roots, there is a need to break it down into as many primary elements as possible at the lowest reachable granularity level. Simon (1996) mentions the concept of complex systems immerged in a total environment where simplicity is hidden under complexity. The apparent chaos reveals itself owing to the identification and sorting of dynamic elements affecting the whole system. The breaking down of complexity into an elementary taxonomy of elements is a fundamental process in physics and live sciences. In his *Lectures on Physics* (1964), Feynman explains that this idea is probably the most important one in the history of sciences. He writes:

> If, in some cataclysm, all scientific knowledge were to be destroyed, and only one sentence passed on to the next generation of creatures, what statement would contain the most information in the fewest words? I believe it is the atomic hypothesis (or the atomic fact, or whatever you wish to call it) that all things are made of atoms- little particles that move around in perpetual motion, attracting each other when they are a little distance apart, but repelling upon being squeezed together.

Greek philosopher Democritus (470–400 BC) introduced, almost involuntarily, atomisation in physics which was then revisited on more scientific grounds by English physicist John Dalton (1766–1844) to give birth to the atomic theory in chemistry in the early 19th century. When looking at risk, the scientific metaphor can sometimes be misleading. Whilst atoms and particles are constitutive of matter, a risk factor is closer to a catalyst. The Cambridge dictionary defines a factor as "a fact or situation that influences the result of something". In other words, a factor contributes to a phenomenon without constituting it. Hence, a factor should not be mistaken with the phenomenon itself, of which it is only a trigger. A factor might accelerate or slow down a phenomenon. It does not make up the 'matter' of the phenomenon. The concept of risk factor in finance is thus not so much related to Democritus' atomic intuition, but rather to Aristotle's causal analysis of phenomenon.

According to this line of thinking, risk exists independently of risk factors which are only contributing to asset returns' volatility without being the risk itself. Risk is a lot more complex than the risk factors. The ambiguity between a factor and a particle, which is common in finance metaphors derived from physics, is not without consequences. It does impact the choice of methodology used to identify factors while sowing confusion about the selection of optimal hedges.

2.3 Factors in financial risk management

Hull (2009) defines factor as a "source of uncertainty", and factorial analysis as an "analysis aimed at finding a small number of factors that describe most of the variation in a large number of correlated variables (similar to Principal Component Analysis)". These definitions underscore the link between factor and risk, and the importance of factors in risk management. Interestingly, they also confirm the confusion surrounding the concept of factor in finance, i.e. the fact that factors are assimilated to sources of risk even though factors' etymology clearly refers to an agent in a process generating uncertainty rather than a source of uncertainty in itself. This somewhat lax understanding of risk factor might have led to a lack of interest for thorough risk models specific to each asset class.

For instance, Charles Fishkin (2006), former Director of the Office of Risk Assessment for the United States Securities and Exchange Commission, proposes a graphic representation of risk into a so-called *shape of risk*. Following Benoit Mandelbrot (1999)'s analysis, he argues that a graphic representation is better than a theoretical model at capturing reality. All models proposed by Fishkin make explicit reference to factors which can be of various origins (biological, physical, molecular...). In one of these models, the model of 'risk particles' which makes a clear reference to Scottish botanist Robert Brown (1773–1858)'s experiment involving pollen of a plant immersed in water under a microscope in 1827, risk is considered as an heteroclite assemblage of particles which swirl in space. Some particles can move in more predictable ways than others, whereas others are purely random. The outcome is a fully random risk. This model suggests that particles are constitutive of uncertainty. The particle metaphor which is part of phenomenological models in finance as categorised by Derman (1996) does not rely on a causal analysis of risk sources and, therefore ignores factors' role as catalyst in the dynamics of complex phenomena.[2]

2.3.1 Nuclear Financial Economics according to William Sharpe (1995): building on Arrow-Debreu securities

In 1995, Sharpe introduced the concept of *Nuclear Financial Economics* underpinned by Kenneth Arrow and Gerard Debreu's work on *contingent contract*. Nuclear financial economics which is concerned with "first principles" should make it possible to analyse risks in the areas of financial engineering, corporate finance, and investment at the lowest possible granular level. Sharpe (1995) writes:

> An important subfield of physics- *Nuclear Physics*- deals with the smallest particles of which matter is composed. Constructs developed by Kenneth Arrow and Gerard Debreu provide a similar foundation for financial economics. With a bit of hyperbole, the approach may be termed nuclear financial economics. [...] The concept of a contingent contract allows for the analysis of risk in simple, yet powerful ways.

According to Debreu (1959), a contingent contract enables the delivery of commodities depending on "an event on the occurrence of which the transfer is conditional". This is equivalent to a contract for the transfer of a commodity whereby the commodity's physical characteristics, location, and event that would trigger the transfer are specified: "a commodity is a good or a service completely specified physically, temporally, and spatially". Debreu (1959) proposes a list of goods covered in his theory, e.g. economic goods such as wheat and truck, as well as services. Noticeably, Debreu mentions the rental market for a range of properties among services. The use of a hotel room or an apartment belongs to a "complex type of services" whose description should be dated and located, and include "a listing of everything which will be performed for the occupant". Likewise, storage services performed in a warehouse should be described "by the type of warehouse (refrigerated or not...), the dates from which to which it is rendered, and the location". Its quantity is expressed by "a real number of cubic feet". In addition to the rental market, Debreu's foray into real estate in his *Theory of Value* focuses on land:

> Land requires special attention. Its condition is described by the nature of the soil and the subsoil (the latter being of importance for construction work), the trees, growing crops and construction on it, etc. A quantity of land with specified condition, location, and date is expressed by a real number of acres.

Hence, Debreu's analysis very much focuses on goods' physical characteristics in a space-time realm, their "characteristics of the world" (Geanakoplos, 2004). These characteristics are quantifiable and observable.[3] The analysis also requires that goods' physicality be readily measured with a specific metric which assumes the commodity is "perfectly divisible".

A special type of contingent contract known as "pure" or "primitive" security (aka Arrow-Debreu security) delivers one monetary unit or a notional amount of commodity at a given date. A complete market enables the purchase and sale of all possible Arrow-Debreu securities. Sharpe (1995) acknowledges that, despite its theoretical relevance, the Arrow-Debreu approach is often ignored in practice to the benefit of Modern Portfolio Theory:

> In the field of investment analysis, both academics and practitioners tend to favour the *mean-variance* approach introduced by Markowitz (1952) over that of Arrow and Debreu. [...] A preferred strategy utilizes the Arrow-Debreu model to develop fundamental ideas, then turns to mean-variance analysis and its use in practice.

However, the Arrow-Debreu approach is useful in risk analysis, by breaking down risks "in term of pattern of payments obtained over different states of the world". In a complete market, it is possible to turn a set of payments into a series of Arrow-Debreu securities with similar present values. Sharpe notes that "the creation and valuation of derivative securities represent direct applications of [the Arrow-Debreu approach]".

Markedly, Arrow-Debreu securities' inherent contingency implies that factors driving uncertainty depend on interactions of a good's physical characteristics with its broad environment. To illustrate how the Arrow-Debreu model of general equilibrium defines a commodity's "characteristics of the world", Geanakoplos (2004) explains:

> A field is better allocated to one productive use than another depending upon how much rain has fallen on it; but it is also better allocated depending on how much rain has fallen on other fields.

Hence, the Arrow-Debreu model implies that risk factors are not static insofar as a "state-of-the-nature" triggers a wide-ranging and potentially complex interaction between a commodity's observable characteristics and the environment, which, in turn, affects an Arrow-Debreu security's pay-out. Conceptually, the process described by Sharpe is very similar to the one underpinning real estate factor hedges. Through atomisation and the search for catalysts driving uncertainty in real estate returns, risk managers can approach real estate risk to its core. In a factor hedge as envisioned by Lecomte (2007), each factorial component serves as underlying to a contingent contract which plays the role of pure security. Pure securities materialise as derivatives with pure factors as underlying. A factor hedge combines as many pure securities as there are factors identified in the asset's risk model. The ability to trade these pure securities separately will depend on the design and structure of the market put in place to exchange factor hedges.

2.3.2 Value at Risk and factors in commercial real estate

Another financial risk management method relying on factors is Value at Risk (VaR). In the preface to his seminal textbook *Value at Risk*, Philippe Jorion (2007) explicitly links VaR with the concept of particles:

> Risk management integrates fixed income markets, currency markets, equity markets, and commodity markets. In each of these, financial instruments must be decomposed into fundamental building blocks and then reassembled for risk measurement purposes. No doubt this is why risk management has been called the "theory of particle finance". All this information then coalesces into one single number, a firm's VAR.

Thus, VaR is the product of a double process of breaking down risk into fundamental elements and reassembling them into a quantifiable measure, i.e. a metric indicating the so-called Value at Risk. The application of VaR supposes that risk managers determine the optimal number of risk factors. This choice is important insofar as "using too many risk factors is unwieldy [while] using too few may create risk holes [or blind spots]" (Jorion, 2007). In its simplest form, a multivariate model applied to a multi-asset portfolio can encompass as many factors as the number of assets in the portfolio. However, for the sake of simplification, the number of factors under consideration is usually inferior to the number of assets due to the aggregation of all or part of positions driven by similar risk factors.

In multifactor models, financial instruments are decomposed in terms of common factors aka general-market risk factors and idiosyncratic (asset-specific) effects "that are uncorrelated with each other". In the context of portfolios, diversification takes care of these idiosyncratic effects. Jorion (2007) presents as an axiom the following "factor model result":

> Assuming that asset returns are driven by a small number of common factors and that residual movements are uncorrelated, the risk of portfolios that are well diversified with a large number of assets will be dominated by the common factors.

Since VaR aims to achieve "aggregation at the highest level", common factors are defined as those affecting the largest number of positions. The objective is not to consider each position individually. Positions are only mapped against a small set of "primitive risk factors". Jorion proposes two methods for identifying common factors: either a parametric approach which "prespecifies factors that we think are important" based on "a good knowledge of markets and economic factors that drive them", or an empirical non-parametric approach that "derives factors from asset returns through statistical techniques" such as Principal Components Analysis (PCA) or factor analysis (FA).

VaR is a paradox. Although the method exemplifies the important role of factorisation in risk management, it does so in such an aggregated way that the method's focus lies almost exclusively on elementary common factors akin to macro-factors in Lecomte (2007). Notwithstanding its multifactorial approach, the underlying risk framework is fundamentally binary in line with modern finance's classic asset pricing models. Hence, VaR does not provide any incentive to probe asset heterogeneity at the granular level.

Commercial real estate has been challenging for Value at Risk due to the scarcity of appropriate data and the non-normality of returns. Researchers have applied the VaR methodology to portfolios of listed commercial real estate assets (e.g. Liow, 2008; Zhou and Anderson, 2012) and more sparsely to private commercial real estate (e.g. Booth et al., 2002; Gordon and Tse 2003). The latter studies tend to deal with real estate risk at the macro-level (i.e. diversified portfolios, broad all country IPD indices), in particular in their exploration of real estate portfolios' leveraged risk. Arguably, researchers have missed a chance to apply the VaR framework to further explore commercial real estate's risk model and break down real estate risk into common and specific components.

2.4 Factors in real estate finance

Real estate finance dominated by the urban economics paradigm has generated many studies identifying macrovariables which impact direct real estate returns. Plazzi, Torous and Valkanov (2008) note that compared to stocks and bonds, "little is known about risk dynamics in the commercial real estate market and their link to prevailing economic conditions". To achieve factor identification and selection, advanced statistical methods are used. Studies on micro-factors are rare, and usually linked to hedonic regression models applied to commercial real estate. The following section presents the methodological issues facing real estate finance researchers as well as their main findings with respect to both macro-factors and micro-factors.

2.4.1 Macro-factors

METHODOLOGICAL ISSUES

Irrespective of the asset class, factor identification and selection are always challenging. In the case of private commercial real estate, the process is even more complex due to the lack of a widely accepted risk model. The first step is to select a methodology to identify relevant macro-factors and to determine their optimal number. Once factors are identified and selected, the important issue of factor stability comes into play.

Factor identification and selection: Macro-factors are customarily identified by applying Factor Loading Model (FLM) or Macro Variable Method (MVM). An example of FLM is Principal Component Analysis (PCA). MVM was developed by Chen, Roll and Ross (1986) in the context of the Asset Pricing Theory (APT) and applied to real estate by Titman and Warga (1986) as well as Chan, Hendershott and Sanders (1990). While FLM is a purely econometric approach which does not give any indication about the true nature of factors involved in the model, MVM enables a qualitative analysis of factors, which are selected ex ante for their supposed impact on asset returns' volatility. With MVM, factors are observable economic variables whose risk premiums can be interpreted within the model. The rationale behind these two methods is very different. Whereas FLM applies a nuclear approach by breaking down risk into single, albeit unidentified components, MVM supposes that external variables impact a complex phenomenon without being part of it.[4] Chen, Hsieh and Jordan (1997) who compare the two methods in the case of listed real estate returns find that MVM is superior to FLM over their study period (1974–1991). They write:

> The primary advantages of the MVM are that the underlying factors are observable economic phenomena and the associated factor sensitivities and risk premiums can be directly interpreted. The primary disadvantage is that no formal economic theory exists guiding the selection of the most appropriate variables to include in the model.

An interesting example of MVM in commercial real estate is the MIT student assignment described by Riddiough (1995). MIT students in a "Real Estate Capital Markets" class are asked to select any basket of three macro-economic variables in order to replicate and hedge real estate risk. These variables come from a wide range of sources, e.g. traded and customised over-the-counter securities such as broad stock market index, US REIT index, macro-economic indicators. Real estate is proxied by Russell/NCREIF (RNI) quarterly appreciation return indices for eight US regions over 1989–1994.[5] The quality of the proposed hedges is assessed by the coefficient of determination R^2: the higher R^2, the better the hedge. The process of synthetic replication is carried out without any reference to a risk model of commercial real estate, which is a major shortcoming of this approach and, more generally a clear limitation of MVM insofar it does not aim for deeper insight into real estate risk.

Factor stability and dynamic hedging: It is well researched that the relationship between financial assets' excess returns and macro-economic risks changes over time. Ghysels (1998) who focuses on NYSE stock returns explains that there is ample empirical evidence that linear factor models are time variant. Because of that, "these models are at the same time sophisticated and fragile". Their fragility stems from the fact "they must deal with time-varying betas and are therefore more prone to sources of misspecification and hence mispricing of assets".

The same shortcoming applies to real estate factor models. For instance, Liow (2004) identifies that expected risk premiums of commercial real estate in Singapore, especially office and retail property markets, are time-varying and dynamically linked to five macro-economic factors (including GDP growth, changes in industrial production and unexpected inflation). This has implication for factor-based real estate derivatives. As noted by Riddiough (1995), there is a need "to employ a dynamic hedging strategy if it appears that replicating portfolio relationships with commercial real estate returns are evolving over time". Hence, factor identification and selection in factor-based real estate derivatives have to be dynamic in order to achieve optimal replication and hedging.

MACRO-FACTORS IN COMMERCIAL REAL ESTATE MODELS: LITERATURE REVIEW

The linkages between macrovariables and commercial real estate have been covered at length in the academic literature. Past research which have mostly focused on US commercial real estate markets explore both listed real estate (Real Estate Investment Trusts) and private real estate (e.g. NCREIF Property Index). Based on empirical findings and almost systematically without any reference to a risk model of commercial real estate, researchers have identified various factors impacting real estate's return and risk. These studies are designed after the classic multifactor model introduced in the Asset Pricing Theory (APT) by Ross (1976). The APT model has been applied to identify macrovariables in the context of equity portfolios. For instance, Chen, Roll and Ross (1986) find that five macrovariables are significant in explaining expected US stock returns: change in expected inflation, unanticipated inflation rate, the unanticipated change in risk premium, and the unanticipated change in growth rate in industrial production.

MVM methodologies are overwhelmingly used by real estate researchers. There are two notable exceptions: Titman and Warga (1986) who apply two FLM-based models (with two-factor and five-factor loadings) in their study of listed US real estate. By the same token, Grissom, Hartzell and Liu (1987) who study the US industrial real estate's risk and return characteristics employ two FLM models designed after the APT: one with 5-factor loadings, the other with 10-factor loadings. Whilst national models fail to capture more than 39% of the return variation in all properties, they identify that priced factors vary across regions and represent major cities with their unique economic bases. They conclude that "constructing city real estate indices according to property type might prove a fruitful endeavour". Interestingly, Grissom et al. refer to Hoag's framework (1980) to develop their APT models of industrial properties' returns, by combining physical and financial characteristics associated with each property. The former include "age, average lease maturity, region of the country, the total amount of square feet, number of tenants and the availability of rail service".

Appendix 1.1 presents a non-exhaustive selection of seminal academic papers, which apply macrovariables to explain commercial real estate returns and risk. For each paper, it lists the macro-factors selected or identified.

As evidenced by the selected papers, researchers choose state variables in their models among a wide range of macrovariables including:

- Stocks: performances and dividend yield,
- Fixed income: yield curve, term and credit spreads, government bonds' short-term rates and long-term rates,
- Nominal interest rate,
- Industrial output,
- Expected inflation and unexpected inflation,
- National and regional employment rates,
- Monetary policy: money supply,
- Household consumption.

Most studies look at combinations of macro-factors among those mentioned above. For instance, Kling and McCue (1987), who study the US office market, single out the importance of nominal interest rates, industrial output, and money supply in explaining office building construction.

Noticeably, some research move away from the classic multifactor approach defined in the APT model: for instance when researchers are focused on singling out the special role of one particular macrovariable. This is the case of Geltner (1989) who underscores the importance of household consumption on commercial real estate, and Liang and McIntosh (1998) who highlight the role of local employment. These macrovariables are sometimes included into multifactor models, e.g. Ling and Naranjo (1999) who build on Geltner (1989) to emphasise the importance of household consumption on commercial real estate markets in the USA.

Models similar to the ones developed for the US markets have been applied to European and Asian markets, in particular the UK commercial real estate markets. Brooks and Tsolacos (1999) identify the impact of yield curve and unexpected inflation on UK markets. Liow (2004) who analyses Singapore's office and retail real estate markets identifies that expected risk premiums on the two markets are not only time-varying, but also impacted by unexpected inflation and short-term interest rates. In addition to national studies, a few researchers adopt an international perspective, usually in a comparative approach. De Wit and Van Dijk (2003) cover 46 major office districts in Asia, Europe, and the USA. They identify that the same macrovariables (GDP growth, unemployment rate, vacancy rate) impact the rate of change in office returns globally.

Among the selection of research in Appendix 1.1, Peng (2016) stands out for its focus on granular data. The researcher has access to the NCREIF database at the property level. His study encompasses capital appreciation returns for 14,115 properties and total returns for 3,633 properties for four property types (apartment, retail, office, and industrial) in all US regions. Factors from well-known multifactor models in finance (Fama & French's three factors coupled with Pastor & Stambaugh's liquidity factor and two bond market factors) are then employed for the analysis, yielding positive loadings on the stock market factor, the size factor, the liquidity factor and credit spread. Interestingly, this research shows the superiority of using disaggregated property level data (i.e. a cross-sectional approach) over real estate price indices (i.e. a time series approach) in assessing commercial real estate returns and macro-factors. Liang explains:

> [...] The cross-sectional approach generally provides more efficient and less biased estimates of factor loadings than the time-series approach. [...] The time series approach is subject to computational difficulties in index estimation when the sample is small, to which the cross-sectional approach is immune.

This finding exemplifies a point made in the introduction of this book: aggregate thinking in real estate finance cannot be the answer to commercial real estate investors' hedging needs. Overlooking commercial real estate returns' extreme granularity simply does not work.

Based on past research, it makes no doubt that macro-factors play an important role in explaining commercial real estate returns and risk. However, their dynamic linkages with individual properties' returns remain somewhat of a mystery in the absence of a comprehensive risk model of real estate. Apart from rare references to Hoag's model (1980), most research select economic risk factors without any reference to a widely accepted theoretical framework modelling the relationships between commercial real estate properties and their economic environment (national, regional, local) over time.

2.4.2 Micro-factors

HEDONIC PRICING MODELS AND THE ART OF MICRO-VARIABLES SELECTION

Factor-based real estate hedges include not only macro-factors but also micro-factors. The Hedonic Price Model (HPM) based on Lancaster's (1966) consumer theory can be helpful in identifying micro-variables factored in commercial real estate prices. The hedonic price model has been used in commercial real estate for two purposes:

- The construction of repeat-sales transaction based indices of commercial real estate (e.g. Fisher, Geltner and Webb, 1994; or Shiller, 1993) to account for fundamental alterations in-between sales, and
- The analysis of real estate return drivers, in particular for a specific property type in a given location, e.g. Brennan, Cannaday and Colwell (1984) who study office rents in the Chicago CBD.

Triplett (1986) explains that

> the [HPM] framework is derived from the idea that production or consumption of heterogeneous goods (or services, for that matter) can be analysed by disaggregating them into more basic, or elemental, units that better measure the dimensions of what is bought and sold- the characteristics.

Characteristics are supposed to be utility-bearing attributes, which are homogeneous and valued by both buyers and sellers.

As the hedonic price theory does not provide any indications with respect to the optimal choice of hedonic variables, the implementation of HPM in commercial real estate has been accompanied with a great diversity of variables in the models applied in past research. Shiller (1993) mentions:

> In constructing such hedonic indices, one is inevitably struck by the arbitrary or judgemental decisions one must inevitably make. Not only is there the decision of which quality variables to include, but there are also decisions to make about allowing nonlinear effects of each and interaction effects (represented, say, by variables equal to products of characteristic variables) between them. [...] There is a fundamental problem of objectivity of such indices.

In his choice of hedonic variables to be included in hedonic repeated-measures indices of commercial real estate, Shiller (1993) focuses on "independent variables that identify the investment", i.e. "identifiers of specific claims on future income or services". Time-varying variables which "naturally change for existing properties" should be excluded even though nothing seems reliably set in stone when it comes to 'normal' hedonic variable selection. For instance, to account for market conditions, Shiller posits that "one might sometimes wish to use hedonic variables" and suggests that "time on the market" be included in the hedonic regression model. This suggestion leads to many troubling questions about the relevance of any hedonic price indices based on "human judgement" and, in turn, derivatives using them as underlyings. Shiller (1993) talks in-depth about hedonic variables in the construction of index numbers feeding a macro-market for commercial real estate assets. But, no references are made to a risk model of commercial real estate underpinning the process of hedonic variable selection. Interaction effects are mentioned in statistical terms but not explained in the context of real estate risk.

Markedly, the hedonic pricing theory is not a risk model. One should not assimilate HPM with proper endeavours to model commercial real estate returns and risk. Besides, HPM was never designed for extremely heterogeneous assets. This inevitably turns hedonic variables selection into an art rather than a science. Pragmatically, Shiller muses that the market will ultimately decide on the value of such model. "If people want to hedge in the market, then the index is a success" in line with the engine versus camera argument made by MacKenzie (2006). But, if they don't, that's another wasted attempt to launch property derivatives until there are none left, that is because market authorities become wary and investors jaded.

LOCATION IN SPATIAL HEDONIC MODELS

One string of academic research combines hedonic modelling with spatial econometrics (e.g. Özyurt, 2014). Location in classic OLS hedonic models such as those presented in Appendix 1.3 customarily assumes that land is a two-dimensional smooth surface on which buildings sit (Pace, Barry and Sirmans, 1998). A myriad of indicator variables in the models embody different parts of the urban area. For instance, Brennan, Cannaday and Colwell (1984) select several location-related regressors such as distance to LaSalle Street in Chicago CBD and positioning of the building in East-West and North-South coordinates.

By employing spatial econometrics, researchers aim to account for each neighbourhood's unique effect while modelling the hedonic price of real estate assets. In doing so, they have identified two spatial effects which impact hedonic pricing models. Wilhelmsson (2002) explains:

> Spatial econometrics explicitly accounts for the influence of space on real estate, urban and regional models. There are two types of spatial effect, namely spatial dependence and spatial heterogeneity.

Spatial dependence derives from "spillover effects such as the impact of the price of one housing on the price of its neighbours [or] spatially correlated variables that have been omitted". Spatial heterogeneity may derive from "spatially varying parameters".

The resulting models are spatial hedonic models. Dubin, Pace and Thibodeau (1999) emphasise that by controlling for omitted variables in real estate price models, spatial techniques can significantly improve the predictive accuracy of hedonic models which would otherwise result in inefficient estimations. One point frequently mentioned is that spatial hedonic models tend to be more parsimonious in independent variables than classic OLS hedonic models. Pace, Barry and Sirmans (1998) assess that the number of variables in a hedonic model increases as a direct proportion to the geographic scope of the study. For a dataset of 10,000 real estate transactions data (n), approximately 500 location-related indicators (n/20) would be needed (corresponding to a separate indicator for each neighbourhood). One way to circumvent the issue is to focus on one specific neighbourhood all the more so if this neighbourhood is dominated by a single economic basis (e.g. Lecomte's (2014) replication and hedging of City of London office buildings).

Although mainly employed in housing studies, spatial hedonic models have also been used for commercial real estate assets, in particular retail properties for which site selection is "a classic spatial problem [...] that can be improved with spatial statistical techniques" (Dubin, et al., 1999). For instance, Desrosiers, Theriault and Menetrier (2005) identify complex interactions between endogenous determinants of shopping centre rents (e.g. agglomeration economies, retail mix and concentration, image and interior design) and exogenous space-related factors. In addition to size, retail mix, and image attributes, spatial determinants linked to neighbourhood and location attributes play a key role in explaining variation in shopping centres' rents in Quebec City, Canada.

More generally, whether spatial econometrics contributes to a more bottom-up approach to commercial real estate modelling than classic OLS hedonic regression by focusing on real estate micro-markets instead of macro-economic markets remains an open question. One would expect spatial determinants to be anchored in their local context. Ideally, spatial effects capture micro-trends at property level, trends which, through complex and dynamic interactions, are ultimately underpinning properties' rents and values.

Practically, spatial techniques can contribute to improving real estate modelling. Dubin et al. (1999) note that spatial autoregression techniques substantially improve "predictive accuracy, change in parameter estimates and their interpretation" in commercial real estate models, whereas OLS methods (e.g. hedonic methodology) in the presence of positive spatial autocorrelation result in "inefficient estimation and literally biased inference".

Hence, in the absence of a widely agreed risk model of commercial real estate, relying on spatial techniques could be an interesting way to reduce the number of variables in factor hedges while improving the instruments' overall hedging effectiveness. Interestingly, the theoretical underpinnings of spatial hedonic models are grounded in urban land economics. By positioning location at the core of commercial real estate analysis, these models support the view that land is central to real estate values, either as a variable with an absolute impact determined by a building's unique location on the surface of the Earth, or as a variable with a relative impact depending on interactions with other factors within a wider external context (be it the immediate or broader neighbourhood, the Metropolitan Statistical Area or beyond).

MILES, COLE AND GUILKEY'S (1990) FIVE DETERMINANTS OF VALUE

Some researchers have been somewhat more conclusive in selecting micro-variables based on HPM, e.g. Miles, Cole and Guilkey (1990) who adopt a very broad approach. Their choice of hedonic variables for commercial real estate sets free from the Hedonic Price Theory's inherent vagaries by shifting the focus to "basic valuation methodology". Their selected variables come from five different categories which are "essential determinants of real property value"[6]:

- *National location* which takes into account "the health of the local market economy in which a particular property is located relative to that of other local markets across the nation".
- *Metropolitan location* such as central business district, major suburban concentration, access to rail line, airport. It is "the most difficult to assess without a personal assessment of each property and its neighbourhood".
- *Physical structure* to assess "how well a particular property is suited for its highest and best use". This includes variables "chosen to proxy for remaining physical usefulness and functional obsolescence" such as physical age, date of last major renovation, number of stories, number of buildings, extra land available, gross and net leasable square footage.
- *Lease structure* to account for the "variability of returns and value attributable to differing lease structures". Four variables can be included: weighted average remaining lease maturity, tenant credit quality, weighted average percentage of expense increases that may be passed through tenants, and number of tenants. Noticeably, whilst in their strictest definition, hedonic variables tend to be structural and static, "lease structure" variables are essentially functional by capturing the dynamic process of income-generating at the asset level.
- *Financial structure* with measurements such as net income, capital improvements, partial sales, and appraised value as a way to measure "the financial operating performance of each property".

These determinants of property value are applicable to a building in its entirety, or to each unit making up the whole building. However, the selected variables are not unsystematic risk factors. Instead, they are "identifiable and observable proxies" selected for their high correlation with unobservable unsystematic factors. This caveat matters because (again) the list of variables is established without any reference to a comprehensive risk model of commercial real estate. Guilkey, Miles and Cole (1989) hypothesise that each of the four main commercial property types should have its own pricing equation built from the above-mentioned five determinants.[7] However, how the five categories of determinants and corresponding hedonic variables fit within a comprehensive and dynamic framework aiming to explain unsystematic risks associated with ownership of real estate property remains a mystery, one that can only be approached by proxy.

REAL ESTATE PRICING MODELS, CAPITALISATION RATES, AND MICRO-VARIABLES

Instead of focusing on sale prices, appraised values, or rents, a few researchers have applied a multifactor approach to disaggregate the determinants of commercial real estate capitalisation rates (cap rates) after pioneering studies by Ambrose and Nourse (1993), Jud and Winkler (1995).

In contrast to the two former studies which are conducted at the macro-level (e.g. Jud and Winkler study cap rates from 21 MSAs in the USA), Crosby, Jackson and Orr (2016) who study a large number of transactions in the London office market (2010–2012) design a multilevel framework which captures at the micro-scale "the variation generated by the characteristics of the real estate, its tenants, its purchaser and how wider macro-economic factors influence the expectations of purchasers with regard to individual investments".

By modelling cap rates at the micro-level, they aim to capture "the impact of attributes specific to the transacted real estate [given] the wider contextual and behavioural factors that can affect the outcome of the pricing decision". Macro- and micro-factors which impact investors' expectations of investment performances belong to four categories: investment and capital markets, real estate market, sector and allocation, stock/asset.

Among the latter category, variables positioned at the micro-end of the risk scale include tenant (credit worthiness), lease (multi/single-let, review/user clause, period to expiry/review), location (micro location/ accessibility), and building (sustainability rating, obsolescence). Furthermore, real estate asset-specific variables cover transaction characteristics broken down into transaction traits (e.g. type of investment transaction, property sold as part of a portfolio) and purchaser traits (e.g. international experience of the buyer, type of buyer). Interestingly, Ratcliff's (1961) real estate analysis specifically recommends a very similar approach. In parallel to each property being "structurally and locationally different and thus subject to certain special influences", the second special circumstance explaining that no two transactions are the same in the real estate market is linked to the parties involved. These parties might have different "motivations, business judgement […] and financial circumstances".

To assess buildings' expected depreciation in their pricing model, the authors select Co-Star building quality rating as an independent variable in the pricing model: from one star (very poor quality building) to five star (landmark building). Crosby et al.'s empirical findings show that real estate specific factors dominate variation in cap rates, even more so than locational differences across submarkets. Yet, surprisingly, building quality does not influence cap rates of London office buildings, which admittedly, might be a special case owing to the focus on London, one of the most sought-after global cities for real estate investment.

2.4.3 Learning from the real estate profession: factors in industry-led research

Past research have rarely combined what this book has identified as macro- and micro-factors so far. Due to the need to position the research within a complex theoretical framework (APT for macrovariables or HPM for micro-factors), academic studies customarily focus on one set of factors only. In that sense, Lecomte's (2007) combinative and factor-based hedge presented before are innovative insofar they aim to combine both families of factors into one single derivative instrument.

The real estate industry has not waited for academia to conduct research on the nature of commercial real estate risk. This section highlights three such research conducted by industry researchers and academics on UK commercial real estate assets.

THE INVESTMENT PROPERTY DATABANK'S PLEA FOR MULTIFACTOR
MODELS IN COMMERCIAL REAL ESTATE

In 1999, the Investment Property Forum (London, UK) commissioned the Investment Property Databank (IPD) to undertake a major survey aimed at "identifying the ways in which risk is understood, assessed and managed within the UK property industry". Based on 124 detailed responses from property investors and advisors, the research (IPF, 2000) identifies 1,590 controllable property specific risks, which are then narrowed down to 57 different aspects of risk at the asset level, at the portfolio level, and in a mixed asset portfolio. Similarly, 20 approaches to risk management are singled out. These 57 risk factors range from cyclical synchronisation through the presence of deleterious materials.[8] Since many of them are not easily quantifiable, they cannot be included into a risk model. However, "this hardly counts as a simple model of risk".

Indeed, IPD outlines that applying conventional models (i.e. CAPM's dichotomous decomposition of risk into market risk and specific risk) does not work for managing the specific risks of commercial real estate. Actually the CAPM is only one of 23 ways for formally assessing or quantifying relevant risks (top 5) mentioned in the survey. Market risk can be disaggregated by component: national non-property, national property, and local property. IPD calls for the development of a property multi-factor risk model which encompasses "all three of the market risk sub-categories [...]", knowing that "a local factor component would perhaps be of greatest value to property investors". With respect to specific risk, IPD asks for "a much tighter measurement framework that is designated to operate [...] at the level of the individual asset rather than one drawn from conventional theory which operates primarily at the portfolio level". This, IPD acknowledges, "remains in the land of property research science fiction".

THE BLUNDELL RISK WEB

Under the umbrella of a joint LaSalle-IPD project, Blundell, Fairchild and Goodchild (2005) map out "a practical way for managing risk in property portfolios" by identifying factors causing volatility in property returns. These factors which have to be managed to control volatility of commercial property returns are categorised into two groups depending on their role in triggering risk for investors:

four fundamental factors and several modulators which have a dampening or intensifying effect on the former. Unfortunately for the analysis conducted here, the focus is on *ex ante* risk at the portfolio level, not single assets. Factors are "based on decomposing the *causes* of volatility". They write:

> Like attribution analysis of return, overall portfolio volatility can be broken down into component parts relating to changes in income (default, re-leasing and rent reviews) and capital (shifts in capitalisation rate and market rent). These changes are driven in turn by a range of factors partly shared in common.

Fundamental risk factors include: tenant credit worthiness (TICCS), exposure to volatile sectors (e.g. City offices), speculative development exposure, weighted lease length, expected income growth, yield level (low is riskier), void rate. By the same token, modulators are: number of properties/ lot size concentration, property type concentration, sector balance, location concentration, leverage, exchange rate mismatch, tenant concentration, lease expiry concentration. Factors can act both individually and in combination. Each fundamental risk factor is given a score which, correlated with the other risk factor scores, defines the Blundell Risk Web (equal weights).

Notwithstanding its focus on portfolios rather than individual buildings, the Blundell web framework epitomises a few interesting ideas for factor-based real estate hedges. First, it does not include any of the macro-factors customarily mentioned in the academic literature. Second, it eschews direct references to buildings' physical dimensions, by focusing instead on their cash flow generating abilities in the money-time realm.

INVESTMENT PROPERTY FORUM (IPF): INDIVIDUAL PROPERTY RISK

In 2015, the IPF commissioned a group of researchers to study "the measurement and explanation of investment risk at the individual property level in the UK commercial market". The research analyses the performance records, property characteristics, and tenancy records of over 1,000 commercial properties held over the period 2002–2013 as well as detailed case studies of 88 commercial properties. Market risk dominates total risk in most individual properties except for a quarter of the properties. For the latter, risk is dominated by asset-specific truly idiosyncratic sources of risk. In particular, properties with relatively small lot sizes, higher yields, fewer tenants and greater exposure to the leasing market and to capital expenditure tend to show high specific risk.

The researchers note that "lease-related [i.e., tenant administration and vacancy following lease expiry] and, to a lesser extent, asset management-related factors are the predominant drivers of high specific risk in individual properties". Macro-economic factors selected in the study (GDP growth surprises, inflation surprises, gilt total return) are not instrumental in explaining the performances and risk of individual properties. The IPF report (2015) concludes by stressing that "in pricing risk in individual properties, investors and researchers need to focus more heavily on the risks related to tenant default, lease events and asset management".

Industry-led research and academic research are seemingly very different in their approaches to commercial real estate risk. In fact, it is difficult to reconcile the various sources and selection of risk factors presented in this section with those selected in academic papers. One striking dimension in industry-led research is the implicit reference to the urban land economics' paradigm of real estate. As mentioned before in this book, urban land economists identify three dimensions to real estate: physical, economic, and legal. Macro-factors and micro-factors as initially thought out in Lecomte (2007) after Hoag (1980) cover a property's economic dimension and physical dimension, respectively, whereas its legal dimension is mostly overlooked in academic models. Notable exceptions are Brennan, Cannaday and Colwell (1984) and Miles, Cole and Guilkey (1990), who explicitly refer to valuation rules.

Conversely, the legal dimension which encapsulates Ratcliff's "legal content of ownership" is predominant among industry researchers' recommendations for a multifactor pricing model of real estate. A bottom-up comprehensive approach to commercial real estate risk at the asset level supposes to start with the property, its physical and legal dimensions, and to progressively move up by extending the scope of the analysis all the way to its local, regional, and national environment. For instance, Brennan, Cannaday and Colwell's (1984) analysis of Chicago CBD office rents is conducted at the office unit level and not at the building level. They posit:

> The use of the building as the unit of observation effectively precludes including the date of lease transaction for each office unit within the building as an independent variable.

Therefore, most studies do not include a variable to account for the fact "transaction rental rates on which the average rate is based may have been negotiated at different points in time when market conditions were significantly different". Brennan et al.'s hedonic model which explains 90% of the variation in the log of rent encompasses: lease features, occupancy rate at the time the lease was executed, physical characteristics of the building, physical characteristics of the unit, location of the building. The complete list of variables is presented in Appendix 1.3.

Considering a building as a set of individual units each with its own lease features and physical characteristics within a building is the ultimate bottom-up approach, which admittedly goes against the mammoth trend of aggregate thinking that gripped real estate finance researchers at approximately the same time. The legal dimension of a property is what modulates the myriad of dynamic relationships between a building and its environment. It acts as a bridge between Graaskamp's two realms of real estate: space-time and money-time. So what is at play here? Has urban land economists' legal dimension been willingly overlooked?

First of all, it is undoubtedly a matter of paradigm. There is no denying that urban economics-driven research cannot easily accommodate the messiness of countless risk factors at the property level. Basically, the scientific bias in real estate research and the tendency for aggregate thinking in real estate finance have resulted in a range of studies on macro-variables in line with seminal papers in financial economics. Meanwhile, an even smaller number of research using the HPM have aimed to identify property-specific factors or micro-factors. The HPT's reliance on human subjectivity partly discredits hedonic variables in the eyes of quantitative research. In the process of defining factor models after the APT, real estate finance researchers have overwhelmingly forgotten about commercial real estate's legal dimension which has been abandoned to appraisers' and surveyors' valuation rules. However, these rules position commercial real estate risk directly into the money-time realm at the most granular level which is exactly where an asset risk should be assessed. Secondly, it is a matter of access to data. Very few researchers have access to the wealth of granular data and property level information accessible to the IPF research team in their 2015 study of individual property risk. The lack of access to data serves as a reinforcing feedback to the scientific bias in real estate studies, which ends up promoting a fragmentary and reductionist view of real estate risk.

2.5 Synthesis: bottom-up versus top-down approaches to factors in commercial real estate

It seems that commercial real estate pricing models based on a strict interpretation of the Asset Pricing Model (macro-variables) and Hedonic Pricing Theory (micro-factors) might have barked at the wrong tree. Industry-led research as well as pricing models inspired after valuation methodologies which adopt a bottom-up approach to real estate risk have managed to cover the full spectrum of real estate risk, i.e. from macro-level risks stemming from the national economy to the most granular micro-scale at the property or even unit level. Such extreme granularity has been more or less overlooked in classic models. Modelling real estate's micro-scale is in fact very straightforward. Identifying relevant variables to be included in models is also straightforward, at least on paper. Dealing with cash flows supposes to select factors potentially affecting a building's income-generating ability, i.e. factors stemming from what Ratcliff identified as the "legal dimension" of real estate.

Noticeably, models which include a micro-scale level of analysis tend to be very parsimonious in macro-variables. For instance, Miles et al. (1990) highlight very few macro-variables from their "national location" category in their models of the four commercial property types, notwithstanding the localness of these variables which are selected at the county level. Likewise, Crosby et al. (2016) only include three macro-variables in their optimal model (risk free rate, anticipated inflation and return on alternative investments) out of 18 variables overall. Does that mean that micro-scale variables have the ability to capture macro-trends at the asset level, i.e. where it matters for investors? A similar point can be raised about spatial hedonic models which position location as a dynamic factor within a complex eco-system whose impact is felt at the most granular level, i.e. the property and its immediate vicinity.

Due to the ever present issue of multicollinearity in factor models, being able to reduce the number of variables in real estate pricing models by fine-tuning variable identification and selection is a great advantage of a bottom-up approach.

It might suppose for real estate finance to find new roots in the valuation paradigm. The fact is that real estate finance has been aiming to develop pricing models without looking in detail at cash flows at the property level even though this information exists and could be readily accessed (under the right conditions of course). In its top-down approach searching for 'normalities', urban economics might have neglected an essential dimension of real estate. From investors' viewpoint, a building is a physical structure built on a unique piece of land in order to generate income. One cannot develop a holistic view of real estate risk without a clear reference to its micro-scale components.

Richard Feynman once jokingly asked: "are bricks essential objects?" (Feynman, 1985). Surely, buildings are not abstract entities even in the perfect world of finance. In line with Ratcliff (1961), they are part of a very material process that turns land into space and ultimately money. What might negatively impact the smooth working of this process whereby the real estate sector transforms bricks into cash flows boils down to risk.

Another noteworthy point is that most real estate pricing models are developed without a clear reference to a risk model of commercial real estate. Valuation-inspired models which, de facto, refer to a conceptual framework anchored in income generation at the most granular level are notable exceptions. Logically, deriving factors from a cap rate perspective rather than a price perspective should contribute to almost naturally adopting a bottom-up approach to variations in returns, and thus risks. The absence of proper structural models of real estate risk is a concern because it means there is no certainty about the choice of variables in factor hedges. Based on academic papers mentioned in Appendices 1.1 and 1.3, one would be hard-pressed to select a small number of macro- and micro-variables, respectively, as underlyings to factor hedges among the myriad mentioned in past studies. Nonetheless, this is what was done in the replication and hedging study of London office buildings reported in Appendix 1.4, out of necessity rather than choice as the desired variables were not publicly available.

This is the paradox of applying a theory designed for financial assets (such as APT) to real estate assets. A top-down approach which ignores the actual nature of commercial real estate as a quintessentially heterogeneous asset class results in anecdotal empirical evidence very far from the normalities the theory would have needed to be fully vindicated in the odd context of real estate. Even the application of ever more sophisticated econometric techniques cannot hide the fact that very little generalisable knowledge comes out of a study which is not underpinned by a model of commercial real estate risk. The following section covers the need for risk models in commercial real estate as a prerequisite to designing relevant and successful property derivatives.

3 Risk models and price dynamics in commercial real estate

Whilst a graduate student in physics at Princeton, American physicist and Nobel Prize Laureate Richard Feynman attended an advanced biology class in which he was asked to discuss an academic paper on cat nerves' impulses which the authors characterised as "sharp, single-pulse phenomena" (Feynman, 1985). As he prepared for his assignment, he reportedly asked Princeton librarians for "a map of the cat". Feynman's first instinct of mapping the underlying physical context of a complex dynamic phenomenon is classic in life sciences. For centuries, many scientists worked on mapping the human body and its various systems through extensive, albeit at times gruesome, dissections of cadavers.

To some extent, modern finance's Capital Asset Pricing Model (CAPM) provides a 'map' of an asset. A relatively simple risk model underpins the single index linear pricing equation. Surprisingly, despite the CAPM's and other financial models' shortcomings in their application to commercial property, real estate finance has not felt the urge to come up with a holistic conceptual framework as a prerequisite to a thorough investigation into commercial real estate asset returns and risks. There are several rational explanations to that neglect. As mentioned before, the import of ready-made models from financial economics has resulted in aggregate thinking and a top-down approach in real estate finance, which does not encourage the granular modelling of property assets. Furthermore, faced with the mammoth task of modelling commercial real estate assets, there is a tendency to think along the lines of "too complicated to bother". The absence of risk models in real estate finance is sometimes justified in the name of practicality: making empirical inferences from historical data should suffice to model real estate price dynamics. Geltner and de Neufville (2018) explain:

> [...] Rather than attempting to model all the possible determinants of [the future value of an asset being built or invested in] in a causal structural model, we content ourselves with modelling the kind of dynamics and randomness that appear in historical data about property price evolution. [...] This does not mean that analysts should not consider, or indeed study and seek to understand, the underlying causal elements that affect prices and values. [...] But an ever-present challenge in effective, practical simulation analysis is to avoid excessive complexity. We must not "get lost in the weeds", and we must not "lose sight of the forest for the trees blocking the view!".

So, does real estate finance actually need to bother about a thorough risk model for commercial property? This book argues that the shortage of research about risk modelling in commercial real estate is one of the main reasons why real estate derivatives have not been successful, especially as hedging instruments for direct property investors. Indeed, it is impossible to hedge an asset whose overwhelmingly idiosyncratic variations in returns cannot be explained at the most granular level.

Risk models matter insofar as they define several crucial conditions which have to be met for real estate derivatives to succeed. Risk models provide the framework underlying any attempts to model factors and their wider interactions. They also underlie the choice of relevant stochastic processes to be used in pricing real estate derivatives. Without a solid risk model, pricing real estate derivatives is approximative at best. Real estate finance should undoubtedly aim to be right in practice about commercial real estate price dynamics. However, forgoing a conceptual approach to risk in commercial property has direct consequences for real estate derivatives.

For instance, one can simply consider US residential real estate derivatives' lack of liquidity (Shiller, 2008). Liquidity in standardised property derivatives markets has been an unsolvable conundrum stemming from property's heterogeneity. Fabozzi, Shiller and Tunaru (2010) assess:

> Derivatives require homogeneity of the underlying for establishing liquidity in their trading. The lack of homogeneity in real estate markets has been one of the main obstacles to the development of property derivatives.

One way to overcome this obstacle is to develop a widely accepted risk model of commercial real estate, which can help make sense of property heterogeneity. A model does not aim for the truth but for a vision of reality that can be widely and systematically adopted by market participants, as CAPM was in the investment industry (Bernstein, 1995). Indeed, a model is an engine, not a camera (MacKenzie, 2006). Short of designing its own models, real estate finance is condemned of having no engine at all or one that does not suit its needs. This section presents two factor-based models: the historical pricing model devised by Hoag in his seminal 1980 paper, and a genetics-inspired risk model proposed by Lecomte (2007). It then shows how the choice of a risk model can affect our understanding of random walk and stochastic process, two important concepts applied to the pricing of commercial real estate derivatives.

3.1 Hoag's (1980) model of commercial real estate

3.1.1 Conceptual framework for index construction from a property valuation function

James W. Hoag is oftentimes credited for introducing the first multifactor asset pricing approach into real estate literature (Miles et al., 1990; Tunaru, 2017). The model presented by Hoag (1980) which focuses on industrial properties is first and foremost a valuation model akin to methods "utilized in common stock risk/ return analysis". Hoag explains:

> The method of analysis [...] leads naturally to a consideration of a property valuation function based on a vector of fundamental microeconomic and macroeconomic variables which affect property value. With certain reasonable approximations, the valuation model leads directly to an estimate of the market rate of return on real estate, the risk and return associated with each property and the market risk.

The full "conceptual framework for index construction from a property valuation function" encompasses the property asset's micro-market defined as buildings' specific characteristics and the broader macro-economic environment captured by national and regional variables. Five categories of variable are represented in the model: national economic, regional economic, locational, temporal, and property-specific characteristics.

Hoag explains that "initially, the list of valuation characteristics should be very broad, but as experience grows, many candidate characteristics will be cast aside". Property-specific characteristics include location, physical characteristics, lease characteristics, financing characteristics, and appraised value. The macro-economic climate, including both regional variables (e.g. regional growth, population changes, regional transportation spending) and national variables (e.g. business inventories, mortgage interest rates and availability), interacts with other fundamental characteristics to impact the valuation function and estimated prices. The supply and demand sides of the real estate market are also part of the model with national variables such as available space/vacancies, commitments, and investment by major participants. Hoag assesses that the locational variables "detract somewhat from the regional economic concomitants since each represent a localized measure of value. [...] Location interacts with specific regional macroeconomic variables such as transportation spending to provide a context for regional valuation [...]". Hence, as mentioned before, locational variables can be a proxy for macro-economic variables at the micro-scale.

Individual risk measures are designed to assess a building's responsiveness to fundamental characteristics.[9] Hoag stresses that the objectivity of the model contrasts with appraisers' subjective estimates of value and thus return. Markedly, the model is determined from an analogy with the "type of fundamental analysis [which] is accomplished on a daily basis by security analysts in the stock market". Among Hoag's objectives is the provision of index numbers that can be used "to utilize current investment technology (the Capital Asset Pricing Model – CAPM) to estimate a real estate investment". In that sense, Hoag's model, although characterised by its innovative use of a multifactor risk model in what is essentially a parametric methodology, is intrinsically biased towards a binary approach to commercial real estate returns and risks.

3.1.2 Hoag's framework and factor-based real estate derivatives

By putting a conceptual framework at the core of the analysis, Hoag's seminal research defines the way multifactor asset-pricing studies for commercial property should be designed. Hoag validates the notion that factors come from two broad categories: macro-variables and micro-variables which are property specific. Property specific does not mean hedonic inasmuch as property-specific factors also include lease and financing characteristics.

National and regional economic variables are designated as "concomitants of value" in the asset valuation function for industrial properties. This implies that economic variables form the context which interacts with fundamental characteristics to determine value. The latter are limited to before-tax equity cash flows and property-specific factors, especially lease characteristics. In that sense, Hoag's framework implicitly follows a bottom-up approach to commercial real estate value. Hoag does not venture into a risk model per se as his framework is essentially designed to estimate a valuation function "at any point in time" (i.e. statically). But, by assessing "the responsiveness of property value to changes in fundamental factors", the framework can double up as a dynamic risk model for commercial property.

3.2 Lecomte's (2007) genetics-based risk model of commercial real estate

3.2.1 Positioning property heterogeneity at the core of real estate finance

It should be clear by now that real estate is refractory to abstraction. This is the crux of a problem which has so far prevented academics and finance experts to successfully design and launch standardised real estate derivatives markets. The over-the-counter format of Total Return Swaps (TRS) can accommodate property heterogeneity. But, standardised markets, as we know them today, simply cannot. Property heterogeneity can be ignored by adopting aggregate thinking in the name of financial economics orthodoxy or for the sake of practicality.

Alternatively, property heterogeneity can become real estate finance's central tenet. The underlying idea is simple. Let's put aside everything financial economics has taught us and think in terms of "what if". The first of a long series of "what if" goes back to the very origins of economics: what if Cambridge economist Alfred Marshall's focus on life sciences had become the dominant paradigm in economics at the turn of the 19th century, instead of physics? What would it mean for real estate?

In his Principles of Economics (1890), Marshall writes:

> The Mecca of the economist lies in economic biology rather than in economic dynamics [...] Frequent use is made of the term "equilibrium", which suggests something of statistical analogy [...] But, in fact [economics] is concerned throughout with the forces that cause movement: and its key-note is that of dynamics rather than statics. [...] Economics cannot be compared with the exact physical sciences: for it deals with the ever-changing and subtle force of human nature. [...] The laws of economics are to be compared with the laws of the tides, rather than with the simple and exact law of gravitation. [...] Economics, like biology, deals with a matter, of which the inner nature and constitution, as well as the outer for, are constantly changing.

3.2.2 Buildings as living organisms

If real estate assets cannot be modelled as abstraction akin to stocks and bonds, they might be amenable to another type of modelling closer to their quintessentially idiosyncratic nature. Scaffolding on Marshall's biological tropism,[10] Lecomte (2007) develops an analogy between risk and a multifactorial disease, and proposes genetics as a modelling paradigm for commercial real estate. Genetics provides a way of thinking about heterogeneity in large populations of similar, yet different, organisms, be they plants, animals, or human beings. Genetics applied to property heterogeneity implies the search for both the commonality in all buildings (what they share in common as a population or sub-group of buildings) and their intrinsic uniqueness (what makes each building idiosyncratic).

The premise of this line of thinking is that buildings are comparable to living organisms immersed in both space and time. Resorting to an analogy with living systems in order to make sense of individual behaviours is not new in social sciences. In their analysis of the urban economics paradigm in real estate research, Clapp and Myers (2000) highlight the link between an economy and "a living system that changes over time", and hint at the living system analogy as an alternative to deductive modes of thought and econometrics in real estate analysis.[11]

A living organism evolves as it interacts with its environment in the space-time realm. One way to look at it is to search for equilibrium after the laws of physics. Another way adopted in the genetics-based model is to centre the analysis on changes and development after Thorstein Veblen's vision of 'evolutionary economics' (Veblen and Boulton, 2010). Whilst physics' laws applied to finance tend to catch the phenomenological dimension of complexity without explaining it (Cartwright, 1980), focusing on a living organism's genetics anchors the model around the conceptual differentiation between what is being observable at the organism level (phenotype) and the organism's fundamental building blocks which, though not directly observable, constantly interact with the environment (genotype). A genetic framework naturally yields a model involving observable features and unobservable factors. Lecomte (2007) stresses that, because of its essentially dynamic nature, real estate risk cannot be properly captured by static variables such as those customarily employed in hedonic pricing models. Risk factors are defined as interactions between the organism's fundamental determinants and its environment. Clapp and Myers (2000) underscore the time-varying dimension of such complex interactions which, to add more complexity, might occur concomitantly:

> In an evolving, living system, any variable that is in the background at any one point in time can assume a prominent position at a later point in time. Thus, a model that assumes that a given variable is in the background may be proved incorrect [...] when that variable later assumes a foreground position. This is a necessary part of the complexity of living systems; many causal conditions may operate simultaneously.

Hence, a genetics-based model which posits buildings as living organisms supposes a decisively dynamic framework of commercial real estate return and risk.[12] Through its dynamism, the model also makes it possible to characterise a stochastic process based on the concept of genetic 'randomness' which would be specific to real estate returns. This point will be presented in detail later in this section. Genetics serves both as a language to structure the thinking about commercial real estate risk (e.g. genotype versus phenotype) and as a source of hypotheses (e.g. stochastic process for commercial property).[13]

3.2.3 Total returns as buildings' complex quantitative trait

The genetics-based model is not an asset pricing model. It is a risk model. As such, it does not aim to explain price levels in a given market, but rather to come to grips with changes in returns (i.e. total return made up of capital appreciation and rental income) affecting a building immersed in a time-space varying environment. Whereas a pricing model tends to be static, a risk model has to be dynamic and accounts for changes at the property level (endogenous) and evolution in the environment (exogenous). Thus, the model presented here aims to decipher a complex phenomenon (i.e. variations in total returns) affecting a population of living organisms (i.e. buildings) as a result of interactions between endogenous and exogenous variables. Lecomte (2007) explains:

> [The model] is aiming at identifying networks of risk factors that modulate the variability of returns in diverse environments.[...] This model [refers to] a branch of genetics known as genetic epidemiology whose goal is to understand the role of specific genes, specific environmental factors and interactions between genes and the environment in determining a particular trait.

As the trait of interest (i.e. a property's ability to generate total returns) potentially involves multiple interactions, it is said to be a complex, though continuous, quantitative trait. Its phenotype materialises as a series of periodic numbers (e.g. quarterly, bi-yearly, or yearly total returns).

3.2.4 Modelling a building's phenotype and genotype

Modelling buildings' combined phenotype and genotype requires that choices be made with respect to what is observable (phenotype) and should be selected in the model, and what is genotype. As said before, the phenotype is easy to identify. It is a building's total return. As far as the genotype is concerned, to adhere to the genetics framework, the model needs to think in terms of genetic makeup of a building, i.e. its chromosomes and genes. How far the model should go in its genetics realism is an important epistemological issue. The criteria of analytical relevance should dominate the selection of the model's structure. Milton Friedman (1966) explains that assumptions in a theory should not be assessed on whether they are "descriptively realistic, for they never are, but whether they are sufficiently good approximations for the purpose in hand". The model's purpose is to devise a factor-based framework that can help analyse real estate risk as a complex dynamic phenomenon. Therefore, the model relies on core genetic concepts such as chromosomes and genes.

A THREE-CHROMOSOME MODEL

Lecomte (2007) starts by modelling a building's fixed components in space-time realm. Two chromosomes are used: one for location, the other for physical structure. The model defines commercial real estate assets as polygenic organisms, i.e. organisms having multiple genes on each chromosome with complex quantitative traits influenced not only by intergenic interactions but also by the environment. Thus, a building's phenotype is influenced by: (i) genetic factors in the form of alternative genotypes of one or more genes and (ii) environmental factors in the form of conditions that are conducive or not to the expression of the trait. It is assumed that all income-producing commercial buildings share the same chromosomes. However, genes on each chromosome and their interactions might differ from one building to another.

The location chromosome which is exogenous channels environmental influences from the global, national, regional, and local economies. In accordance with Ratcliff (1961) and Weimer and Hoyt (1966), the model considers that location is a highly dynamic concept which acts as a vector to many disturbing factors. Conversely, the physical structure chromosome is endogenous. To some extent, its genes can be altered by the property owner and through property management, for instance in response to the direct impact of time on the building's physical structure. Time impacts not only the building's physical structure (physical obsolescence), but also the interactions between genes within a chromosome and between genes on different chromosomes (technological and economic obsolescence).

Modelling a property's total return over time implies the ability to capture the environment interacting with the property at different scales. The environment is not a separate conceptual entity from the property's intrinsic structural dimension. The environment, from local to global, is part of a building's genetic makeup. Indeed, as the second chromosome is location-based, the model underscores the central role of land (i.e. location) as an embedded vector of dynamic environmental interactions in the complex process that leads to total return at the property level.

A realistic model should probably limit itself to these two chromosomes (as done in Lecomte (2007)). However, it is obvious that one crucial dimension affecting a property's ability to deliver total returns would be missing should the model be only focused on real estate's structural and locational dimensions.[14] Real estate's space-time realm should also encompass functional variables related to the actual use of space in a building. Thus, an additional chromosome should cover this important dimension of a building's riskiness for investors. This chromosome includes the micro-scale variables presented previously as part of lease structure in factor models, e.g. occupancy rate, tenant creditworthiness, weighted average lease expiration. Based on these considerations, a third chromosome for space usage is added to Lecomte (2007)'s initial two-chromosome model. Figure 1.4 presents a generic representation of this three-chromosome model.[15] Lecomte (2007) calls these chromosomes "riskosomes".

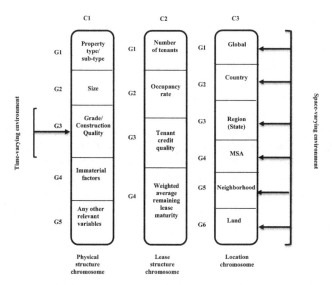

Figure 1.4 The three-chromosome model of commercial real estate after Lecomte (2007).

Notes: In Lecomte (2007), chromosomes are labelled 'riskosomes'. The specific number and positioning of genes on the chromosomes have to be determined. Genotypes are specific for each type of property. Likewise, the size of bars on the above figure are not representative of individual genes' dominance on each chromosome or within chromosomes.

- Physical structure:
  - C1G1 (property type) identified as dominant over location in various studies (e.g.,Miles and McCue, 1982; Hamelink, Hoesli, Lizieri and MacGregor, 2000; Lecomte and McIntosh, 2006 ; Pai and Geltner, 2007)
  - C1G2 (size) includes gross and net leasable square footage, building footprint, number of stories.
  - C1G4 (immaterial factors) includes a property's historical background as well as its aesthetic and architectural attributes. It is a subjective gene altered by changes in taste. The notion of grade already captures some of its impact. Standardized classifications such as the Costar building classification for offices (Crosby et al., 2016) can be used.
  - The physical structure chromosome and location chromosome are potentially subjected to Acts of God.
- Lease structure:
  - Lease structure genes are defined after Miles, Cole and Guikley (1990).
- Location: examples of space-varying variables impacting interactions with location-related genes
  - C3G1 (global)/ C3G2 (country): interest rates, inflation rates, unemployment, industrial production, productivity, financial market index, foreign direct investment, institutional investing, demographics, legal environment, property rights, transparency, taxes,
  - C3G3 (region/state): regional economic and real estate market indicators, demographics,
  - C3G4 (MSA)/ C3G5 (neighbourhood): local economic and real estate market indicators (e.g., institutional property investment), economic base, demographics (e.g., age groups, household formation), socio-economic factors, infrastructures, schools, universities, sport facilities, hospital, retail outlets, entertainment, proximity to airports, highways, pollution
  - C3G6 (land): quality of land, zoning, entitlement, environmental contamination, immediate surroundings,
  - The location chromosome is modelled after Ratcliff's (1961) three dimensional concept of property location in a global context.

Genes on each chromosome are selected from past research on macro- and micro-variables presented in a previous section of this chapter. Each gene embodies one important characteristic and might be proxied by several variables. For instance, in the model reproduced in Figure 1.4, the physical structure's gene related to size contains three single variables. Besides, as granularity increases on the location chromosome (i.e. from global to local), one could expect genes to interact with more variables linked to local real estate markets rather than broad macro-economic indicators.

Practically, to generalise the model's application, proforma genotypes should be developed. That is, each property type can define a proforma 'physical structural' chromosome. Similarly, each location can define a proforma 'locational' chromosome. And finally, each type of lease structure can define a proforma 'space usage' chromosome. The combination of the three chromosomes defines a proforma genotype for a property type in a given location with a standardised set of functional characteristics. The process can be conducted at all levels of chromosome granularity if need be, resulting in targeted standardised proforma genotypes readily available for real estate researchers to fine-tune. The use of geographic clusters based, for instance, on spatial hedonic models to sort out buildings could also allow for more parsimonious models with regard to location linked risk factors.[16]

GENE EXPRESSION AND INTERACTIONS

The genetic framework offers the possibility to qualify the way a gene interacts with other genes in influencing the phenotype. In the model, a gene might be (Ahluwalia, 2009):

- *Dominant*: when one gene completely controls total return, by superseding other genes,[17]
- *Complimentary*: when two genes must be present together for a certain level of total return to materialise,
- *Duplicate*: when two or more genes have the same effect on total return,
- *Polymeric*: when genes' effect on total return is additive,
- *Modifying*: when some of the many genes involved in generating total return are acting as 'modifiers' impacting the activity of other genes,
- *Lethal*: when a gene prevents a property from generating any returns.

Noticeably, two buildings sharing the same genetic structure do not a priori share the same ability to generate total return insofar as the type of gene interactions as well as their degree of expression (i.e. expressivity) ultimately condition the complex phenomenon at play. Hence, contrary to a static model, such as the hedonic regression model, in which spatial proximity as well as common structural characteristics are usually enough to cluster real estate assets together, risk factors in a genetics-based model derive from gene interactions whose expressivity might fluctuate. Being able to qualify these interactions' expressivity is as important as identifying the relevant genes for each specific property under study. Such variability embedded at the very core of the model builds on Graaskamp's view that in answering real estate questions, there might be "no necessary connections, only some degree of associations between variables" (Kummerow, 2000).[18]

Time intervenes in the model as an external variable directly affecting the 'grade' gene on the physical structure chromosome and indirectly impacting gene interactions and their expressivity for all other genes in the space-time varying environment. Lecomte (2007) explains:

> Physical deterioration and obsolescence show up in the interactions between genes on both chromosomes. They disturb the causal relationships between the structure chromosome and the space chromosome either by modifying their impact on the phenotype, or by creating new relationships which might be age-dependent.

A hypothetical gene regulatory network can be drawn up to graph functional relationships among various genes in the genotype and their various interactions with the space-time varying environment. Unless it is dominant, a gene works with others within a network of identified interactions to achieve a property's total return. Each network is built from the viewpoint of one gene only as an undirected, albeit partially oriented, dependency graph. To get a full picture of the phenomenon at play, without prejudging the causal relationships involved (if any), single gene networks should be assembled together to build a "synchronicity map" that gives a full picture of total return risk for the commercial property under study. Such wide-ranging non-hierarchical representations of real estate risk inspired by undirected dependency graphs in biostatistics (Shipley, 2016) can help generate interesting hypotheses concerning causal processes involved. Practically, they can also serve as repositories of past research interactions linked to a given property type in a specific location and available for all researchers to fine-tune their own models. Figure 1.5 presents a hypothetical gene network of occupancy rate in terms of polygenic interactions with physical structure and other lease structure genes.

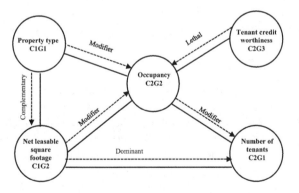

Notes: This figure symbolizes polygenic interactions of occupancy with physical structure and other lease structure genes. It is an undirected dependency graph: straight line arrows represent undirected relationships between two genes. Dotted line arrows designate the hypothetical direction of relationships between two genes. These relationships are qualified in reference to genetics' taxonomy of genotypic interactions. For instance, property type and net leasable area are complementary in impacting occupancy (and total return) while tenant credit worthiness is lethal in its interaction with occupancy (i.e. a building full of bankrupt tenants does not generate total return). All genes are impacted by location genes at different levels of granularity (not represented in the figure above).

Figure 1.5 Hypothetical gene regulatory network.

The genetics-based model of commercial real estate fosters synchronicity thinking in real estate analysis. Synchronicity refers to parallel non-causal relationships.[19] Static components of real estate are immersed into a wider and complex system that links space-time and money-time. This polymorphic and dynamic system is both physical and abstract, observable and unobservable as underlying forces are constantly and silently at work to disrupt properties' return-generating abilities over time.

BOX 1.1: Genetics-based model of real estate risk

- Premise: buildings are akin to living organisms immersed in a time-space varying environment.
- A commercial property asset is made up of three dimensions: physical structure, lease structure, and location. Location is the vector of exogenous influences by channelling macro-economic exogenous effects (from the local real estate market to the global economy).
- The model is a dynamic risk model. It aims to explain variations in a property's total returns.
- Risk factors are not static variables, but interactions of two or more variables selected in the model framework.
- Time affects the quality and type of variable interactions at three levels: (i) variables involved in the interaction, (ii) variables interactions with the environment, and (iii) the environment itself.
- The genetics-based model provides the conceptual foundations for a new random walk specific to direct commercial real estate at the property level. The process can be used to quantify micro-scale return dynamics and to price factor-based real estate derivatives.

3.2.5 Methodologies for modelling risk factors as interactions

Progresses in genetics have been accompanied by parallel progresses in methodologies applied by geneticists and biostatisticians to identify genes and decipher complex polygenic traits. The genetics-based model opens the door to many exciting methodologies, at least in principle. It makes no doubt that their application to a purely theoretical model such as the one presented above requires some adapting.

In his presentation of factor-based macro-markets for hedging real estate and other assets, Shiller (1993) specifically mentions MIMIC (multiple indicators, multiple cause) models to "estimate factors as functions of other variables". These models which are applied in economics (e.g. in studies of factors contributing to economic performance) bring us back to genetics inasmuch as they originated in methodologies initially developed by genetics pioneer Sewall Wright (1889–1988).

Shiller notes that applying multivariate modelling techniques to identify factors is not devoid of problems:

> In practice, the idea of such modelling would have to be pursued with care, since the methods might produce factors that have no simple intuitive base, and there may be scepticism that an estimated factor structure will continue to hold up in the indefinite future. A less formal approach to identifying factors on which to base markets [...] may suffice.

It is interesting to note that among the shortcomings of factor-based hedging instruments for real estate assets, Shiller singles out the potential lack of dynamism of the underlying model. This chapter addresses this important point in the next section. Another point raised by Shiller (1993) with respect to factor-analytic models is the impact of interaction effects. Because of them, "the quality of the property would have different effect on price in different dates". Indeed, identifying and qualifying interactions among variables (in pairs, threes, or more) should be central in any selected methodologies. It is also part of the model's dynamism.

Another issue facing researchers derives from the fact that hypothesis testing in economics has to rely on uncontrolled experiments (Friedman, 1966). In an uncontrolled experimental environment, establishing causal connections cannot be easily achieved compared to the way biologists customarily carry out controlled experiments in line with 19th-century physiologist Claude Bernard's seminal *Study of Experimental Medicine* (Shipley, 2016). Mindful of "the basic confusion between descriptive accuracy and analytical relevance", Friedman (1966) insists that in economics, "[a meaningful scientific hypothesis or theory] cannot be tested by comparing its assumptions directly with reality", but by putting it in the context of "other hypotheses dealing with related phenomena".[20]

Methodologies presented in this book are derived from methods customarily applied in quantitative genetics (variance partitioning) and population genetics (path analysis). The trait under study (i.e. Total Return) is a continuous quantitative trait. The objective is to shed some light on variations in this trait over time (i.e. same building over time) and in space (comparative analysis of different buildings in different locations). The following section introduces Variance Partitioning. Path analysis is presented in Appendix 1.5.

FUNDAMENTALS OF TOTAL RETURN VARIANCE DECOMPOSITION
AT POPULATION LEVEL

To deal with risk factors which are essentially interaction effects, the genetics-based model of real estate risk relies on a parametric approach. It analyses property assets according to its own proforma framework (e.g. the genotype/ phenotype dichotomy) and proposed structural models (e.g. 3 chromosomes × 15 genes × environment), which ought to be adapted depending on each property's idiosyncrasies. In the process, the genetics-based model turns commercial real estate into a highly idiosyncratic, though conceptually homogeneous, abstraction interacting with the environment. The aim here is to qualify and explain selected genes' interactions (i.e. risk factors in the model) in driving variations in total return.

Variance decomposition is well suited to identify interaction effects at the core of the model's dynamism. It has been applied in quantitative genetics to study variation in the genetics of a metric character at the population level (i.e. large sample of buildings in a neighbourhood). The basic idea is to partition variation into components attainable to different causes.

In the genetics-based model, the only determinants of a property's total return (P) are the genotype (G) and the environment (E):

$$P = G + E \tag{1}$$

Environment encapsulates "all the non-genetic circumstances that influence the phenotypic value" (Falconer and Mackay, 1996). A property asset's genotypic value G is itself made up of several components:

- The *Genotypic value* of each gene involved in the phenotype: the genotypic value of two genes is supposed to be additive. A is the sum of all genotypic values attributable to separate genes;
- The *Dominance deviation* D in case one or more genes are dominant over other genes involved in the interaction;
- The *Interaction deviation* I if genes interactions affect the phenotype. I is the "deviation from additive combination of these genotypic values" involved in A above. If I = 0, then the genes in pairs, threes or higher numbers are purely additive.

$$\text{Hence,} \quad G = A + D + I \tag{2}$$

In terms of variance, the model yields:

$$V_P = V_G + V_E \tag{3}$$
$$\text{Or } V_P = V_A + V_D + V_I + V_E \tag{4}$$

The ratio V_G/V_P gives an estimation of genetic determination in the population, i.e. similarity of physical structure, lease characteristics, and location. V_A, the additive variance, is an indication of the degree of resemblance between properties in an experimental population.

V_I, the interaction variance, captures the variance of the interaction deviations. In the simple case of two genes involved in an interaction, there are three sorts of two-factor interactions:

- Additive (A) Additive (A) if the two genes are additive
- Additive (A) Dominant (D) if one gene is additive and the other dominant
- Dominant (D) Dominant (D) if both genes are dominant

$$\text{With } V_I = V_{AA} + V_{AD} + V_{DD} \tag{5}$$

Considering that in the genetics-based model, risk factors are interactions, one can expect V_I to account for the bulk of V_G, and ultimately V_P.

CORRELATION AND INTERACTION BETWEEN A PROPERTY ASSET'S GENOTYPE AND THE ENVIRONMENT

It is highly likely that there is a correlation between genotypic value and environmental deviation in the model. That is, the better buildings in terms of physical structure tend to be built in the better environment. Furthermore, the better buildings in terms of total return for investors will tend to attract more development of buildings with similar characteristics in similar environments, thereby improving the overall quality of the correlation between genotype and environment.

As a result, $V_P = V_G + V_E + 2COV_{GE}$ (6)

Falconer and Mackay (1996) explain that when this occurs for human phenotypes, as the covariance is unknown in practice, "an individual's environment can be thought of as part of its genotype", which is in effect the case in the genetics model where location, in the broad acceptance of the term, is part of a property asset's genotype.

In Equation 1, we assume that interactions between genotype and the environment are same irrespective of the genotypes on which the latter acts. This is obviously not realistic. In practice, specific differences in environmental factors might have different effects on various phenotypes depending on the environmental sensitivity of a genotype (aka "reaction norm"). For instance, an office building located in the City of London might show larger total return than another seemingly similar office building in the City, but smaller returns than another similar building in Paris' Golden Triangle. Thus, Equation 1 should be rewritten as follows:

$$P = G + E + I_{GE} \qquad (7)$$

where I_{GE} captures interaction effects between the genotype and the environment,

and $V_P = V_G + V_E + 2COV_{GE} + V_{GE}$ (8)

To qualify whether specific environments are more or less favourable for expression of the total return trait in a property, one can compute the *environmental sensitivity*, by regressing the genotype value (G) on the environmental value (equal to the mean of all genotypes in that environment).

APPLICATION OF VARIANCE ANALYSIS AT THE PROPERTY LEVEL

Variance decomposition can also be applied at the property level by breaking down variance in total returns into a component written within each property (*within-property component*) and another component measuring differences be-tween properties (*between-property component*). The within-property component is due to changes in the environment (all other things being equal in terms of genotype) whereas the between-property component measures the permanent differences between properties in a population.

Falconer and Mackay (1996) notes that "by this analysis, the variance due to temporary environmental circumstances is separated from the rest, and can be measured". The within-property variance fully results from the environment ow-ing to temporary or localised circumstances. It is called the *Special Environment Variance*, V_{ES}.

In parallel, V_{EG}, the *General Environment Variance*, captures the variance of the permanent between-property component with:

$$V_E = V_{ES} + V_{EG} \tag{9}$$

The ratio in eq (10) is known as the repeatability of the character, r with

$$r = (V_G + V_{EG}) / V_P \tag{10}$$

The repeatability measures the proportion of the variance in total return due to the permanent, non-localised differences between properties, both genetic and environmental. This type of analysis could be applied at the MSA level. In the genetics-based model, V_{ES} refers to the space-time varying environment of the individual property level at the micro-scale.

To separate V_{EG}, the general environment variance, from V_G, the genotypic variance, Falconer et al. suggest to calculate repeatability in a genetically uni-form group (i.e. similar buildings in the same neighbourhood with similar physical and lease structures). The between-property variance of this group of buildings is equal to the general environment component V_{EG} since V_G of a genetically uniform sample of buildings is close or equal to zero. Hence,

$$\text{If } V_G = 0 \text{ and } V_P = V_E = V_{EG} + V_{ES} \tag{11}$$
$$\text{and the repeatability ratio } r = V_{EG} / (V_{EG} + V_{ES}) \tag{12}$$

Partitioning the environment variance into general and specific environments makes it possible to focus on property level interactions with the environment. V_{ES} expresses the micro-scale dimension of location which involves the more granular locational variables (including the local real estate market's impact on individual properties), whilst V_{EG} expresses the broader spatial dimension of the environment linked to less granular levels of location-related genes in the model.

Variance decomposition of a property negatively affected by time (obsoles-cence) can be expected to express many interactions with the grade gene on the physical structure chromosome. This gene might become dominant to the point of being lethal to the building. In particular, whenever environmental variance shifts from special (ES) to permanent (EG), this can spell disaster for unfit prop-erties such as an ageing building.[21]

Variance decomposition can help design effective factor-based hedges for commercial real estate assets, by deciphering the role played by each category of variables in explaining total return variance at the property level. Properties where V_E dominates are easier to hedge than those where V_G dominates. The latter type might have structural issues whose origins can widely vary, from physical structure to location. Moreover, if V_{ES} dominates, one can expect more local real estate market related factors in optimal hedges. Conversely, if V_{EG} dominates V_E, one can expect more macro-variables in optimal hedges.

To design effective hedging instruments, researchers can use variance partitioning as a guiding tool for factor selection in factor-based real estate derivatives. Although not mainstream, variance decomposition is not new in commercial real estate studies, e.g. Wheaton (2015) who partitions the volatility in vacancy into demand/supply contributions for four property types in US MSAs. The methodology, a staple method in quantitative genetics, is well suited to real estate derivatives insofar as it focuses on the very phenomenon the genetics-based model aims to capture, i.e. variation in total return as a result of interactions.

Other methodologies derived from genetics and biological sciences such as path analysis and structural equation modelling based on maximum likelihood techniques (Shipley, 2016) are also worth considering for implementing the genetics-based model. Appendix 1.5 presents an application of path analysis.

3.3 Price dynamics in commercial real estate

Now that we have introduced a risk model of commercial real estate and discussed methodologies to implement it, identifying real estate price dynamics to quantify uncertainty is the next step in the analysis. This point is especially important for deriving the 'correct' price of real estate derivatives. One fundamental issue here is to explore whether real estate follows a random walk, akin to financial assets, which would make it possible to apply well-known stochastic processes, such as the Brownian motion, for pricing real estate derivatives.

The concept of classical random walk introduced by Louis Bachelier (1900) and popularised by Burton Malkiel (1973) posits that asset prices exhibit a random walk whereby "successive price changes in individual securities are independent [...] A series of random walks implies that a series of stock price changes has no memory – the past history of the series cannot be used to predict the future in any meaningful way" (Fama, 1965).

This section starts by introducing models employed in the academic literature to simulate price dynamics in real estate markets. It then explores the random walk hypothesis in light of the genetics-based model.

3.3.1 Price dynamics in the absence of a risk model of commercial real estate

Since real estate derivatives were reintroduced in the early 2000s, real estate finance researchers have looked for reliable models to capture real estate market price dynamics in view of quantifying real estate uncertainty and pricing real estate derivatives. This section briefly introduces two main categories of models:

models derived from financial engineering, mathematics or econometrics, and models opting for a pragmatic approach of real estate risk (e.g. Geltner and de Neufville, 2018). These methodologies have in common not to rely on a risk model of real estate while assuming that real estate prices follow some kind of random walk.

METHODOLOGIES DERIVED FROM FINANCIAL ENGINEERING,
MATHEMATICS, AND ECONOMETRICS

Although the literature on pricing models of real estate derivatives is limited, Tunaru (2017) identifies three categories of models customarily applied in academic research:

- Equilibrium models pricing contingent claims on a real estate index (e.g. Geltner and Fisher, 2007),
- No-arbitrage models based on the no-arbitrage valuation principle which is applicable in markets assumed to be complete (e.g. Syz, 2008),
- Econometric and mathematical based models which focus on econometric specifications rather than financial engineering specifications (e.g. Fabozzi, Shiller and Tunaru, 2009, 2012).

These models are designed for index-based derivatives, i.e. the most aggregated level in real estate analysis. Among the three categories, the third one is undoubtedly the most interesting insofar as it takes into account real estate prices' empirical characteristics (i.e. serial correlation) whilst the other two categories are simply trying to make real estate fit into conceptual frameworks developed for other asset classes. Interestingly, all three categories of models tend to refer to a random walk process (e.g. Van Bragt et al., 2015 who mention a random walk with a drift).

Markedly, these models consider real estate in its financial dimension only. Fabozzi et al. (2012) affirm that "for a commercial real estate index describing the market in aggregate, it is better to model this asset as a financial asset". When it comes to the hedonic value methodology and the related hedonic variables, they add: "In contrast [to residential property], commercial property prices are driven mainly by their investment attributes and the resulting economic value is related to both general and local economic conditions". Hence, according to these models, one should not worry about underlying commercial properties' characteristics such as size, age, location, and quality.

Considering real estate price dynamics at the aggregate level as a totally abstract process oblivious of actual physical assets and their space markets makes these three categories of models appear disconnected from the reality of real estate risk. Abstraction cannot make up for the lack of a comprehensive risk model of real estate informing these pricing models. In effect, notwithstanding their commendable search for scientific rigor, most models struggle to price real estate derivatives in a satisfactory manner. Case in point: no-arbitrage models assume a complete real estate market, which is notoriously not the case in practice since commercial real estate markets are inherently incomplete (Tunaru, 2017).

GELTNER AND DE NEUFVILLE (2018)'S EIGHT-FACTOR REAL ESTATE PRICE DYNAMICS

In contrast to the previous models' extreme abstraction, Geltner and de Neufville (2018) propose an eight-factor model whose interest stems for its non-dogmatic approach to real estate market price dynamics. It is "as much an art as a science" affirm the authors.

The eight components are: (1) long-term trend rate, (2) volatility, (3) cyclicality, (4) mean reversion, (5) inertia (autoregression), (6) price dispersion (noise), (7) idiosyncratic shift, and (8) black swans. Components 1–5 as well as component 8 occur at the aggregate (index) level. They are systematic whereas components 6 and 7 occur at the property level and do not appear in indices. Once identified and modelled, these eight components can be put together to simulate real estate market price dynamics aiming for "the generation of future pricing scenarios that 'look' realistic and plausible [...]". It is interesting to go over each component individually and point out important assumptions made by the authors:

1   *Long-term trend rate*: Structure depreciation affects property value negatively but might be more than offset by land value over time;
2   *Volatility*: It "refers to the way prices change randomly, unpredictably from one period to the next". It supposes that some degree of "memoryless" random walk type influence applies to real estate price dynamics;
3   *Cyclicality*: Real estate asset markets are notorious for their cyclicality which might or might not reflect the space market;
4   *Mean-reversion*: Prices tend to 'auto-correct' and revert back towards the long-term trend in component 1 above. Powerful economic fundamentals in terms of structure and land might be at play;
5   *Inertia*: Price changes in one period tend to echo price changes in the previous period though "autoregression";
6   *Price dispersion or noise* which occurs at the property level (individual transactions);
7   *Idiosyncratic shift*: It occurs at the property level when "individual property paths evolve separate from and independent of the market value index";
8   *Black swans*: Also known as 'fat tail events' which rarely happen, and contrary to volatility, result in unexpected losses.

This combination of eight components yields a model-free methodology with many strong points. First, the model is firmly rooted in the behaviour of real estate markets and assets, especially assets' physicality over time (component 1), and the asset market's well-identified characteristics (components 3, 4, 5). Second, it accommodates property idiosyncrasies at the property level as a result of a transaction (component 6: impact on local real estate market) or a property's uniqueness (component 7). But, it paradoxically combines a memoryless random walk (component 2) and long memory/memory-laden processes (components 1, 4, 5), which questions the actual nature of uncertainty in real estate. Geltner and de Neufville (2018) assert: "our pricing factors substantially enhance the traditional random walk process, by recognizing the special features of the dynamics of real estate markets". It is undoubtedly the case. However, what does the eight-factor model mean with respect to the type of random walk applicable to commercial real estate assets?

When put together, the eight components seem to point at the impact of investment horizon on uncertainty with risk decreasing over long horizons.[22] Indeed, real estate price dynamics appears a lot more uncertain in the short run than in the long run. So, does commercial real estate follow a time-varying enhanced random walk, i.e. relatively strong degree of randomness in the short run but mitigated by other potent processes in the long run? Notwithstanding its practicality and in the absence of an underlying risk model, the methodology cannot answer these questions, nor does it help in terms of risk factors to be used in order to hedge real estate risk.

3.3.2   The genetics-based model and the irrelevance of classical random walk for commercial properties

In contrast to the models presented so far, the genetics-based model can help explain the nature of real estate price dynamics at the property level. The main contribution of the genetics framework is to fill in the gap left by the other models which almost exclusively focus on the macro-scale. As pointed out by Pai and Geltner (2007), the real estate industry understands "fairly well the big picture of what the typical or average real estate investment return should be – but not very well how a given property's or market segment's expected return should differ from that average". Aggregate-level studies are fine for index-based derivatives, but they are of little value for property-level risk hedging. The analysis below focuses on the random walk at the micro-scale.

The classical random walk hypothesis which underpins the efficient market hypothesis has been applied to commercial real estate. Following in the footsteps of Alfred Cowles's (1933) seminal study, Ling (2005) goes on "a random walk down main street" where he finds no evidence to support the predictability of private commercial real estate returns in US institutional-quality commercial properties. However, there is no decisive and consistent evidence in the literature to support the random walk hypothesis in real estate finance. First-order autocorrelation of appraised returns is a well-researched issue in real estate finance, an issue amply covered in the academic literature (e.g. Geltner, 1989). Private property markets are notoriously inefficient, plagued by asymmetry of information, illiquidity, and high transaction costs.

As a matter of fact, the random walk hypothesis, no matter how much one refines it (e.g. geometric random walk) is not conceptually compatible with direct commercial real estate. In its various incarnations (Ibe, 2013), the random walk hypothesis embodies a clear-cut disconnect between the 'walker' and the environment. This is the exact opposite to real estate where the environment is an integral part of a building's ability to produce returns, and vice versa. The Brownian motion, as the continuous-time analogue of the random walk, might be a well suited diffusion process for liquid markets, but not for an illiquid and heterogeneous asset as physically and sociologically immersed in its environment as commercial real estate.

Nineteenth-century economists who questioned the use of physics, in particular equilibrium thermodynamics, in analysing economic systems shed an interesting light on this issue. For instance, Veblen (1898) suggests that the only rational approach to economic system is to consider they orderly unfold through "a cumulative process of adaptation of means to ends that cumulatively change as the process goes on, both the agent and his environment being at any point the outcomes of the past". More concretely, Shiller (2008) who describes derivative markets for home prices explains that "other markets for liquid assets are nearly random walks" but not property which is so different "because there [might be] expectations of big price change".

In this context, the genetics-based model proposes an alternative to the classical concept of random walk. In genetics, there is no ambiguity: the expression of a polygenic complex trait in a given genotype is not random. Lecomte (2007) explains:

> Prices depend on assets' genes, some of which cannot be easily altered or modified (e.g., land which is at the core of real estate's physical dimension). Hence, what is randomness of assets whose returns are defined with what is essentially a deterministic model? [...] The concept of unqualified random walk in real estate is an aberration. Genetics defines randomness in a way that is not fortuitous but causal since linkages have known impact on traits.

Because of their essential physicality, real estate assets require a specific definition of randomness anchored in the space-time realm. Arrow (1951) brings an interesting perspective on the issue of uncertainty in real estate when identifying three classes of economic phenomena linked with uncertainty: (i) phenomena which are inherently concerned with uncertainty, such as gambling or insurance, (ii) phenomena "which are not related to uncertainty but nevertheless have no other conceivable explanation", and (iii) phenomena "whose relation to uncertainty is more remote and disputable". According to Arrow, contractual obligations such as leases fall in the second class.

One could argue that the application of the random walk in real estate is a misinterpretation of Arrow's stance on uncertainty. Pricing models at the aggregate level treat real estate as a class one phenomenon (e.g. by proxying real estate uncertainty with ready-made stochastic processes and diffusion processes taken straight out of mathematics textbooks). More realistically, Geltner and de Neufville (2018) opt for a class two phenomenon whereby the random walk anchored in a few of real estate's specific characteristics is enhanced and controlled. The genetics-based model selects the third class, arguing after Fisher (1930) that "risk varies inversely with knowledge".

Lecomte (2007) asserts that genetics

> has the potential to be to real assets what the Brownian motion is to finan-
> cial assets, by defining and modelling randomness in process. [...] For any
> given environment, variability in [total] returns is deterministic, dependent
> on complex, though identifiable, patterns.

Thus, real estate follows a multifactorial causal walk, which is highly idiosyncratic, but not random. There is unquestionably the possibility that extreme idio-
syncrasy at the property level be mistaken for randomness at the aggregate level.

The key to modelling real estate price dynamics at the property level is the
ability to accommodate the changing nature of interactions between a building's
genotype and the space-time varying environment, i.e. to encapsulate real estate's
paradox of apparent stability amid constant changes. Kummerow (2000) sums it
up as follows:

> Processes [in real estate] are not strictly stationary in the long run, but they
> do have some structural stability and in normal times evolve slowly enough
> to allow imprecise forecasts. For these disorderly systems, parsimonious gen-
> eral models are more likely to fail than those that take account of local
> circumstances.

Hence, whatever process is selected should avoid a 'one-size-fits-all' solution.
Ad-hoc micro-scale stochastic processes derived from the genetics-based model
should replace a systematic top-down approach modelled after stochastic processes employed for pricing standardised financial derivatives. In that respect, the
genetics-based model provides a fully consistent approach which encompasses a
risk model as well as a wide-ranging notion of price dynamics to be used in real estate derivatives pricing. It is new in real estate finance, and unusual in finance to
underpin a stochastic process by a risk model concerned with veracity in reflect-
ing a particular asset's behaviour inclusive of its environment at the micro-scale
(e.g. property type and sub-type, local market). After all, the Brownian motion
was originally inferred by Scottish botanist Robert Brown from observing small
pollen particles in a drop of water, not the stock market (Ibe, 2013).

That said, the fact a stochastic process is disconnected from an asset's true nature is not a problem in itself. Noticeably, according to Fama (1965), the random
walk is unlikely to provide an exact description of the behaviour of stock market
prices. But, it is still acceptable for practical purposes "even though it does not fit
the facts exactly".

Monte Carlo simulations of the genetics-based model can be run to infer a
reasonable portrayal of price dynamics for a given property in a specific environment through simulated future scenarios. The 'eyeball test' of price paths mentioned by Geltner and de Neufville (2018) does matter here. Thus, the danger of
this micro-scale experimental methodology is to claim generalisation that it is
not entitled to. Simulation results are highly idiosyncratic and represent plausible

asset-level price dynamics. To infer aggregate level price dynamics, interactions between proforma property type genotypes (standardised physical structure C1 and lease structure C2) and the least granular levels of location (G1 global, G2 country, G3 region on C3) would have to be selected instead and simulated within the confines of the model. Irrespective of the simulations' aggregation level, interactions between genotype x environment will have to be defined through parametric rules part of genetics-based models. The complexity of these rules might range from simple (e.g. dominance of one gene not directly impacted by the environment) to complex (e.g. dominant genes directly impacted by modifiers and the environment) and extremely complex (e.g. polygenic and indirect environmental interactions with time effect). Comparative scenario-based simulations of total return paths under different controlled hypotheses (e.g. same building in different environments, different buildings in same environment) could then be envisioned. These pro forma models known as 'avatars' could serve as underlying to real estate derivatives. A market for pro forma genotypes in controlled environments known as 'Market for Avatars' is introduced in the section below. Suffice to say that a lot of research work will be needed to turn the genetics-based model from a conceptual framework to a practical tool catering to industry professionals' hedging needs.

4 Markets for trading factor-based real estate derivatives

4.1 Theoretical background and challenges

To become tradable instruments, factor-based real estate derivatives will have to come with a specific apparatus enabling their efficient trading on sustainable and transparent markets. Contrary to index-based real estate derivatives which can easily fit within the well-oiled format of cash-settled financial derivatives markets, factor-based property derivatives pose a challenge for existing markets. The section below presents three new formats that a market for factor-based derivatives could adopt. These formats (i) combine privately exchanged derivatives on over-the-counter markets and publicly traded derivatives on standardised markets (*market for factors*), (ii) radically redesign the way derivatives are traded on public markets (*market for hedging effectiveness*), or (iii) propose to trade truly synthetic property derivatives (*market for avatars*).

As pointed out by Shiller (2004a), "historic changes in our risk management institutions are less frequent than historical innovations in science or engineering". There is undoubtedly a certain level of inertia from market authorities when it comes to creating new alternative platforms for trading assets and derivatives. Numerous layers of regulation and market leaderships' rightful concern about any new contracts' profitability are valid reasons for this apparent conservatism.

However, markets are not a universal truth set in stone. Existing markets are social phenomena or "accidents of history" (Shiller, 1993). They were originally created to facilitate the workings of the economy at a given time. Societal needs coupled with legal and regulatory constraints led to the market formats that we know today. But, fundamentally, as underscored by MacKenzie (2006), "markets are means to be tinkered with, modified, redesigned, improved [...]. They are not forces of nature, but human creations". Concretely, markets should evolve with technological progresses and access to new resources such as large databases powered by big data. Undoubtedly, information technology will play an even bigger role in the design and efficient operation of new markets for complex financial contracts in the future (Shiller, 2004b).

Hedging effectiveness is an important factor in the success of a new derivatives market. Hedging is indeed the 'basic function' of a derivatives market (Shiller, 2004b). Achieving high levels of hedging effectiveness has long been a hurdle for commercial real estate derivatives, especially at the micro-scale (Lecomte and Mcintosh, 2006). Under the existing index-based market format, the problem is inherently structural and cannot be solved. According to Fabozzi, Shiller and Tunaru (2009, 2010), property heterogeneity which is a source of market incompleteness for index-based real estate derivatives market is responsible for less than optimal hedging effectiveness. Due to the lack of homogeneity in the underlying assets, it is very difficult to establish a liquid property derivatives market. Hence, the litmus test of any alternative real estate derivatives market boils down to hedging effectiveness and liquidity that should come with it. It is, of course, easier said than done.

To pass this test, derivatives markets should cater to two types of market participants: hedgers and speculators. Duffie and Rahi (1995) stress that both hedgers and speculators are required for the long-term viability of a new security. A market needs to target both groups insofar as speculators depend on hedgers for trading opportunities while hedgers need speculators to create exchange-wide liquidity necessary for the efficient transfer of risk, i.e. price discovery owing to transparent pricing and hedging effectiveness thanks to a wide range of liquid instruments being available for trading. Markets presented here aim to provide effective hedging for real estate investors while not impeding speculators' ability to intervene.

Beyond market structure and technology, innovation supposes to change mindsets. Psychological framing will play a crucial role in the way stakeholders view a market for factor-based hedges. Whether a real estate 'micro market' is major enough to create a "sound frame [for] long term risk management vehicles" or just an incremental improvement within "consumers' habitual frame of reference" (Shiller, 2004b) can only be assessed in retrospect.

The three market formats explored below have in common to adopt the notion of property heterogeneity as their driving principle. Whilst most financial markets implicitly cater to a 'top-down' approach of risk, markets proposed here are 'bottom-up' markets which accommodate commercial real estate's multivariate risk structure. They frame real estate risk in a markedly different manner from that usually applied in real estate finance. These markets aim to look at property heterogeneity not as an undecipherable riddle, but instead as the fundamental tenet of commercial real estate risk which, positioned at the core of factor-based derivatives markets, should define markets' ability to provide effective hedging at all scales.

4.2 Cash-settled market for factor derivatives

The first market microstructure susceptible to accommodate factor-based derivatives is a market for cash-settled factor derivatives. This market finds its roots in Shiller's writings about real estate derivatives and derivative markets over the years. In *Macro Markets* (1993), he mentions contracts that could cash-settle on the basis of factors identified from "data on service flows (or prices) of real estate of narrowly defined kinds, or in tiny geographical areas". Ten years later, in *The New Financial Order* (2003), Shiller asks for "pure markets, markets for conceptually simple claims, not a hodgepodge of claims".

Lecomte (2007) suggests the creation of a hybrid market for cash-settled pure factors "whose values are not derived from some cash market's underlying price but from their contribution to the asset's total risk". In theory, pure factors are equivalent to risk factors in the genetics-based model. However, in practice, the market for factors boils down to two parallel markets: one for macro-factors and one for micro-factors.

4.2.1 Cash-settled macro-factor derivatives

The market for macro-factors can be modelled after the market for economic derivatives introduced in 2002 by Goldman Sachs and Deutsche Bank and transferred to the Chicago Mercantile Exchange in 2005. The economic derivatives market relies on the parimutuel mechanism described by Lange and Economides (2005). The parimutuel mechanism is a "call auction rather than a continuous auction". The technique used is called Parimutuel Digital Call Auction. Instruments are traded through a universal Dutch auction format (Barrau et al., 2005).

Economic derivatives are essentially over-the-counter contracts with economic indicators serving as underlyings. In his foreword to Baron and Lange's (2007) book on parimutuel future markets, Shiller mentions that:

> creating such a market is a radical departure from our normal ways of managing risks [...] The parimutuel structure for financial markets is an important invention in part because it deals with some of the barriers to achieving liquidity that stymied would-be founders of markets.

Digital options, vanilla options, and forwards on an array of underlyings were offered for auctions. The non-farm payroll market was the first to open in October 2002, followed by contingent claims on retail sales, levels of Institute for Supply Management's manufacturing diffusion index, initial employment claims, and the Eurozone harmonised CPI (Gürkaynak and Wolfers, 2007).

Although based on auctions, the market uses the same trading conventions as classic OTC markets where participants can buy and sell derivatives through an Interdealer broker. The market is essentially a prediction market (Chen and Pennock, 2010; Wolfers and Zitzewitz, 2010). Auctions deal with future unknown events. The organisers offer a series of different states (or events) to potential bidders. States are mutually exclusive, i.e. only one state can occur ex post. Once the outcome is made public, bidders with the winning state are paid off a certain amount of money which depends on the number of accepted orders. Barrau et al. (2005) underscore that the parimutuel auction mechanism should enable agents to "know beforehand their cash flow if the bid-event happens, which makes hedging easier".

In 2007, the CME decided to shutter the economics derivatives market because of low level of investor participation (Swidler, 2010). So what went wrong? When the partnership between Goldman Sachs and the CME was announced in June 2005, their joint press release boasted about "the wide variety of instruments available for trading [allowing] investors to tailor very precise hedges or exposures to economic indicator". Underlyings were indeed not the problem of this market. Besides, Barrau et al. (2005) show that when the parimutuel mechanism allows both long and short positions, market liquidity is not a problem either. It does not depend on the number of players in the auctions contrary to what would happen in a classic market for index-based derivatives. Something else in the market design did not quite work as planned. In line with this book's thesis against aggregate thinking in real estate finance, it seems that the market microstructure forgot one important point: hedgers did not view economic derivatives as an efficient way to hedge their portfolios.

As explained by Gadanecz, Moessner and Upper (2007), economic derivatives are first attractive to sophisticated traders "looking to speculate on data releases". Conversely, hedgers who think in terms of overall portfolio value and not economic indicators might not be so keen on "unbundling the sensitivity of asset prices to macroeconomic data". As a result of the market's limited attractiveness to hedgers, its growth was very constrained, ending up in a still-born market when the CME pulled the plugs.[23] Notwithstanding the high hopes initially raised by economics derivatives, the market could not survive the litmus test of hedging, not because it did not suit its purpose but simply because hedgers did not think they could benefit from such instruments.

In the case of factor-based real estate derivatives, this is where framing a new mindset by moving away from aggregate thinking will be instrumental in enabling a market for macro-factors to take off. Interestingly, a centrally organised contingent claims market for macro-factors, as part of larger risk management apparatus, is not asset class specific. It can apply across a wide range of assets, from financial assets to alternative assets like commodities, infrastructure, commercial real estate, and even art. Hence, provided 'nuclear financial economics' becomes sufficiently mainstream, its appeal could be wide and large, ensuring demand from both sophisticated traders and hedgers. But, this theorist dream of 'micro markets' might well be wishful thinking given the massive imprint of aggregate thinking on finance.

An interesting lesson to be learned from economic derivatives' untimely demise is the fact that hedgers have to be involved in the design and implementation of a new market. This involves optimal microstructure as well as selection of underlyings, i.e. in the case of commercial real estate, developers, property owners (e.g. REITs, Real Estate Operating Companies), real estate investors, and private equity fund managers have to be closely associated with any endeavour to create a market for factors. Alfred Marshall (1890) states that modification brought upon by inventors, organisers or financiers to the economy can only be sustainable if they "bring to a head a broad constructive movement which had long been in preparation". A market for macro-factors will therefore need time to build a broad consensus of all market players.

4.2.2 Cash-settled micro-factor derivatives

The parimutuel market mechanism can also apply to micro-factors. Markedly, with such specialised underlyings, the market's appeal would be significantly narrower than that of macro-factors. One can reasonably expect demand stemming from hedgers but very little interest from speculators under normal circumstances in the commercial real estate markets. This would obviously be a major constraint on the micro-factors market's growth potential. To overcome such hurdles, a market for micro-factors should: (i) pay extra attention to underlyings' definition and selection in order to meet hedgers' needs, (ii) focus on generic underlyings applicable to a large array of real estate players and assets in order to spur liquidity, and (iii) allow buy and short positions in the same way as the market for macro-factors.

4.2.3 Intrinsic shortcoming of a market for factor derivatives

A market for factor derivatives could potentially encompass a myriad of factorial underlyings and lead to an exuberance of instruments available for trading. This might be Arrow's ultimate objective of "a market for every risk and a price for every state of nature" (Shiller, 2004a). However, in practice, it is not necessarily optimal. Too many open contracts, be they on different underlyings or a range of expiration dates, may destabilise the market for factor derivatives and prevent it from gaining momentum. In a very stylised model, Brock, Hommes and Wagener (2009) show that when traders are heterogeneous, more hedging instruments represented by Arrow Debreu securities can increase volatility and negatively impact average welfare. Although the long-term horizon involved in commercial real estate risk hedging could help assuage this negative effect, it is still a concern.

Furthermore, economic derivatives exchanged through the parimutuel mechanism are customarily daily settlement contracts. Hence, they suppose very active management of the hedge, which is obviously time-consuming and costly for hedgers. Notwithstanding market completeness' theoretical importance, Geanakoplos (2004) notes that Arrow Debreu commodities are rarely traded as single "pure" securities, but instead as "unbreakable bundles [...] in second best transactions". He explains, "the more finely the commodities are described, the less likely are the commodity markets to have many buyers and sellers [...]". Arrow Debreu's model of separate markets for each commodity simultaneously meeting is therefore an idealisation, "the benchmark against which the real economy can be measured".

For real estate derivatives, cash-settled factor derivatives are not realistic. An alternative mode of trading factors should be devised. This is the purpose of the combinative real estate derivative model.

4.2.4 Combinative model of factor-based real estate derivatives

The combinative model of real estate derivatives embodies what Lecomte and McIntosh (2005) call "standardized customisation". An example of combinative derivative trading is reproduced in Appendix 1.6. To allow for standardisation necessary to foster market liquidity, all risk factors are bundled together in an aggregate hedge customised for a particular asset from a set of tradable factors. With standardised customisation, a real estate derivatives market captures as closely as possible real estate assets' unique risk while supporting a sustainable and liquid market for real estate derivatives.

Furthermore, a combinative derivative model provides the right format to implement multi-factor models of real estate risk which are dominated by one overriding factor (i.e. akin to first factor hedging in fixed income risk management in Appendix 1.2) and several others of lesser significance (e.g. Eichholtz et al., 1995). Miles and McCue (1982) and Hamelink et al. (2000) show that property type dominates other variables (e.g. geographic factors) in explaining US and UK real estate markets, respectively. Location can then be incorporated through economic bases capturing the importance of local economic activities on real estate returns.

The model in Lecomte (2007) supposes the combination of a futures contract on a specific property type or sub-type (appraised) price index with options linked to economic base, MSA, and an ad-hoc selection of macro-factors. A similar approach is used in the case study of London City office buildings presented in Appendix 1.4. All variables are standardised enough to make it impossible to directly identify a specific physical property and/or location so as to alleviate market authorities' fear of potential cash market manipulation. Pricing of a combinative hedge is equivalent to the pricing of a futures contract on an appraised real estate index (property type sub-index) with add-on options modifying the derivatives' payoff to better replicate a building's cash flows.

4.3 Market for hedging effectiveness

The second market format presented in this book is the market for hedging effectiveness. This market is meant to provide a "robust psychological framing [...] outside consumers' habitual frame of reference" (Shiller, 2004b). Instead of considering hedging effectiveness as the outcome of the hedging process, this market introduced in Lecomte (2007) positions hedging effectiveness as the central variable in selecting a hedge. In accordance with traditional hedging theory, the aim is to minimise basis risk, ideally reducing changes to basis to zero when spot price and derivative price move. If the change in basis is zero, then the hedge is perfect according to Ederington (1979). The market also aims to enable dynamic hedging strategies by enabling periodic rebalancing of the hedges depending on changes in the environment. Hedging is a basic rationale for derivatives markets. However, with heterogeneous assets, it is a challenge. This innovative market which is a high-tech variation on the cash-settled market for factors makes it possible to overcome this hurdle for commercial real estate.

4.3.1 Basic principles

The market is conceived with the same non-prescriptive use of factors as Riddiough's (1995) MIT exercise, but with the important addition of a multi-scale risk model of commercial real estate. Customarily, hedging effectiveness results from the choice of hedging instruments. It is a collateral measure on which users have no direct impact. Hedgers have to cope with basis risk which might be very large, e.g. when hedging with index-based real estate derivatives at the micro-scale level.

In the market for hedging effectiveness, hedging effectiveness is not a desirable 'side effect' of the choice of derivatives but the central criterion entered by users when they initiate their hedges. The desired level of hedging effectiveness, along with hedgers' time horizon, conditions the selection of factors among macro- and micro-factors. Such a market is essentially a market for hedgers although, with the proper market microstructure described below, it might appeal to traders as well. The initial factor selection at inception and dynamic rebalancing throughout the hedge's life are carried out owing to a risk engine which aggregates data about individual assets as well as all macro- and micro-factors.

4.3.2 Risk mapping and risk scans

The first step in the hedging process is to map risk factors for a particular property or portfolios of properties whose returns are to be hedged. The concept of mapping risk factors is borrowed from Value-at-Risk systems (Jorion, 2007). Lecomte (2007) explains that "though an iterative process, the system would map the risk profile of the asset(s) to be hedged and determine a risk scan". A risk scan is a disaggregation of a building's return volatility into macro- and micro-factors. It identifies each factor's contribution (in %) at time t when mapping takes place. As a risk scan provides a snapshot, risk mapping has to be conducted not only at the hedge's inception, but also on a periodic basis (e.g. daily) to allow for dynamic hedging strategies. Risk scans can actually be carried out on a continuous basis in order to capture any changes in the asset(s)' risk profile given exogenous changes in the environment over time and alert hedgers accordingly

4.3.3 Periodic rebalancing for dynamic hedging strategies

If after mapping risk factors for a property or portfolio of properties at the hedge's inception, the risk engine identifies that the desired level of hedging effectiveness is not achievable, it proposes the next best achievable level of hedging effectiveness given an ad-hoc selection of macro- and micro-factors. This initial factor combination enabling optimal level of hedging effectiveness at inception has then to be rebalanced periodically to capture changes in factors and cash asset's risk. The process supposes to have access to a lot of data such as time series of returns on individual assets. This would clearly be a problem for new buildings even though studies of comparable buildings could help make up for the lack of long-run time series.

Periodic rebalancing of factor combinations to optimise hedging effectiveness supposes that hedges be adjusted throughout their lives. At the time of each rebalancing, users can either (i) keep their hedges unchanged irrespective of changes in basis, (ii) decide to automatically adjust the factor combination to the new optimal hedge identified by the risk engine in order to maintain their initial hedging effectiveness (in which case the hedge is said to be *marked to basis*), or (iii) choose a new optimal factor combination among a selection proposed by the risk engine at slightly lower levels of hedging effectiveness than the optimal hedge in (ii) so as to reduce the cost of rebalancing. The price of a hedge quoted in terms of each US$1 million of underlying hedged asset(s) is affected by the desired level of hedging effectiveness, optimal factor combination and hedge's time horizon. The risk engine's output lists the optimal selection of factors as well as a confidence level for the desired level of hedging effectiveness at time t.

4.3.4 A market for hedgers

The market for hedging effectiveness is primarily a market for hedgers. Physical property owners looking to hedge their cash exposure would be short derivatives, say futures, on factor aggregates exchanged on such a market. As pointed out by Lecomte (2007), "tailor-made factor hedges would create a market with no-cross hedge basis risk, no mismatch of maturity, and no risk of manipulation in the underlying cash market". In theory, a market where it is all about managing basis should be a hedger's paradise. In practice, it would suppose that buildings' returns can be easily replicated by factors on offer, and that investors' time horizons perfectly fit with the periodicity of data releases (e.g. monthly or quarterly releases of most macro-variables).

Furthermore, for the market to succeed, it also needs to attract speculators. Hence, a cash-settled market for factors as described previously could operate in parallel to the digital platform powering the market for hedging effectiveness, the two being complementary segments of the same factor market. That is, the same factors selected by the risk engine in optimal hedges on the digital platform are listed concomitantly on the OTC market where all market participants can trade them.

Rebalancing hedges on the market for hedging effectiveness is frictionless (though not costless) compared with rebalancing hedges traded on traditional derivatives markets. As exemplified in Lecomte (2014) presented in Appendix 1.4, the frequency of underlying rebalancing for some buildings or portfolios of buildings can be so large that single index-based derivative instruments are preferred for the sake of cost and efficiency. Trading factors as part of aggregates driven by an overriding measure such as hedging effectiveness is a simple, though effective, way to overcome the hurdle of factors' selection and periodic rebalancing.

Figure 1.6 represents the workings of the market for hedging effectiveness with a risk engine gathering data, running risk scans and continuously assessing optimal hedges in view of optimising hedging effectiveness. The market requires a sophisticated technology platform with access to real-time data analytics capabilities. When the concept of this market was first introduced in Lecomte (2007), this point might have seemed a little far-fetched. With the rapid emergence of data analytics, this market seems much more reachable than ever, at least technically.

Box 1.2 summarises the main points underpinning the market for hedging effectiveness.

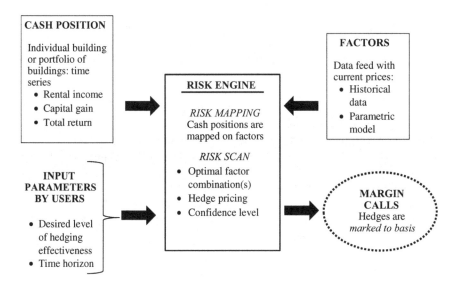

Figure 1.6 Factor-based market for hedging effectiveness – risk engine.

BOX 1.2: Factor-based market for hedging effectiveness

- Factors are not traded as Arrow-Debreu commodities but as bundles in an innovative way reversing the role of hedging effectiveness in the hedging process.
- The focus is not on derivatives' underlyings but on hedging effectiveness. Factors combine as hedge components in view of achieving a desired level of hedging effectiveness.
- The price of a hedge depends on the desired level of hedging effectiveness and hedge's time horizon entered by hedgers at the inception of the hedge.
- Risk scans are periodically conducted to determine the optimal factor combination(s) enabling the desired level of hedging effectiveness.
- Derivative positions are periodically 'marked to basis' in order to account for changes in optimal factor combinations over the hedge's life.
- The market is powered by a risk engine which enables dynamic hedging strategies.
- A cash-settled market for factors operates in parallel to the digital platform supporting the market for hedging effectiveness in order to attract both hedgers and speculators.

4.4 Market for property avatars

The third market presented in this chapter is called 'market for property avatars'. This new concept of market for real estate derivatives is a model-based market which implements the genetics framework of commercial real estate. It might sound like pipedreams, but the stars are slowly aligning for this market to materialise.

The principle underpinning the market microstructure is the basic idea that market completeness should not be gauged at the factor level but at the property level. Only the property level is truly representative of the cash market's idiosyncrasies. The market for avatars is designed to overcome property's lack of homogeneity.

By leveraging on a digital platform powered by digital technologies, it enables hedgers to have access to customised underlyings (with all their idiosyncratic physical, locational, and lease characteristics) covering the wide array of buildings they can potentially own either as stand-alone property or as part of property portfolios. Thus, a market for avatar properties is complete at the property level.

4.4.1 Putting flesh to the genetics-based model

Avatars are factor-based synthetic properties modelled according to the genetics framework. They serve as underlyings to real estate derivatives. In effect, avatar property derivatives act as alternatives to single property derivatives whose prospects as widely traded derivatives on standardised markets are limited due to the risk of "manipulation of the futures market via sales in the cash market" in commercial real estate (Shiller, 1993).

Avatars are engineered assets based on the chromosome model. Hedgers are able to select chromosomes and genes as well as genotypic and environmental interactions at inception of the hedge. Their selection defines an avatar property built to replicate as closely as possible their cash asset(s). Avatars are not frozen assets: the physical structure chromosome, the lease structure chromosome, and the location chromosome make up dynamic avatars akin to living organisms which interact with their space-time varying environment. Hence, avatars provide dynamic underlyings to real estate derivatives. An avatar property takes shape in its environment over time.

4.4.2 Hedging with property avatar derivatives

The avatar market does not rely on macro- and micro-variables contrary to the market for hedging effectiveness. Factors involved in avatars are similar to those in the genetics-based model. Avatars enable the process of synthetic replication of a property in all its dimensions and at all scales (from local to global). There are potentially two types of avatar underlyings: single property avatars and portfolio avatars (for portfolios of synthetic properties replicating portfolios of actual buildings). In essence, avatar underlyings are akin to extremely customised property-level indices of real estate assets.

The avatar market microstructure could be twofold:

- First, a public market for standardised avatars representing major archetypical property types and sub-types in large well-researched locations (neighbourhood, MSA, region, country);
- Second, in parallel to the public market, a private market for highly customised avatar hedges.

One would expect buildings falling into the average category to be hedged on the public segment of the market, and outliers to be hedged on the private segment of the market. The market for avatars is a market aimed at hedgers. To deal with basis, optimal avatars would be automatically selected by the market's risk engine for their hedging effectiveness with physical asset(s) whose returns are to be hedged. Avatars quoted in US$1 million units of underlying synthetic property would be tradable as bundles of chromosomes, but also ideally as independent chromosomes provided one is capable of pricing the relative contribution of each set of genes in the model. This is where variance partitioning presented before in this chapter might help build a market.

4.4.3 Pricing property avatars

One can envision that private real estate index providers who manage some of the largest databases of private commercial properties supply to avatar market promoters index components which can be used as building blocks to avatar derivatives' underlyings. Simulations of avatar properties' behaviours in actual real estate market conditions will have to be conducted. Taxonomies of avatars' behaviours and market conditions could be established in order to systematise the process. Real estate economists and valuers will play a central role in modelling the avatar market's numerous blocks. Without doubt, it would be a monumental undertaking. Some might even say sheer madness. Actually, the process towards property avatars has already started. Progresses in automated valuation models (AVMs) based on artificial intelligence, deep learning, and big data developments (RICS, 2017) are part of the trend leading to synthetic properties. Replication and hedging are a natural evolution for these models.

4.4.4 Property avatars and controlled experiments in real estate finance

The concept of avatar in real estate finance paves the way to sophisticated simulations in controlled environments akin to life sciences' experiments (Shipley, 2016). In particular, experiments controlling for exogenous environmental variables would make it possible to adopt a micro-scale approach to commercial real estate risk by testing causal hypotheses at the property level. Avatars' sensitivities to changes in physical structure, lease structure or location could be used to compare assets and portfolios, and to hedge risks derived from these three dimensions in the genetics-based model (e.g. options based on avatar total returns' sensitivities to changes in each of these dimensions, capturing physical obsolescence, vacancy risk, or location-induced economic risk, respectively).

4.4.5 Castles in the sky? Yes, but…

The market for hedging effectiveness and the market for avatars propose two different ways to aggregate factors into tradable derivative instruments. Both are the product of 'Ivory Tower' imagination. With the market for avatars, the analysis presented in this first chapter has gone full circle. It started with index-based real estate derivatives, and concludes with markets for factors traded as bundles or synthetic properties. The journey from theory to reality will undoubtedly be arduous and unpredictable if past attempts to launch real estate derivatives can tell us anything about a successful path to real estate finance innovations. Let's find solace in the fact that castles in the sky are nonetheless useful to 'think out of the box' and wonder about 'what could be'.

Notes

1 Physical settlement of index-based futures contracts as an alternative to cash settlement was initially explored by the Chicago Board of Trade to circumvent the law of Illinois prohibiting gambling (Brine and Poovey, 2017). In December 1981, the Commodity Futures Trading Commission and the Securities Exchange Commission eventually approved cash settlement of futures contracts on a stock index provided that the underlying index is broad enough.

2 Derman (1996) identifies three different classes of models in finance: fundamental models, phenomenological models, and statistical models, with the former two classes embodying "some sort of cause and effect". The genetics-based model of commercial real estate is a phenomenological model which "provides a description or an analogy to help visualize something that cannot be directly observed". But, it also acts as a fundamental model which sets "a system of postulates and data together with a means of drawing dynamical inferences from them".

3 Geanakoplos (2004) notes that "Arrow-Debreu characteristics of the world" may be intrinsically connected to the objet itself (e.g. geographical and temporal locations), or not (e.g. name of final consumer in Arrow, 1969) as long as they are observable.

4 Regarding the use of Asset Pricing Theory-APT in real estate (Fundamental Valuation Model of which FLM is a variation), Draper and Findlay (1982) point out that

> though the factors are' located' statistically, they are not identified with real-world variables (i.e., the methodology of APT is aimed at estimating return, not providing an exhaustive list of factors). […] An application of the APT to real estate does not require all the individual property micro-data or the general economy data.

5 Riddiough (1995) explains that "[As] real estate risk and return are derived in good part from local economic activity, […], focusing at a regionally refined level may better focus the replicating security selection process and therefore provide better overall results". Markedly, as pointed out by Brown and Brown (1996) who apply this hedging framework to UK Commercial real estate markets (MIT Thesis), the MIT exercise is an extension of earlier research. Papers by Giliberto (1990, 1992, 1993) and Kerson

(1994) already explore the "idea of linking private real estate returns [Russell/NCREIF Index] to traded security returns, especially REIT returns" as part of dynamic hedging strategies. Giliberto's hedge (1993) combines a long position in the National Association of Real Estate Investment Trusts Equity index (NAREIT) and a short position in the S&P 500 in order to eliminate systematic risk. Kerson (1994) constructs "Market-hedged Real Estate Index" (MaREI) by using the Wilshire Real Estate Securities Index (WRE) and a short position in the Russell 2000.

6 Miles, Cole and Guilkey (1990) explain that

> the logic behind the pricing equations [of their model] follows basic valuation methodology. This methodology holds that the value of an income-producing property is a positive function of its stabilized net income and a negative function of a market capitalization rate, with adjustments for the variety of factors that make each property unique.

7 Guilkey, Miles and Cole's (1989) pricing equations include different variables "proxying for each determinant [of value] to reflect differences among property types". For instance:

- *office buildings*: the number of stories (market location), change in county population (market's location relative to the nation as a whole: in-nation location), historic property cash flows (operating history), the amount of capital improvements and the holding period (physical condition) and the number of major credit tenants and percentage of pass-throughs relative to lease maturity (impact of existing leases)
- *retail properties*: change in per capita income (in-nation location)
- *industrial properties*: distance to an interstate highway (market location), wholesale earnings (in-nation location).

8 The top 15 aspects of risk identified in the IPD survey of risk assessment and management in the UK property industry (2000) are: income/structures, covenant strength, economic obsolescence, liquidity, location, management issues, economic context, national market factors, contamination/ environment, local market factors, sector bias, yield level/ shift/ relativity, market/portfolio/asset volatility, diversification issues, and lettability/ occupier potential.

9 "Fundamental valuation characteristics" in Hoag (1980) include location, property type, size, and age. This information is combined with economic and demographic variables (such as business inventories, construction costs, transportation access, and population), transaction prices and cash flows to estimate a valuation function "composed of weights for the value of each fundamental characteristics". These weights represent "the responsiveness of property value to changes in the fundamental factors". The fundamental factors are used to "objectively estimate the value of a property at any point in time".

10 For Cambridge economist Alfred Marshall (1890), "economics is a branch of biology broadly interpreted", which deals with "a matter of which the inner nature and constitution, as well as the outer form, are constantly changing".

11 The notion of buildings as conscious living organisms and the reference to biological concepts have been employed in the smart building literature in order to characterise smart buildings' intelligence as well as their bidirectional interactions with occupants and the broader environment (e.g. Warwick, 2013; Turner, 2016).

12 The genetics-based model's embedded dichotomy between phenotype and genotype as well as its inherent dynamism are consistent with Graaskamp's (1970) view that the physical nature of real estate is misleading insofar as "real estate is essentially a very dynamic process. We see brick and mortar when we look, rather than perceiving these static elements as a manifestation of a very dynamic process underlying the tangible property".

13 As explained by Milton Friedman (1966) quoting Alfred Marshall,

> a theory is, in general, a complex intermixture of two elements. In part, it is a "language" designed to promote 'systematic and organized methods of reasoning'. In part, it is a body of substantive hypotheses designed to abstract essential features of complex reality.

14 For a model primarily anchored in the money-time realm, two metric traits (e.g. income return and capital appreciation) can form the phenotype under study in the genetics-based model. They are considered as 'correlated characters' whose observed values display phenotypic correlation. Genetics of correlated characters would have to be employed in modelling the two traits (Falconer and Mackay, 1996). The risk model considers total return as a single phenotype for the sake of efficiency since the trait of interest is actually total return.

15 One of the main questions to address when designing a genetics-based model of commercial real estate is how to account for the multiplicity of genotypes in a population of buildings. In effect, the model must deal with extreme heterogeneity within one species only. How to do so? In a genetics context, buildings form a single species and share most of their genetic makeup notwithstanding extreme phenotypic diversity. In terms of genotype, diversity comes from the three chromosomes: (i) structural diversity per property type and within each property type, (ii) locational diversity, (iii) space usage diversity. Amusingly, animals such as dogs display very similar phenotypic diversity to buildings: one species with a myriad of different breeds. In fact, dogs are so diverse that Darwin wrongly suggested they might have been founded from more than one species. Yet dogs are not necessarily the easiest model to get inspiration from in order to design a structural model for building's DNA as they come with 78 chromosomes (compared with 46 for humans). The generic model presented here contains three chromosomes only. As research develops over time, one could envision a more complex genotypic framework for buildings.

16 The need to narrow down the scope of such model either functionally or geographically is mentioned by Shiller (1993) who suggests the use of "narrowly defined kinds" or "tiny geographical areas" for factor-based cash-settled macro-markets.

17 As an illustration of the concept of gene dominance in the genetics-based model, Lecomte (2007) explains: "Research shows that property type is more important than region for explaining returns in US commercial real estate. Hence, for US commercial real estate, the property type gene is dominant over the region gene (structure over location). Interestingly, genetics makes it possible to qualify this dominance. An application is shown in Appendix 1.5 with the concept of gene regulatory network and synchronicity map.

18 Kummerow (2000) highlights that for Graaskamp,

> the answer to a real estate question is always 'it depends'. [...] Generalizations are risky. Relationships that hold in one context may not in another. Theory provides little useful guidance; one has to look at the details to see what is feasible in a particular case.

19 The concept of synchronicity used in the genetics-based model is a direct reference to Swiss psychiatrist Carl G. Jung (1875–1961) who defined synchronicity as an "acausal connecting principle". Synchronicity allows scholars to think broadly about complex phenomena and free themselves from the diktat of causality.

20 Friedman (1966) explains that due to the reliance on uncontrolled experience, 'assumptions' play an especially important role in economic analysis. In particular, there might be more than a unique set of assumptions to explain a certain class of phenomena. As a result, choices have to be made

> on the grounds of the resulting economy, clarity, and precision in presenting the hypothesis; their capacity to bring indirect evidence to bear on the validity of the

hypothesis [...] by bringing out its connection with other hypotheses dealing with related phenomena [...].

21 Variance partitioning can be applied to the study of a single building by considering a time series of periodic total return at the property level as a series of observations of the same character immersed in a space-time varying environment. The mean of these measurements is the phenotypic value of the individual building P(n), where n is the number of measurements made (Falconer and Mackay, 1996). Then, $V_{P(n)} = V_G + V_{EG} + V_{ES}/n$. As n increases, $V_{P(n)} \to V_G + V_{EG}$.

Given that the measurements are taken from the same building, the genotypic structure of the building might change only marginally from one period to the next. Changes might involve observable changes to lease structure genes and unobservable changes to the grade gene on the physical structure chromosome (C_1G_3) due to its interaction with time in the model. Hence, over short time periods, an individual building's V_G captures the impact of time on variation in periodic total return while V_{EG} and V_{ES} can be assumed to be constant ($\Delta V_{EG} = \Delta V_{ES} = 0$). Thus, $\Delta V_{P(n)} = \Delta V_G$ = impact of time on total return through the grade gene. Conversely, in case there are important changes in a building's genotype (e.g. lease expiration) and/or environment over time, a period-by-period variance partitioning at the property level could be useful to unbundle the dynamic impact that these changes might have on a property's ability to generate total return. This is as close as one can get to a controlled experimental environment in (ex post) real estate studies.

22 The implicit differentiation between short-run and long-run uncertainty in Geltner and de Neufville (2018)'s eight factor model is consistent with the literature. MacKinnon and Al-Zaman (2009) who study the predictability of direct real estate returns assess that due to mean-reversion, risk decreases with horizon even though investors with long investment horizons (over 10 years) are dealing with weaker mean reversion for real estate than for stocks.

23 The most popular underlying economic indicator traded on the CME economic derivatives market was US Non-Farm Payrolls. It averaged only US$9 million per auction, which was obviously not sufficient to justify a full-blown market (Gadanecz et al., 2007).

References

Ahluwalia K. (2009) *Genetics*, New Delhi: New Age International Publisher.

Ambrose B., and Nourse H. (1993) Factors influencing capitalization rates, *Journal of Real Estate Research*, 8:2, pp. 221–238.

Arrow K. (1951) Alternative approaches to the theory of choice in risk-taking situations, *Econometrica*, 19:4, pp. 404–437.

Arrow K. (1964) The role of securities in the optimal allocation of risk bearing, *Review of Economic Studies*, 31:2, pp. 91–96.

Arrow K., (1969), The organization of economic activity: Issues pertinent to the choice of market vs. non-market allocation, Joint economic committee, The analysis of public expenditure: The PPB system, Government Printing Office, Washington, DC (1969), pp. 47–64.

Bachelier L. (1900) *Théorie de la speculation, in Louis Bachelier's Theory of Speculation: The Origins of Modern Finance*, edited and translated by M. Davis and A. Etheridge, Princeton, Oxford: Princeton University Press, 2006.

Baron K, and Lange J. (2007) *Parimutuel Applications in Finance: New Markets for New Risks*, New York: Palgrave-Macmillan.

Barrau G., Zerda A., Wang J., and Argaiz V. (2005) Analysis of an economic option market based on parimutuel auctions, *Stanford University, Department of Management Science & Engineering, Working Paper.*

Baum A. (2015) Property derivatives, in *Real Estate Investment: A Strategic Approach*, 3rd edition (Baum A., ed), London: Routledge.

Bell D. (1980) Models and reality in economic discourse, *Public Interest* (special issue).

Bernstein P. (1995) Risk as a history of ideas, *Financial Analysts Journal*, 51:1, pp. 7–11.

Blundell G., Fairchild S., and Goodchild R. (2005) Managing portfolio risk in real estate, *Journal of Property Research*, 22:2 & 3, pp. 115–136.

Booth P., Matysiak G., and Ormerod P. (2002) *Risk Measurement and Management for Real Estate Portfolios*, Report for the Investment Property Forum (IPF), London.

Breitung J., and Eickmeier S. (2005) Dynamic factor models, *Deutsche Bundesbank, Discussion Paper*, Series 1: Economic Studies, 38.

Brennan T., Cannaday R., and Colwell P. (1984) Office rent in the Chicago CBD, *Real Estate Economics*, 12:3, pp. 243–260.

Brine K., and Poovey M. (2017) *Finance in America: An Unfinished Story*, Chicago: University of Chicago Press.

Brock W., Hommes C., and Wagener F. (2009) More hedging instruments may destabilize markets, *Journal of Economic Dynamics and Control*, 33:1, pp. 1912–1928.

Brooks C., and Tsolacos S. (1999) The impact of economic and financial factors on UK property performance, *Journal of Property Research*, 16:2, pp. 139–152.

Brown C., and Brown T. (1996) *Liquefying Risk in the UK Commercial Real Estate Market*, MIT Department of Architecture, MSc Real Estate Development thesis (T. Riddiough, advisor), September.

Brown G., and Matysiak G. (2000) *Real Estate Investment*, London: Financial Times/Prentice Hall, 708 p.

Bruggemann W., Chen A., and Thibodeau T. (1984) Real estate investment funds: Performance and portfolio considerations, *Journal of the American Real Estate and Urban Economics Association*, 12:3, pp. 333–354.

Carlton D. (1984) Futures markets: Their purpose, their history, their growth, their successes and failures, *Journal of Futures Markets*, 4:3, pp. 237–271.

Cartwright N. (1980) Do the laws of physics state the facts? *Pacific Philosophical Quarterly*, 61:1–2, pp. 75–84.

Chan K., Hendershott P., and Sanders A. (1990) Risk and return on real estate: Evidence from equity REITs, *Journal of the American Real Estate and Urban Economics Association*, 18:4, pp. 431–451.

Chen S., Hsieh C., and Jordan B. (1997) Real estate and the arbitrage pricing theory: Macrovariables vs. derived factors, *Real Estate Economics*, 25:3, pp. 505–523.

Chen Y., and Pennock D. (2010) Designing markets for prediction, *AI Magazine*, 31:4, pp. 42–52.

Chen N., Roll R., and Ross S. (1986) Economic forces and the stock market, *Journal of Business*, 59:3, pp. 383–403.

Clapp J. (1980) The intermetropolitan location of office activities, *Journal of Regional Science*, 20, pp. 387–399.

Clapp J., Goldberg M., and Myers D. (1994) Crisis in methodology: Paradigms vs. practice in real estate research, in *Appraisal, Market Analysis, and Public Policy in Real Estate: Essays in Honor of James Graaskamp* (DeLisle J. and Sa-Aadu J., eds), Boston: Kluwer Academic Publishers, pp. 107–132.

Clapp J., and Myers D. (2000) Graaskamp and the definition of rigorous research, in *Essays in Honor of James Graaskamp: Ten Years Later* (DeLisle J. and Worzala E., eds), Boston: Kluwer Academic Publishers, pp. 341–364.

Cowles A. (1933) Can stock market forecasters forecast? *Econometrica*, 1:3, pp. 309–324.

Crosby N., Jackson C., and Orr A. (2016) Refining the real estate pricing model, *Journal of Property Research*, 33:4, pp. 332–358.

De Wit I., and Van Dijk R. (2003) The global determinants of direct office real estate returns, *The Journal of Real Estate Finance and Economics*, 26:1, pp. 27–45.

Debreu G. (1959) *Theory of Value: An Axiomatic Analysis of Economic Equilibrium.* Cowles Foundation Monograph 17, New Haven: Yale University Press.

DeLisle J. (2000) Graaskamp: A holistic perspective, in *Essays in Honor of James Graaskamp: Ten Years Later* (DeLisle J. and Worzala E., eds), Boston: Kluwer Academic Publishers, pp. 51–85.

Derman E. (1996) *Model Risk*, Goldman Sachs, Quantitative Strategies Research Notes, April.

DesRosiers F., Theriault M., and Menetrier L. (2005) Spatial versus non-spatial determinants of shopping center rents: Modelling location and neighbourhood-related factors, *Journal of Real Estate Research*, 27:3, pp. 293–320.

Draper D., and Findlay M. (1982) Capital asset pricing and real estate valuation, *Journal of the American Real Estate Association and Urban Economics*, 10, pp. 152–183.

Dubin R., Pace R., and Thibodeau T. (1999) Spatial autoregresion techniques for real estate data, *Journal of Real Estate Literature*, 7, pp. 79–96.

Duffie D., and Rahi R. (1995) Financial market innovation and security design: An introduction, *Journal of Economic Theory*, 65, pp. 1–42.

Ederington L. (1979) The hedging performance of new futures markets, *Journal of Finance*, 34:1, pp. 157–170.

Eichholtz P., Hoesli M., MacGregor B., and Nanthakumaran N. (1995) Real estate portfolio diversification of property type and region, *Journal of Property Finance*, 6:3, pp. 39–59.

Fabozzi F., Shiller R., and Tunaru R. (2009) Hedging real estate risk, *Journal of Portfolio Management*, 35:5, pp. 92–103.

Fabozzi F., Shiller R., and Tunaru R. (2010) Property derivatives for managing European real estate risk, *European Financial Management*, 16:1, pp. 8–26.

Fabozzi F., Shiller R., and Tunaru R. (2012) A pricing framework for real estate derivatives, *European Financial Management*, 18:5, pp. 762–789.

Falconer D., and Mackay T. (1996) *Introduction to Quantitative Genetics*, 4th edition, England: Pearson.

Fama E. (1965) Random walks in stock market prices, *Financial Analysts Journal*, 21:5, pp. 55–59.

Feynman R. (1964) *Lectures on Physics*, Reading: Addison Wesley Longman, 1552 p.

Feynman R. (1985) *Surely, You are Joking, Mr. Feynman: Adventures of a Curious Character*, New York: W.W. Norton & Company.

Figlewski S. (1984) Hedging performance and basis risk in stock index futures, *Journal of Finance*, 39:3, pp. 657–669.

Fisher I. (1930) *The Theory of Interest*, New York: The Macmillan Company.

Fisher J. (2005) New strategies for commercial real estate investment and risk management, *Journal of Portfolio Management – Special Real Estate Issue*, 32, pp. 154–162.

Fisher J., Geltner D., and Webb R. (1994) Value indices of commercial real estate: A comparison of index construction methods, *Journal of Real Estate Finance and Economics*, 9, pp. 137–164.

Fishkin C. (2006) *The Shape of Risk*, Basingstoke: Palgrave Macmillan.

Friedman M. (1966) The methodology of positive economics, in *Essays in Positive Economics* (Friedman M., ed), Chicago: University of Chicago Press, pp. 3–16, 30–43.

Gadanecz B., Moessner R., and Upper C. (2007) Economic derivatives, *BIS Quarterly*, March, pp. 69–81.

Gay G., and Kolb R. (1983) The management of interest rate risk, *Journal of Portfolio Management*, 9:2, p. 4.

Geanakoplos J. (2004) The Arrow-Debreu model of general equilibrium, *Cowles Foundation for Research in Economics at Yale University*, Cowles Foundation Paper No. 1090.

Geltner D. (1989) Estimating real estate's systematic risk from aggregate level appraisal-based returns, *Journal of the American Real Estate and Urban Economics Association*, 17:4, pp. 463–481.

Geltner D., and de Neufville R. (2018) *Flexibility and Real Estate Valuation under Uncertainty: A Practical Guide for Developers*, Cambridge: Wiley-Blackwell.

Ghysels E. (1998) On stable factor structures in pricing of risk: Do time-varying betas help or hurt? *Journal of Finance*, 53:2, pp. 549–573.

Giliberto S.M. (1990) Equity real estate investment trusts and real estate returns, *Journal of Real Estate Research*, Summer, pp. 259–263.

Giliberto S.M. (1992) Measuring real estate returns: The hedged REIT index, *Salomon Brothers Real Estate Investment Report*, January 7.

Giliberto S.M. (1993) Measuring real estate returns: The hedged REIT index, *Journal of Portfolio Management*, Spring, pp. 94–99.

Gordon J., and Tse E. (2003) VaR: A tool to measure leverage risk, *Journal of Portfolio Management*, Special Real Estate Issue.

Graaskamp J.A. (1970) The role of investment real estate in portfolio management, in *Graaskamp on Real Estate*, Urban Land Institute (Jarchow S., ed), 1991, pp. 310–363.

Graaskamp J. (1976) An approach to real estate finance education by analogy to risk management principles, in *Recent Perspectives in Urban Land Economics Essays in honor of Richard U. Ratcliff and Paul F. Wendt* (M. Goldberg, ed), Vancouver: University of British Columbia (Faculty of Commerce and Business Administration, Urban Land Economics Division). ISBN 0920198015 9780920198018.

Grissom T., Hartzell D., and Liu C. (1987) An approach to industrial real estate market segmentation and valuation using the arbitrage pricing paradigm, *Journal of the American Real Estate and Urban Economics Association*, 3, pp. 199–219.

Grissom T., and Liu C. (1993) The search for a discipline: The philosophy and the paradigms, in *Appraisal, Market Analysis, and Public Policy in Real Estate: Essays in Honor of James Graaskamp* (DeLisle J. and Sa-Aadu J., eds), Boston: Kluwer Academic Publishers, pp. 65–106.

Guilkey D., Miles M., and Cole R. (1989) The motivation for institutional real estate sales and implications for asset class return, *AREUEA Journal*, 17:1, pp. 70–86.

Gürkaynak R., and Wolfers J. (2007) Macroeconomic derivatives: An initial analysis of market-based macro forecasts, uncertainty, and risk, in *NBER International Seminar on Macroeconomics* (Frankel J. and Pissarides C., ed), Boston: MIT Press, pp. 11–50.

Hamelink F., Hoesli M., Lizieri C., and MacGregor B. (2000) Homogeneous property market groupings and portfolio strategies in the U.K., *Environment and Planning A*, 32, pp. 323–344.

Hartzell D., Hekman J., and Miles M. (1986) Diversification categories in investment real estate, *Journal of the American Real Estate and Urban Economics Association*, 14:2, pp. 230–254.

Hekman J. (1985) Rental price adjustment and investment in the office market, *Journal of the American Real Estate and Urban Economics Association*, 13:1, pp. 32–47.

Hoag J. (1980) Towards indices of real estate value and return, *Journal of Finance*, 35:2, pp. 569–580.

Hough D.E., and Kratz G. (1983) Can "good" architecture meet the market test? *Journal of Urban Economics*, 14:1, pp. 40–54.

Hull J. (2009) *Options, Futures, and Other Derivatives*, 7th edition, Upper Saddle River: Pearson International-Prentice Hall, 814 p.

Ibe O. (2013) *Elements of Random Walk and Diffusion Process*, Hoboken: Wiley.

IPF (2000) *The Assessment and Management of Risk in the Property Investment Industry*, a survey by IPD for the Investment Property Forum Risk Working Party (March).

IPF (2015) *Individual Property Risk*, a report written by Paul Mitchell Real Estate Consultancy for the Investment Property Forum (July).

Jayeola O. (2020) Inefficiencies in trade reporting for over-the-counter derivatives: Is blockchain the solution? *Capital Markets Law Journal*, 15:1, pp. 48–69.

Jorion P. (2007) *Value at Risk: The New Benchmark for Managing Financial Risk*, 3rd edition, Boston: McGraw Hill, 602 p.

Jud G., and Winkler D. (1995) The capitalization rate of commercial properties and market returns, *Journal of Real Estate Research*, 10:5, pp. 509–518.

Jud G., and Winkler D. (2009) The housing futures market, *Journal of Real Estate Literature*, 17:2, pp. 181–203.

Jung C. (1950) Foreword to *The I Ching, or, Book of Changes*, translated by R. Wilhelm and C. Baynes, New York: Pantheon Books/Bollingen Series XIX.

Karlin S., Cameron E., and Chakraborty R. (1983) Path analysis in genetic epidemiology: A critique, *American Journal of Human Genetics*, 35:4, pp. 695–732.

Karolyi G., and Sanders A. (1998) The variation of economic risk premiums in real estate returns, *Journal of Real Estate Finance and Economics*, 17:3, pp. 245–262.

Kerson J. (1994) Trading in fundamental real estate risk with market-hedged equity indexes, *Bankers Trust Research-Derivatives Focus* (September 1).

Kling J., and McCue T. (1987) Office building investment and the macroeconomy: Empirical evidence 1973–1985, *Real Estate Economics*, 15:3, pp. 234–255.

Kummerow M. (2000) Graaskamp on research methods, in *Essays in Honor of James Graaskamp: Ten Years After* (DeLisle J. and Worzala E., eds), Boston: Kluwer Academic Publishers, pp. 365–384.

Lancaster K.J. (1966) A new approach to consumer theory, *The Journal of Political Economy*, 74:2, pp. 132–157.

Lange J., and Economides N. (2005) A parimutuel market microstructure for contingent claims, *European Financial Management*, 11:1, pp. 25–49.

Lecomte P. (2007) Beyond index-based hedging: Can real estate trigger a new breed of derivatives market? *Journal of Real Estate Portfolio Management*, 13:4, pp. 345–378.

Lecomte P., (2013) Tiptoe past the dragon: Replicating and hedging Chinese direct real estate, *Journal of Real Estate Portfolio Management*, 19:1, pp. 49–72.

Lecomte P. (2014) Testing alternative models of property derivatives: The case of the City of London, *Journal of Property Investment and Finance*, 32:2, pp. 107–153.

Lecomte P., and McIntosh W. (2005) Going synthetic, *The Institutional Real Estate Letter*, 17:11.

Lecomte P., and McIntosh W. (2006) Designing property futures and options based on NCREIF property indices, *Journal of Real Estate Portfolio Management*, 12:2, pp. 199–153.

Leschhorn H. (2001) Managing yield-curve risk with combination hedges, *Financial Analysts Journal*, May/June, pp. 63–75.

Liang Y., and McIntosh W. (1998) Employment growth and real estate return: Are they linked? *Journal of Real Estate Portfolio Management*, 4:2, pp. 125–133.

Ling D. (2005) A random walk down main street: Can experts predict returns on commercial real estate? *Journal of Real Estate Research*, 27:2, pp. 137–154.

Ling D., and Naranjo A. (1997) Economic risk factors and commercial real estate returns, *Journal of Real Estate Finance and Economics*, 14:3, pp. 283–301.

Ling D., and Naranjo A. (1999) The integration of commercial real estate markets and stock markets, *Real Estate Economics*, 27:3, pp. 483–515.

Liow K. (2004) Time-varying macroeconomic risk and commercial real estate: An asset pricing perspective, *Journal of Real Estate Portfolio Management*, 10:1.

Liow K. (2008) Extreme returns and value at risk in international securitized real estate markets, *Journal of Property Investment & Finance*, 26:5, pp. 418–446.

Litterman R., and Scheinkman J. (1991) Common factors affecting bond returns, *Journal of Fixed Income*, June, pp. 54–61.

MacKenzie D. (2006) *An Engine Not a Camera*, Boston: The MIT Press.

MacKinnon G., and Al Zaman A., (2009) Real estate for the long term: The effect of return predictability on long-horizons allocation, *Real Estate Economics*, 37:1, pp. 117–153.

Malkiel B. (1973) *A Random Walk Down Wall Street*, New York: W.W. Norton & Company, 456 p.

Mandelbrot B. (1999) *Les Objets Fractals: Forme, Hasard et Dimension, Survol du Langage Fractal*, Paris: Flammarion.

Markowitz H. (1993) unpublished quotes drawn verbatim from transcribed comments of a Modern Portfolio Theory Roundtable, A. Reinbach (moderator), Buildings Magazine (sponsor). Quoted in *Essays in Honor of James A. Graaskamp: Ten years After*, Chapter 3 (Delisle J. author), Dordrecht: Kluwer Academic Publishers, 2000, p. 55.

Marshall A. (1890) *Principles of Economics*, London: Macmillan.

McCue T., and Kling J. (1994) Real estate returns and the macroeconomy: Some evidence from real estate investment trust data, 1972–1991, *Journal of Real Estate Research*, 9:3, pp. 277–287.

McNamara G. (2010) Chapter 8: Property derivatives: The story so far, in *Global Trends in Real Estate Finance* (Newell G. and Sieracki K., eds), Hoboken: Wiley-Blackwell.

Miles M., Cole R., and Guilkey D. (1990) A different look at commercial real estate returns, *Journal of the American Real Estate and Urban Economics Association*, 18:4, pp. 403–430.

Miles M., Eppli M., and Kummerow M. (1998) The Graaskamp legacy, *Real Estate Finance*, 15:1, pp. 84–91.

Miles M., and McCue T. (1982) Historic returns and institutional real estate portfolios, *Journal of the American Real Estate and Urban Economics Association*, 10:2, pp. 184–199.

Miles M., and McCue T. (1984) Commercial real estate returns, *Journal of the American Real Estate and Urban Economics Association*, 12:3, pp. 355–377.

Mills E. (1992) Office rent determinants in the Chicago area, *Real Estate Economics*, 20:2, pp. 273–287.

Morgan L. (2008) Combination hedges applied to US markets, *Financial Analysts Journal*, 64:1, pp. 74–84.

Morini M. (2017) Managing derivatives on a blockchain: A financial market professional implementation, unpublished paper.

Mueller G. (1993) Redefining economic diversification strategies for real estate portfolios, *Journal of Real Estate Research*, 8:1, pp. 55–68.

Mueller G., and Ziering B. (1992) Real estate portfolio diversification using economic diversification, *Journal of Real Estate Research*, 7:4, pp. 375–386.

Munneke H., and Slade B. (2000) An empirical study of sample-selection bias in indices of commercial real estate, *Journal of Real Estate Finance and Economics*, 21:1, pp. 45–64.

Neiderhoffer V., and Zeckhauser R. (1980) Market index futures contracts, *Financial Analysts Journal*, 36:1, pp. 49–55.

Özyurt S. (2014) *Spatial Dependence in Commercial Property Prices: Micro Evidence from the Netherlands*, Working Paper No 1627, European Central Bank.

Pace R., Barry R., and Sirmans C.F. (1998) Spatial statistics and real estate, *Journal of Real Estate Finance and Economics*, 17:1, pp. 5–13.

Pai A., and Geltner D. (2007) Stocks are from Mars, real estate is from Venus, *The Journal of Portfolio Management*, Special Real Estate Issue, 33:5, pp. 134–144.

Patel K. (1994) Lessons from the FOX residential property futures and mortgage interest rate futures, *Housing Policy Debate*, 5:3, pp. 343–360.

Peng L. (2016) The risk and return of commercial real estate: A property level analysis, *Real Estate Economics*, 44:3, pp. 555–583.

Plazzi A., Torous W., and Valkanov R. (2008) The cross-sectional dispersion of commercial real estate returns and rent growth: Time variation and economic fluctuations, *Real Estate Economics*, 36:3, pp. 403–439.

Priem R. (2020) Distributed ledger technology for securities clearing and settlement: Benefits, risks, and regulatory implications, *Financial Innovation*, 6:1, pp. 1–25.

Rao D., and Rice T. (2005) Path analysis in genetics, in *Encyclopedia of Biostatistics* (Armitage P., and Colton T., eds), Chichester: John Wiley & Sons.

Rao D., and Rice T. (2006) Path analysis in genetic epidemiology, in *Encyclopedia of Life Sciences*, Chichester: Wiley-Blackwell.

Ratcliff R.U. (1949) *Urban Land Economics*, New York: McGraw-Hill Book Company.

Ratcliff R.U. (1961) *Real Estate Analysis*, New York: McGraw-Hill Book Company.

RICS (2017) *Artificial Intelligence: What it Means for the Built Environment*, Royal Institution of Chartered Surveyors, London.

Riddiough T. (1995) Replicating and hedging real estate risk, *Real Estate Finance*, 12, pp. 88–95.

Ross S. (1976) The arbitrage theory of capital asset pricing, *Journal of Economic Theory*, 13:3, pp. 341–360.

Roulac S. (1995) Individual vs. institutional real estate investing strategies, in *Alternative Ideas in Real Estate Investment* (Schwartz A. and Kapplin S., eds), Boston: Kluwer Academic Publishers, pp. 35–58.

Seldin M. (2000) The legacy in *Essays in Honor of James Graaskamp: 10 years After*, edited by J. DeLisle and E. Worzala, Boston: Kluwer Academic Publishers, pp. 41–50.

Sharpe W. (1995) Nuclear financial economics, in *Risk Management: Problems and Solutions* (Beaver W. and Parker G., eds), New York: McGaw-Hill, 1995.

Shiller R. (1993) *Macro Markets: Creating Institutions for Managing Society's Largest Economic Risks*, Oxford: Oxford University Press.

Shiller R. (2004a) Radical financial innovation, *Cowles Foundation Discussion Papers 1461*, Yale University.

Shiller R. (2004b) *The New Financial Order: Risk in the 21st Century*, Princeton: Princeton University Press.

Shiller R. (2008) Derivatives markets for home prices, *Cowles Foundation Discussion Papers 1648, Yale University.*

Shilton L., and Zaccaria A. (1994) The avenue effect, landmark externalities, and cubic transformation: Manhattan office valuation, *Journal of Real Estate Finance and Economics*, 8, pp. 151–165.

Shipley B. (2016) *Cause and Correlation in Biology*, 2nd edition, Cambridge: Cambridge University Press.

Simon H. (1996) *The Science of the Artificial*, Boston: The MIT Press.

Swan E. (2000) *Building the Global Market: A 4000 Year History of Derivatives*, Boston: Kluwer Law.

Swidler S. (2010) Chapter 12: Emerging derivatives in *Financial Derivatives: Pricing and Risk Management* (Kolb R. and Overdahl J., eds), Wiley, pp. 221–230.

Syz J. (2008) *Property Derivatives: Pricing, Hedging and Applications*, The Wiley Finance Series, Hoboken: John Wiley & Sons.

Titman S., and Warga A. (1986) Risk and the performance of real estate investment trusts: A multiple index approach, *Journal of the American Real Estate and Urban Economics Association*, 14:3, pp. 414–431.

Torous W. (2017) *History of Commercial Property Derivatives*, MIT Center for Real Estate and Sloan School (presentation dated 13 October).

Triplett J. (1986) The economic interpretation of hedonic models, *Survey of Current Business, Federal Reserve of St. Louis.*

Tu Y., Yu S., and Sun H. (2004) Transaction-based office price indexes: A spatiotemporal modeling approach, *Real Estate Economics*, 32:2, pp. 297–328.

Tunaru R. (2017) *Real Estate Derivatives*, Oxford: Oxford University Press.

Tunaru R., and Fabozzi F. (2017) Commercial real estate derivatives: The end or the beginning? *The Journal of Portfolio Management, Special Real Estate issue*, 43:6, pp. 179–186.

Turner J. S., (2016) Homeostasis is the key to the intelligent building, *Intelligent Buildings International*, 8:2, pp. 150–154.

Van Bragt D., Francke M., Singor S., and Pelsser A. (2015) Risk-neutral valuation of real estate derivatives, *Journal of Derivatives*, 23:1, pp. 89–110.

Veblen T. (1898) Why is economics not an evolutionary science? *Quarterly Journal of Economics*, 12:4, pp. 373–397.

Veblen T., and Boulton J. (2010) Why is economics not an evolutionary science? *Emergence: Complexity and Organization*, 12:2, pp. 41–69.

Warwick K (2013) Conscious buildings? *Intelligent buildings International*, 5:4, pp. 199–203.

Weimer A. (1966) Real estate decisions are different, *Harvard Business Review*, 44, pp. 105–112.

Weimer A., and Hoyt H. (1966) *Real Estate*, 5th edition, New York: The Ronald Press Company.

Wheaton W. (2015) The volatility of real estate markets: A decomposition, *The Journal of Portfolio Management, Special Real Estate Issue*, 41, pp. 140–150.

Wheaton W., and Torto R. (1994) Office rent indices and their behaviour over time, *Journal of Urban Economics*, 35:2, pp. 121–139.

Wilhelmsson M. (2002) Spatial models in real estate economics, *Housing, Theory and Society*, 19:2, pp. 92–100.

Wright S. (1921) Correlation and causation, *Journal of Agricultural Research*, 20, pp. 557–585.

Wright S. (1983) On "path analysis in genetic epidemiology: A critique", *American Journal of Human Genetics*, 35:4, pp. 757–768.

Wolfers J., and Zitzewitz E. (2010) Chapter 12: Event derivatives, in *Financial Derivatives: Pricing and Risk Management* (Kolb R. and Overdahl J., eds), Hoboken: Wiley, pp. 157–176.

Young, M. S., and Graff, R. A. (1996) Systematic behavior in real estate investment risk: Performance persistence in NCREIF returns, *Journal of Real Estate Research*, 12:3, pp. 369–381.

Zhou J., and Anderson R. (2012) Extreme risk measures for international REIT markets, *Journal of Real Estate Finance and Economics*, 45:1, pp. 152–170.

2 The digitalisation of commercial real estate

Smart space as real estate finance's new asset

Introduction: the emergence of smart space

This chapter deals with an ongoing process: the digitalisation of commercial real estate under the combined effects of smart technology embedded into the very fabric of the built environment and the implementation of pervasive computing, a sweeping concept in computer sciences (Weiser, 1991).

While the introduction of Internet of Thing (IoT) devices and other cyber-physical systems in the built environment has been widely publicised, few out of computer sciences specialists might have heard about pervasive computing, the information technology (IT) conceptual framework which underpins the implementation of smart technologies in the built environment. Pervasive computing originated in the early 1990s when Xerox PARC's Chief Technology Officer Mark Weiser and his team invented the third era of computing in human-computer interactions.

The premise is straightforward: instead of humans actively engaging with computers (e.g. sitting at a desk to use a software), computers should be calmly and transparently interacting with humans in space without the latter being even aware of computers' presence. Thus, computers can remain in the background at the periphery of human attention at all time and everywhere (Weiser and Brown, 1996). Computing becomes a 'calm technology'. Due to its quest for ubiquity, pervasive computing is also known as ubiquitous computing (ubicomp). Without the seamless human-computer interactions enabled by ubicomp, smart cities and smart buildings would not be possible. Ubicomp whose apparent simplicity should not hide the drastic consequences on human lives lies at the core of commercial real estate's digitalisation.

As cities and buildings are slowly moving towards Weiser's vision, social scientists have labelled the unprecedented level of cyber-physical systems pervading physical space in smart environments a "tectonic shift" (Hayles, 2014). These systems turn buildings into cognitive assemblages characterised as "complex interactions between humans and nonhuman cognizers and their abilities to enlist material forces" (Hayles, 2017). For commercial real estate, the so-called fourth industrial revolution (Schwab, 2016) is therefore a lot more than technological gimmickry and entrepreneurial fever exemplified by massive investments in proptech.

Fundamentally, the digitalisation of commercial real estate has a paradigm-shifting impact on space, a crucial dimension of real estate which is admittedly invisible, thus oftentimes taken for granted or flatly ignored in real estate finance. However, in Graaskamp (1970)'s own words, "the essence of real estate is [...] space, for this is the usable commodity created by the intersection of land, wall, floor, and roof planes". With smart technologies, the nature of space in the built environment is changing. Thus, the very commodity that real estate finance has to contend with is being transformed.

Not only are buildings evolving towards smart buildings, but the urban environments they sit in are also mutating into smart cities. A digital skin is literally donning cities and buildings, serving as the backbone to their new-found smartness (Gross, 1999; Rabari and Storper, 2015). The resulting smart cities are "cities of bits and atoms" (Mitchell, 1995) while smart buildings exemplify "the intense interaction between the occupants and the built environment" (Liu and Gulliver, 2013).

The concept of a new space opening up owing to information technology (IT) is not new, but it has rapidly materialised in recent years as technology pervades always ever more aspects of the built environment. In the 1970s, French sociologist Henri Lefebvre (1974) had the intuition that the rapid rise of information technology would lead to a new specific type of space dominated by technology although he could not define it. Over the years, this space has taken many names in the computing sciences literature: cybernetic space, pervasive space, intelligent space.

In the context of commercial real estate, Lecomte (2019a) calls it "smart space". Smart space sits at the intersect of digital space and physical space. It embodies "the congruence of real and virtual in smart environments". Lecomte (2019a) explains:

> Space has traditionally been a silent component of real estate. Smart technologies powered by ubiquitous computing are turning space into an active part of real estate, and to some extent into real estate itself. [...] The whole real estate discipline is challenged by what amounts to a paradigm shift.

In particular, space users' mode of relation to buildings shifts from a relational ontology to a phenomenological one whereby space in real estate becomes a highly personal experience (Lecomte, 2019a). In addition to Graaskamp's classic four dimensions of real estate (length, width, height, and time), a fifth dimension of real estate emerges in the form of digital which unfolds in the digital-time realm, a new realm in real estate analysis (Lecomte, 2020).

Concretely, the emergence of smart space bears important consequences for the real estate industry. Buildings immersed in smart environments have to leverage on synergies between digital and physical in order to create value for space users (Lecomte, 2019b). As buildings serve as platforms to digital, they are no longer the focus of value creation, but tools powered by technology and ubicomp. Smart buildings have to be proactive, rather than reactive. They are context-aware and display bi-directional consciousness. As pointed out by Ratti and Haw (2012), smart buildings are "living bits and bricks" which embody "a feedback fuelled world where we don't just inhabit our architecture but integrate with it".

Furthermore, with smart buildings, commercial real estate moves from asset provision to service provision (RICS, 2017). Smart buildings, nicknamed 'ibuildings' (Carvalho, 2015), enable the commercial real estate industry to broaden its value chain by linking the built environment with IT applications (e.g. cyber-physical systems, software, data analytics). Consequently, commercial real estate's value drivers are changing, which questions the relevance for smart buildings of pricing models initially developed for non-smart buildings, such as hedonic regression models anchored in classic physical structure and location characteristics.

Case in point: in smart cities, physical location is no longer the key to a building's value (Berman et al., 2016). By contrast, what matters in smart buildings is their digital positionality, i.e. access to "interactive loci or gateways where human tasks are mediated and value created" (Lecomte, 2019b). One can safely forecast that over the coming decade, digital will play an increasingly important role in pricing models of commercial real estate in smart cities.

Noticeably, models should account for the fact identified by William Mitchell in his seminal book *Me++: The Cyborg and the Networked City* (2003) that smart cities cater to hyper individualised space users. Highly personalised user-centric digital services available in smart buildings create a "market of one" (Curry and Sheth, 2018). The wide array of Gibsonian affordances in smart buildings questions the classic concept of property heterogeneity derived from physical structure and location, and the best way for real estate finance to deal with it.[1]

This chapter presents two new pricing models applicable to smart buildings in smart cities. They build on the hedonic pricing theory to design methodologies taking into account smart commercial real estate's digital realm. They accommodate smart space' extreme experiential diversity underpinned by smart buildings' user centricity.

This chapter also introduces a new concept of property rights in smart cities: digital rights. As smart buildings are externally covered by smart cities' digital skin and internally laden with an Information and Communication Technology (ICT) infrastructure that turns ubicomp into reality, smart space is likely to mediate a growing number of human activities in the years to come.

By entering into a building's physical space, building occupants step into smart space. Whilst relations in physical space are regulated by property rights, what rights, if any, should regulate smart space? Who should own access to and/or have control over the new digital realm? Is smart space dependent on physical space, or is it independent from any physical structure, by existing as a fully fledged legal entity with its own set of rights?

Since Tudor enclosures in 13th-century England, property rights and technology have traditionally been closely intertwined. Thus, unsurprisingly, the digitalisation of commercial real estate carries with it a natural evolution in the concept of property rights. Ratcliff (1961) provides a good summary of the situation real estate is facing with smart technologies:

> Down through the centuries property has been moulded and fitted to the needs of the social organization, needs that are ever-changing through the

broadening of knowledge, the surges of social movements, the slow changes in the social mind, and the advances in technology. [...] Changes in the property concept have been associated with changes in man's way of life and with advances in technology.

The thesis presented in this book is that smart space should come with a set of rights encapsulating space users' relations in smart environments. These rights are called digital rights. Similarly to property rights in physical space, digital rights are rights to smart space. Defining rights that match smart buildings' digital dimension in smart urban environments is important but not sufficient. How should these digital rights be valued and exchanged? And ultimately, what does it mean to own a building in a smart city? This chapter explores these questions. It analyses the nature of property rights in smart urban environments, lays out a series of axioms defining the economic foundations of digital rights, and proposes a market template for exchanging these rights. The issue of digital rights arises in commercial real estate because of the potential economic value of smart space for the real estate sector.

As demonstrated in the following chapter, aggregate thinking seems unfit to analyse smart real estate assets. Instead, approaches presented in this chapter rely on micro-scale analysis and micro markets. Many concepts presented here might seem a little abstract. Like the other ideas introduced in this book, they map out a vision of what the future could be for real estate finance in the context of radical technological innovation. They are exploratory in nature and meant to foster a healthy debate among academics and industry researchers.

1 Pricing models of smart buildings in smart environments

1.1 Smart buildings as interactions

Classic hedonic pricing models in real estate finance rely on physical structure, location and, in some rare cases illustrated in Chapter 1 of this book on lease characteristics to derive prices of commercial real estate assets. In doing so, models focus on two realms of real estate highlighted by James A. Graaskamp (1981): the space-time realm (physical structure and location) and the money-time realm (lease structure).

In smart environments, there is a third realm of real estate that models should take into account: the digital-time realm which emerges for smart buildings. In their usual formulations, hedonic pricing models do not account for smart buildings' digital dimension. There are two possible ways to incorporate real estate's digital-time realm in pricing models:

– First, by adopting a technological approach where the objective measurements of technologies embedded in the built environment (e.g. number of cyber-physical devices in a building) are used, as additional layers of a building's physical structure.

- Second, by considering a functionalist approach where interactions between buildings and their occupants are assumed to be value drivers in the built environment. Technology underpins these interactions but only as a tool towards a means which, in the context of ubicomp, should be transparent to the end-users.

The first approach does not represent a major conceptual challenge, provided that there are objective measurements available to assess the 'quantity' of technology embedded into smart buildings. An industry consensus on these measurements would of course be essential. Conversely, the second approach supposes to develop a taxonomy of interactions in smart space applicable to all buildings (Lecomte, 2019a).

Methods presented in this section rely on the second approach which can be characterised as functionalist. The premise of this approach hinges on a new take on what constitutes a building. In addition to bricks and mortars, technology fuelled space enables interactions between a building and its occupants, thus triggering the emergence of intelligent pervasive spaces. Liu and Gulliver (2013) explain:

> [The built environment] provides a context within which social spaces can be constructed, allowing the value of the built environment to be quantified through services and interactions that it provides to users. [...] The building can be seen as a set of designed interaction scripts, which the users evoke when they interact with the space.

1.2 Hedonic pricing model of smart buildings based on smart space's layered structure

The first pricing model adopts an holistic approach to smart buildings' digital dimension by including into the pricing model the smart environment's overall contribution to a building's smartness (i.e. its ability to be smart).

Smartness in buildings is the product of an urban system including the smart grid, ICT infrastructure, and the digital skin. Smart buildings come with "new boundaries" that extend beyond their physical structures and follow smart space's layered structure. In that sense, smart buildings bring back to the fore pioneer real estate academics' view on land as multidimensional space underpinning the physical foundation of real estate value (e.g. Fisher and Fisher, 1954). Ratcliff (1961) asserts: "The essence of location derives from one of the elemental physical facts of life, the reality of space". This was true in 1960s America. And it is still true in smart cities except that the reality of space has changed with the emergence of smart space.

The methodology presented here supposes a holistic approach to commercial real estate value. To encompass the reality of space in smart buildings, it implements a micro-scale analysis of each layer of smart space. According to Lecomte (2019b), smart space is made up of four layers constitutive of physical space (smart grid, building's physical structure) and digital space (embedded ICT in the built environment, cloud/fog). Figure 2.1 represents the four layers of smart space. Each of these four layers contributes to a building's smartness.

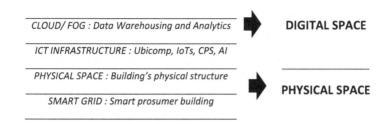

Figure 2.1 The four layers of smart space after Lecomte (2019a).

To capture the complex synergies among the four layers in enabling smartness in the built environment, Lecomte (2019a) designs an indicator of a building's smartness after smart space's layered structure. This indicator is called the Smart Index Matrix (SIM). The SIM is used as an engine to a hedonic pricing model of smart real estate.

- **The Smart Index Matrix (SIM)**

The Smart Index Matrix (SIM) is a scoring methodology for smart real estate which includes (i) a physical score broken down into a smart grid coefficient and a smart building score and (ii) a digital score capturing digital space's ICT and data analytics capabilities.

Interactions between the physical score and digital score determine a building's performances in smart space, which are captured in the SIM (Lecomte, 2019a). The mathematical formulation of the SIM follows a simple matrix equation:

$$SIM = xA(BC)$$

where xA is the physical score (x is a scalar parameter capturing the smart grid's performance and A is a NxK matrix with entries for smart-enabling factors at the building level).

And BC is the digital score (B is a KxN matrix capturing smart-enabling factors in the built environment's ICT infrastructure and C is a NxK matrix capturing the cloud/ fog's data warehousing and analytics capabilities). SIM is compatible with the two generic models of smart city: ubiquitous city and augmented city (Lecomte, 2019b). In ubiquitous cities (Aurigi, 2009; Anttiroiko, 2013), matrices B and C are constant irrespective of the building's location whereas in augmented cities where the digital skin is uneven, B and C are location specific and, possibly, property-type specific.

When adding the digital realm's micro-scales to commercial real estate analysis, new dimensions of granularity emerge in smart urban environments. As technology becomes "the dominating factor of heterogeneity and the main value driver for commercial real estate in smart cities" (Lecomte, 2019b), pricing models of smart buildings have to account for property heterogeneity stemming from the pervasive implementation of smart technologies in commercial real estate. Technological heterogeneity as a source of smart property heterogeneity materialises at two levels in the SIM: first, at the urban infrastructure level where not all MSAs and neighbourhoods within a city might offer the same quality of ICT infrastructure; second at the level of buildings whose smartness within a given property type and/or geographic area might display great diversity.

Therefore, whilst commercial real estate indices are traditionally segmented by property types and geographic locations, indices of smart buildings can be segmented according to smart space' layers:

- The overall smartness of the building's physical environment (xA),
- The building's intrinsic smartness based on its physical structure (matrix A),
- The overall smartness of the building's digital environment (BC),
- The assessed quality of the ICT infrastructure accessible to the building (matrix B),
- The cloud/fog's data warehousing and analytics capabilities (matrix C).

- **Hedonic pricing model of smart buildings based on the Smart Index Matrix**

The premise of the model is that interactions between occupants and a smart building define the property's value. In smart environments, these interactions are underpinned by smart space's four layers captured in the SIM. Combinations of constituent characteristics linked to these four layers contribute to the property's value depending on estimated coefficients indicative of the weights that occupants place on the various dimensions of a building's smartness. Noticeably, environmental attributes which originate in technology have to be identified and standardised.

This methodology redefines the boundaries of value in commercial real estate by providing a broad vision of property pricing, which is anchored in the complex nature of smart environments' spatial components. Figure 2.2 illustrates this vision of a smart building in its smart urban environment.

In mathematical form, let Yt be the building's (ln) price at time t such that:

$$Y_t = SIM_t y_t + \varepsilon_t$$

where yt denotes a Kx1 estimated coefficient vector and ε_t is the regression error term.

Hence, property price is directly linked to the four strata of smart space in a model that fully acknowledges smart real estate's positioning amid an urban ecosystem fostering smartness through synergetic interactions at the property level. The micro-scales involved here are not user-centric, nor experiential but structural in both physical and digital spaces. These micro-scales' scopes depend on the selection of quality variables in matrices A, B and C reported in the SIM.

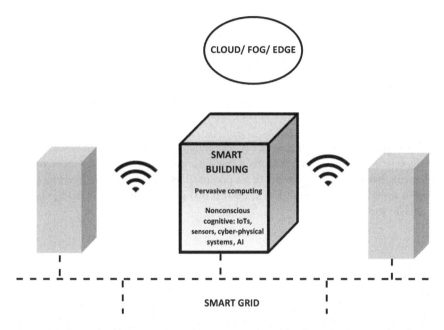

Figure 2.2 Smart building in smart urban environment (cloud computing paradigm).

It is assumed that space users have preferences with respect to these smart-enabling technological characteristics in a building and its broader environment. It is also assumed that all components as well as their complex interactions can be objectively and reliably measured. A lot of technical expertise will obviously be required in order to set up and effectively run such model.

As smart technologies become more pervasive and keep evolving towards ever more widespread interactions in cities and buildings, quality variables along with their coefficients in the pricing model will have to be regularly re-assessed and calibrated.

1.3 Activity-based hedonic pricing model of smart buildings

The second model presented in this book focuses on an essential dimension of smart space: its user-centricity. Smart buildings are totally focused on their occupants, thereby turning real estate space into "iSpace" (Lecomte, 2020). This is in sharp contrast to the previous model which does not incorporate user centricity in its formulation as interactions between occupants and buildings are purely captured in terms of smart space's four strata.

Known as activity-based hedonic pricing model of smart real estate, this second model accommodates coded space's user centricity by pricing individual interactions between space users and a building. In doing so, it echoes Liu and Gulliver's

(2013) definition of a smart building as the sum of individual interactions with its occupants in smart space. Lecomte (2020) asserts:

> In smart buildings, real estate merges with technology to form cognitive assemblages [...] User-centric interactions with real estate are primarily designed by code and mediated by non-conscious cognitive. Hence, smart space becomes real estate's main productive component, whereas its physical characteristics move to the periphery of space users' attention.

Whilst the previous pricing model is very much rooted in physical space, an activity-based model solidly positions a building into smart space. In order to implement this model, a taxonomy of all potential smart interactions has first to be drawn up (Lecomte, 2019a). Let Y_t be the (ln) price of the building (dependent variable) such that:

$$Y_t = w_t Z_t \beta_t + \varepsilon_t$$

where $w_t = \Sigma w_{it}$ with w_{it} is the weight of activity i in the building's use at date t. Coefficients w_{it} are derived from actual smart use of the building (e.g. average use over a period). Z_t is the matrix of independent quality variables representing the interactions in smart space related to all activities in the building. β_t is the estimated coefficient vector for these interactions. ε_t is the regression error term.

If the building encompasses N activities for K interactions[2] then:

- w_t is a 1xN vector of N activities' weights in the building's actual smart use at date t with the sum of all weights w_i (from 1 = 1 to N) being equal to 1;
- β_t is a Kx1 vector of K estimated coefficients;
- and Z_t is a NxK matrix of N activities in the building's taxonomy triggering K independent pre-defined interactions in smart space. Z_t's ith row consists of a vector of K interactions for activity i (z_{ik} for k = 1 to K). Z_t is such that:

$$Z_t = \begin{bmatrix} z11 & \cdots & z1K \\ \vdots & \ddots & \vdots \\ zN1 & \cdots & zNK \end{bmatrix}$$

To implement the model, the following elements are required:

- a comprehensive taxonomy of activities and pre-defined interactions in smart space,
- a very dynamic formulation and calibration of these activities and interactions so as to take care of omitted variables and changes in the building's usage patterns over time, which might outdate the current taxonomy of activities, and
- the ability to assess space users' preferences at an extremely granular level and in terms of technology-driven experiences (linked to activities).

In this model, a smart building is akin to a set of on-demand services which are individually experienced by occupants in coded space. It is hypothesised that pre-defined interactions in matrix Z_t can be experienced both successively and concomitantly with potentially synergistic effects while an activity takes place. By contrast, modelled activities are supposed to be exclusive (e.g. a building occupant is either working or shopping but not doing two activities at the same time).

Hence, one can expect that most interactions will occur as a succession of events rather than concomitant occurrences within an activity. Major exceptions to this rule are interactions pertaining to the building's environment which truly remain in the background at all times. By definition, environmental interactions will be overwhelmingly concomitant (e.g. HVAC system, lighting), whereas activity-supporting interactions are conceptualised to occur individually and sequentially as activities unfold in digital-time. That is, smart space is inherently a specialised space. It might be an omni-use space (Lecomte, 2019a), albeit in a series of very specialised interactions matching with each modelled activity carried out in the building. Selection of quality variables in Z_t should reflect the fact that smart space has both scope and depth.

Another dimension concurring to space specialisation is the presence of two generic types of interactions: (i) standard interactions shared by all tenants in a smart building and (ii) specific interactions which are idiosyncratic to a particular tenant. The latter might stem from Built-To-Order requirements, or result from the implementation of proprietary technologies.[3] These assumptions about activities and interactions correspond to a new model of space user in smart real estate known as the cyber-dasein (Lecomte, 2019a). As pointed out by Dourish and Bell (2011), "new technologies inherently cause people to reencounter space". The cyber-dasein purposefully engages in smart space in view of achieving tasks, one task at a time. His concernful absorption in carrying out his daily tasks in smart space is characteristic of pervasive computing's phenomenology (Lecomte, 2020).[4]

Lecomte (2019a) describes a variant of the activity-based hedonic pricing model of smart buildings, by superimposing a behavioural map of space users' patterns of activities in smart space. Such maps at the intersection of psychology and geography, called "preoccupation maps", derive from psychogeography, a concept defined by French Situationist philosophers in the 1950s. Similar maps can be found in the pervasive computing literature where user-generated classifications of space are implemented (e.g. Calabrese et al., 2010). In the same line of thinking, Batty (2002) suggests to "conceive cities as being clusters of spatial events, events that take place in time and space, where the event is characterised by its duration, intensity, volatility and location". The resulting model known as "behavioural spatial hedonic model of smart real estate" accounts for spatial effects in smart cities, especially spatial heterogeneity as smart buildings become more widespread in increasingly smart urban environments.[5]

1.4 Defining utility in smart real estate: decision or experienced?

Hedonic pricing models are based on the fundamental assumption that a good's observed market can be linked to observed utility-bearing characteristics

(Lancaster, 1966). Price differences among goods are explained by "the economic content of the relationship between observed prices and observed characteristics" (Rosen, 1974). Edmonds (1984) explains that a hedonic price model provides "a distinct, homogenous marketable tied bundle of characteristics [which are] objectively measurable, utility affecting attributes".

In hedonic pricing models applied in real estate (see Chapter 1 of this book), utilities attached to a property's characteristics are decision utilities. Their formation is underpinned by logical criteria assessed by a system of preferences, assuming that agents are rational. In smart environments where buildings are equivalent to a series of activities translated into interactions experienced in smart space, does a concept of utility disconnected from space users' actual experience make sense for pricing smart buildings? Alternatively, should the concept of experienced utility introduced by Nobel Prize laureate Daniel Kahneman be applied instead?

Kahneman (1994) defines experienced utility as "the measure of the hedonic experience of [an] outcome" whereas "the decision utility of an outcome [...] is the weight assigned to that outcome in a decision". Experience utility differs from decision utility insofar as it is "the rewards we realize once the choices are made" (Robson and Samuelson, 2011).

Lancaster (1966) who invented the hedonic pricing theory propounds "the objective nature of the goods-characteristics relationship" in a hedonic model, i.e. "the characteristics possessed by a good or a combination of goods are the same for all consumers, and [...] are in the same quantities". Therefore, there is no need for involving the subjectivity of individual experiences in utility formation. Indeed, Robson and Samuelson (2011) explain:

> Experienced utilities are of no interest to a fiercely neoclassical economist. Decision utilities suffice to describe behaviour. However, if we are to consider welfare questions, the difference may be important. If experienced utilities do not match decision utilities, should we persevere with the standard economists' presumption that decision utilities are an appropriate guide to well-being?

In smart real estate where space is coded, utility should encompass smart space's three realms: the space-time, money-time, and digital-time realms. When considering smart space as the good to be priced in a model of smart buildings, it is obvious that Lancaster's assumption cannot hold. Each space user experiences real estate in a unique manner resulting in what Curry and Sheth (2018) call "a market-of-one". To describe space users' unique surrounding worlds in smart space, Lecomte (2019a, 2020) refers to "Umwelt", a concept borrowed from Heidegger's phenomenology (see Appendix 2.1). To paraphrase Situationist precursor Chtcheglow (1933–1998) in his Formulary of a New Urbanism, in a smart building "everyone will live in his own cathedral".

Hence, due to its experiential dimensions and focus on building occupants' well-being, smart space questions the use of decision utilities in hedonic pricing models of smart real estate. Furthermore, smart buildings' occupants do not make every decision impacting their well-being in smart space since ubicomp coupled with non-conscious cognitive instruments transparently and continuously act on their behalf as soon as they step into a smart environment. Defining the scope of decision utility is therefore problematic in a smart building.

Indeed, decision utility would struggle to gauge the full spectrum of subtle utilities involved in human-building interactions in smart environments. As mentioned before, decision utility also supposes that smart building occupants are capable of making rational choices on a range of utility-bearing characteristics which are technological in essence. This seems quite unrealistic in practice.

Despite its irrelevance for hedonic pricing models of smart buildings, decision utility can serve a useful purpose when analysed in comparison with experienced utility. The difference between the two utilities may even become an important indicator in smart real estate analysis at the micro-scale.

• **The difference between decision utility and experienced utility in smart space as an indicator of affordances in smart buildings**

The difference between decision utility and experienced utility, customarily known as "focusing illusion" in economics, can be of great interest to smart buildings' owners provided they have a way to derive it. This is a granular indicator at the building level, which focuses on occupants rather than physical or digital structures. Let's define the difference D by

$$D_t = \sum_{t=1}^{n} U \text{ decision} - U \text{ experienced}$$

where n is the total number of building occupants at a given time t (instant utility) or over a period of time t (concept of extended utility mentioned in Kahneman, Wakker and Sarin, 1997).

D_t is the difference between decision utility and experienced utility for a specific interaction (or series of interactions attached to an activity) in a smart building.

Pervasive computing and non-conscious cognitive systems in smart real estate impose on space users' pre-defined decision utilities inferred from revealed preferences in smart space (and derived from space users' Umwelt). In that sense, in smart environments, decision utility is ubicomp's modelled utility. It is an ex-ante utility whose technicalities might elude building occupants.

However, space users' highly customised interactions with the built environment produce utilities which are first and foremost experiential, i.e. experienced utilities which quantify the actual amount of pleasure and pain evoked while interacting with the building. D, the difference between decision utility and experienced utility in smart buildings, measures the degree of 'non-predictability' of building occupants' experiences in smart space. It indicates how their own unique ways of experiencing space are not yet fully calibrated by the built environment's embedded technological apparatus. As technology becomes smarter and space users' personal surrounding worlds (Umwelt) take shape in smart space, one can envision decision utility and experienced utility to converge (D = 0) to the point where space users' experiences in space are perfectly forecasted by technology.[6]

Until this point is reached, the ability of embedded technologies to optimise space users' utility will affect the price of utility-bearing characteristics in the two proposed models of smart buildings. A negative difference (D < 0) hints at affordances in smart space which are not properly modelled in the building's technological apparatus. It is a good sign for any smart building owners inasmuch as more value can be accounted for than the building's enterprise currently does (e.g. obsolete taxonomy of activities, accrued synergies among existing interactions).

Conversely, a positive D (i.e. experienced utility is less than decision utility) hints at misaffordances in smart space. These could stem from an array of causes, such as (i) dysfunction at one or several of smart space's four layers, (ii) a disconnect between a building's physical structure and its digital infrastructure resulting in failed synergies among pre-defined human-building interactions, or (iii) mismatches with the changing ways that space users perceive and/or consume smart space and its characteristics such as level of monitoring, respect for privacy, memory duration, and overall trust in context-aware environments. In any case, it is a warning signal for smart property owners.

Thus, it makes no doubt that unless D = 0, basing a hedonic pricing model of smart real estate on decision utility is inherently faulty. It would result in wrong estimates of a building's price, with either underestimation if D < 0 or overestimation if D > 0. Experienced utility in hedonic pricing models of smart buildings is another break from aggregate thinking in real estate finance. Utilities in smart buildings are no longer deemed to be homogeneous. On the contrary, after 18th-century English economist Jeremy Bentham, experienced utility acknowledges the uniqueness of human interactions with the built environment in terms of their "intensity, duration, certainty and propinquity" (Stigler, 1950).

2 Property rights in smart environments: the advent of digital rights for smart buildings

This section explores another consequence of the emergence of smart space in real estate analysis: the changing nature of property rights in smart urban environments. Property rights are a fundamental tenet of real estate, its legal dimension. Alongside land and building, property rights are a major real estate resource which represents "income or income potentials [for] the people who own, use, produce, finance or market them" (Weimer and Hoyt, 1966).

In his Fundamentals of Real Estate Development (1981), James A. Graaskamp elaborates further:

> Individual and collective use of space-time resources and land has always been regulated by society, in part through law and in the larger part through political administration of the laws [...] The rights to use or abuse, to provide expertise or choose contractors, the rights to prohibit or to condition use in

certain ways or to transfer rights from one person to another are defined as property rights. Society creates, and continually modifies the allocation of property rights among private ownership, public institutional ownership, and common ownership indivisible among all members of society.

In the four-dimensional framework of real estate (height, length, width, and time), rights for "space-time resources" are well captured by the classic concept of property rights. However, in smart buildings, there is a fifth dimension of real estate, that of digital (Lecomte, 2020). In parallel to Graaskamp's space-time and money-time realms of real estate, a new digital-time realm emerges. Given this sweeping evolution, are property rights defined in the classic framework of non-smart buildings in non-smart cities applicable to smart buildings in smart cities? Or is there a need for a new definition of property rights pertaining to smart buildings in smart cities? If so, how should these new rights be defined, valued and exchanged? What are the implications for owners of smart buildings?

These are the main questions that this section addresses by exploring:

– the nature of property rights in smart environments,
– the economic foundations of property rights attached to smart buildings,
– the economic analysis (and pricing) of these property rights through a series of axioms underpinned by Henri Lefebvre (1974)'s seminal analysis of urban space's appropriation in *The Production of Space*.

In this book, smart real estate's new property rights are introduced as "digital rights", a term explained in the following section.

2.1 The advent of digital rights for smart buildings

• **Embedded technology as a trigger for a new type of property rights in smart real estate**

Pervasive computing's impact on real estate's legal dimension should not be overlooked. As a new spatial dimension opens up in smart environments, an increasing number of human activities are mediated by smart technologies, thereby taking over the usual role of buildings in cities (Ratti and Claudel, 2014). Property rights are rights in the space-time and money-time realms. What about rights pertaining to property ownership in the digital-time realm?

From property owners' standpoint, does controlling access to smart space have value? By the same token, does controlling the use of smart space have value? To both questions, the answer is undoubtedly yes. As smart buildings are akin to a series of interactions at the intersection of physical and digital spaces, controlling access and use of smart space does have value. Hence, property rights attached to access and use of smart space should be properly ascertained and assessed. The term 'digital rights' has been coined to describe these new rights. Digital rights are property rights in smart space. The very concept of a new type of property rights resulting from the emergence of a new technology is nothing new. This is a natural process: property rights evolve over time. As pointed out by Ratcliff (1949):

> Since society is dynamic, so must be the institution of property, to be subjected to constant alteration as man's notions of the general welfare shift and evolve and as technological advance calls for new patterns of social organization. [...] Property in the sense of ownership has been defined as 'the exclusive right to control an economic good'. Property has no significance when the property object has no economic value. Property raises a wall about ownership to exclude all others.

Studies conducted by property rights scholars support a similar view that technological innovation should trigger an evolution in property rights. Furthermore, according to Demsetz (1967) who pioneered the academic study of rights creation, "new rights are created in response to new economic forces that increase the value of the rights" (Barzel, 1997).

In the case of smart space, these new economic forces are numerous and only starting to appear. Property rights cover all activities involving non-conscious cognitive devices and pervasive computing in smart buildings. These encompass:

- Embedded technology (e.g. IoTs, sensors, actuators),
- Human-smart space interactions,
- Data collection, warehousing, and analytics.

Potential liabilities pertaining to security, privacy, and behavioural control in smart real estate come with digital rights. Noticeably, rights related to the smart grid (e.g. the right for property owners/tenants to sell energy produced in smart prosumer buildings) are not within the scope of digital rights. Instead, they are treated as an extension of property rights inasmuch as they do not materialise in smart space but in physical space.

There are many instances when smart technologies create opportunities to generate value in smart real estate and thus many instances when digital rights would be extremely valuable. To make the argument in favour of digital rights more concrete, let's look at a few seemingly straightforward situations arising when shoppers visit a smart shopping mall. In these situations, agreeing on property rights' ownership in smart space would be extremely difficult without a well-defined regime of digital rights.

For instance, who should own the data collected when shoppers evolve in a mall? Who should have the right to install and exploit cyber-physical systems (e.g. based on facial recognition systems) in the mall, or within limited and well-defined areas of the mall? Who should have the right to use smart technology to entice shoppers towards one retail outlet/ area of the mall rather than another? Whenever shoppers enter into a particular retail outlet, who should own the data collected during their visits in the store? Do the data belong to the mall operator or to the tenants? Should data ownership be divided depending on which interactions in smart space are concerned (e.g. environmental interactions for the mall operator, all other interactions for the tenants depending on where they take place in the mall)? If the data belong to the mall operator, can data collected in a retail outlet be used to drive sales in other potentially competing outlets located in the same mall? Does a retail outlet have the right to digitally interact with shoppers while they are visiting or simply walking by competing brands' outlets? Who should decide? If cyber-physical systems embedded in the mall's physical structure enable interactions in common areas, who should benefit from them in order to attract footfall and generate sales, for instance in case of two neighbouring retail outlets? Can tenants decide to opt out from the mall's smart ICT infrastructure (e.g. face-recognition-free retail spaces) or pledge to restrict their in-store data collection on shoppers' behaviours (e.g. anonymous data only or disclosed time limit on all data uses) at the expense of the mall's overall ability to optimise returns in smart space over time?[7]

Similar issues to those identified here in the case of retail properties apply to other commercial property types (e.g. office buildings). In sum, who owns access to smart space and determine space users' interactions in smart space? Who owns the right to exert control on space users' experiences in smart space? Concretely in tenanted smart buildings, should property owners own these economic rights? Or should they rest with tenants, e.g. proportionately to their usage rights for physical space as contractually agreed in leases? The institution of digital rights can help address the myriad of questions that will inevitably pop up as smart technologies become ever more pervasive in the built environment, while enabling the real estate sector to capture as much value as possible from smart space.

- **Lockean Proviso and digital rights in smart buildings**

Although obviously linked to value creation in real estate, digital rights in smart space do not necessarily require the formation of privately owned property rights. Commons could be the optimal solution for smart space. The litmus test applied by property rights scholars to determine whether a market should be regulated by commons or private property rights is known as the Lockean Proviso. The Lockean Proviso is named after 17th-century philosopher John Locke who, in his *Second Treatise of Government*, analyses land appropriation by using the famous phrase "still enough and as good as left". Schmidtz (1994) explains:

> Locke's idea seems to have been that any residual common [...] claim to the land could be met if a person could appropriate it without prejudice to other people, in other words, if person could leave enough and as good for others.

In practice, the Lockean Proviso is exceedingly difficult to meet. The main criteria in applying the Proviso is the scarcity of resources inherent to capitalist economies. As pointed out by Alchian and Demsetz (1973), "capitalism relies heavily on markets and private property rights to resolve conflicts over the use of scarce resources".

Schmidtz (1994) assesses:

> When resources are not scarce, the Lockean Proviso permits appropriation; when resources are scarce, the Proviso requires appropriation [...] When resources are scarce, it is leaving in the commons that would be prejudicial to future generations.

So, the question boils down to: is smart space scarce? If so, the Lockean Proviso would prescribe the creation of specific property rights in smart real estate. Conversely, commons would suffice to manage access and use of smart space in smart buildings.

Smart space sits at the intersect of physical space and digital space: it is a hybrid space. Therefore, there are two potential drivers of scarcity for smart space: physical space, and digital space. Of these two spaces, physical space is the most likely to be limited insofar as digital space depends on technologies whose progresses are not limited in the long run. Physical space in any property is a finite resource captured in areal surface measurements. As such, whenever a space user is in physical space, he/she might prevent others to consume smart space: due to its physicality, smart space is subject to exclusion.

Likewise, the number and capacity of non-conscious cognitive instruments (e.g. IoTs, cyber-physical systems) embedded in physical space are also finite. One square meter in any building can embed so many sensors and captors which, irrespective of how large technological progresses enable them to be, are not unlimited. Furthermore, these devices are also limited in terms of their usage capacity. Whilst an actuator is involved in implementing a pre-defined interaction in smart space, it cannot take care of an unlimited number of other interactions, notwithstanding its extreme versatility.[8] Therefore, whenever a space user interacts with technology in physical space, he/she uses up smart space resources: smart space is a rival good.

In that sense, technology-embedded physical space within the structural confines of a smart building is a private good and a scarce resource.[9] By dominating space, technology allows property owners to create property rights that regulate interactions in smart space. To paraphrase Weimer and Hoyt (1966), in smart urban environments, real estate resources include land (with smart grid), smart buildings (physical structure and embedded ICT infrastructure) plus property rights. These rights are of a dual nature: property rights for the physical space and digital rights for the smart space component of real estate.

Technology influences property rights, but the reverse is also true (Pejovich, 1996). Without a proper regime of rights in smart space, there will be little incentive for the real estate industry to invest in future proofing their properties and bear the legal liabilities and regulatory requirements that will increasingly come with the implementation of embedded pervasive technologies in the built environment.[10] Digital rights appear like the necessary complement to the two hedonic pricing models of smart buildings, by creating and protecting value for investors. It does not take a crystal ball to see that digital rights are bound to play an instrumental role in the digitalisation of commercial real estate.[11]

- **Digital rights and the notion of boundaries in smart space**

For new rights to emerge, they need to be delineated. Barzel (1997) explains that

> what causes an imperfect delineation of rights is the choice of owners not to exercise all their rights. [As] describing what the property is and protecting it consume resources [...], the delineation of property rights is in itself subject to individuals' optimization.

Non-exercised rights move into the public domain. In the case of digital rights, the technology involved in creating new rights adds an important dimension to consider. Digital rights are rights to a hybrid space, partly physical, partly digital. Furthermore, digital rights are the by-product of pervasive computing. Without ubicomp, the question of right delineation in smart space would not be so acute since all human-computer interactions would take place in fixed locations in physical space. However, ubicomp is by definition ubiquitous. It is calm and transparent to its users. It promotes fluidity and seamless continuity of spatial experiences. How can such characteristics be compatible with the emergence of digital rights? To delineate rights, boundaries are necessary.

Pervasive computing researchers have analysed the question of boundaries in pervasive intelligent space and asserted that one fundamental tenet of ubicomp is the "boundary principle". According to Ma et al. (2005), although "boundaries in smart space are not necessarily related to a boundary in the physical world, spatial features of a smart space must be clearly drawn". These researchers assess that boundaries are essential as a smart world will consist of many ubiquitous systems rather than one single system. The same is true of a smart building which might have to accommodate multiple tenants with potentially very different requirements with respect to smart space (a situation exemplified by the notion of standard and specific interactions mentioned previously). Therefore, what should define a workable system of boundary and maintenance in smart space? Should boundaries in smart space derive from physical space or digital space, or both?

To emerge, property rights need enclosure. Umbeck (1981) propounds that "all private ownership rights are ultimately founded upon the ability to forcefully exclude potential competitors". Achieving this martial ideal in smart space will involve delineations not only in physical space (e.g. clearly delineated surface area in a building) but also in digital space (e.g. cyber-physical systems, data analytics, AI).

Defining rights underpinned by use in digital space is not easy. The issue of boundaries in cyberspace has been dividing law scholars since the World Wide Web appeared in the 1990s. Cyberspace is sometimes considered as a place with delineated borders defining property rights (Reeves, 1996), or as a placeless space where commons should prevail (Hunter, 2003). Beyond the debate about the legal nature of cyberspace, the issue at stake here is whether smart space is a legal place whose boundaries can be perfectly defined or a placeless space as far as law making is concerned.[12]

According to Johnson and Post (1996), "cyberspace challenges the law's traditional reliance on territorial borders; it is a "space" bounded by screens and passwords rather than physical markers". For geographic boundaries to apply for law making, four conditions have to be met:

i   *power* (i.e. "control over physical space and the people and things located in that space"),
ii   *effects* (i.e. "the correspondence between physical boundaries and 'law space' boundaries [reflecting] a deeply rooted relationship between physical proximity and the effects of any particular behaviour"),
iii *legitimacy* (i.e. "persons within a geographically defined border are the ultimate source of law-making authority for activities within that border"),
iv   *notice* (i.e. "physical boundaries are appropriate for the delineation of 'law space' in the physical world because they can give notice that rules change when the boundaries are crossed. Proper boundaries have signposts that provide warning that will be required after crossing, to abide by different rules [...]").

In light of these four conditions, are geographic boundaries applicable to rights in smart space? Or is smart space more akin to cyberspace? Noticeably, contrary to cyberspace whose "power to control activities has only the most tenuous connections to physical location" (Johnson and Post, 1996), smart space gives control over physical space, either owned or tenanted. Its effects are deeply rooted in physical space, whether it is about footfall in a shopping mall or hot-desking in an office building. By the same token, digital rights are not property rights in cyberspace. A property owner is legitimate as the ultimate source of authority in dealing with the building's smart space. And, physical boundaries in a property (e.g. physical separation between a retail outlet and its neighbours) are appropriate for the delineation of smart space regimes (i.e. changes of rules). Hence, smart space can meet the four above-mentioned conditions. As such, territorial boundaries are relevant for 'law-making' in smart space and, in turn, for delineating digital rights.

Digital rights are fundamentally bounded by physical space. The boundary "made up of screens and passwords" mentioned in Johnson and Post (1996) no longer exists with ubicomp. In smart real estate, space users mesh with buildings' infrastructure in what smart building researchers call bi-directional consciousness (e.g. Warwick, 2013), which paradoxically roots digital rights in smart space's physical component.

An interesting framework for analysing digital rights in smart properties with multiple owners and/or tenants is that of containers in cyberspace introduced by a joint group of Harvard Law School and MIT students as part of the MIT Internet

Policy Initiative (Adida et al., 1998). A container is a metaphor for ownership in cyberspace. They write:

> Each container has an owner [...] who has control over the contents and the permissions of the container. Each container consists of a barrier or set of barriers between its contents and the outside world [...] Ownership of containers includes the entitlement to exclude third parties, the right to possess and control access to a container, and the right to determine what actions or behaviors are allowed with a container.

Smart space can be called a container whose access is permitted unless technical barriers attempt to prevent it. Besides, despite the existence of privately owned and managed containers, users have a right to public digital space. For instance, a shopping mall manager should not be allowed to prevent space users in a mall from visiting public cyberspace (legit websites) while they are in the property. By the same token, a brand represented in a mall should not prevent shoppers from looking at a competing brand's website while they are in its retail outlet, but it can prevent shoppers from receiving promotional messages from a competing brand while they are physically located in its retail outlet's smart space (which would be equivalent to a form of 'digital trespass'). Containers in smart space which are anchored in physical space embody the fact that boundaries in smart space should be based on territorial boundaries in a building (e.g. a building owner has control over smart space in his/her building, but not in neighbouring buildings).

In sum, the principle of territorial delineation for digital rights in smart buildings is consistent with ubicomp's boundary principle and smart space's hybrid nature as both physical and digital spaces. Beyond the legal argument presented here, boundaries in smart space will ultimately have to be consistent with the way smart space is produced and consumed by real estate players and space users, respectively. Delineation is also important in defining trespass in smart space. In that respect, boundaries will need to be easy to identify and enforce, lest costly and unclear delineation results in negative externalities for all.

- **Divided ownership of digital rights in smart buildings**

According to Graaskamp (1970), there are two basic issues to consider with real estate space's legal dimension: access and claims. Access refers to "decision-making prerogatives arising out of the right to occupy the land or to control its use", and claims to "the benefits or income arising out of ownership".

Similarly, smart space encompasses two distinct sets of rights:

- Rights to access and control smart space: for instance by implementing smart technologies in the built environment and/or by setting up interactions between space users and the building. These rights are called *Digital Access Rights*;
- Rights to use smart space, for instance to generate revenues. These rights are called *Digital Usage Rights*.

Should these two sets of rights be owned by a unique stakeholder in a smart building? Or should these new rights' ownership be divided among different stakeholders in a smart building (e.g. owners, tenants, technology providers)? If so, on which grounds should the attribution take place?

Whoever owns Digital Access Rights can decide on which technologies and interactions to implement in a building, where to position them and how to use them. Whoever owns Digital Usage Rights is entitled to employ smart space to create value in space. Barzel (1997) explains that

> the structure of rights is expected to be designed so as to allocate ownership of individual attributes such that the parties who have a comparative advantage in affecting the income flow over the attributes that are susceptible to common-property problem will obtain rights over them.

Let's apply this principle to smart buildings, by first defining the scope of the two sets of rights. Digital Access Rights should apply to the whole of smart space within the confines of a smart building (common areas, tenanted space, non-tenanted space). By contrast, Digital Usage Rights should only apply to tenanted spaces and be defined as part of contractual agreements between property owners and tenants. If a tenant wants to modify smart space access in his or her tenanted space (e.g. specific interactions), then he/she needs to get the owner's approval since the latter controls smart space owing to full and undivided ownership of access rights. Maintenance of technologies will also fall under property owners. By the same token, the implementation of standard and specific interactions discussed previously is regulated by Digital Access Rights. As owners hold all Digital Access Rights, implementing specific interactions and maintaining smart technologies underpinning these interactions is under their responsibility. Incidentally, owners should have the right to refuse tenants' request for specific interactions that they consider as non-appropriate or non-compatible with their strategic vision of their properties.

By controlling access to smart space, property owners make sure of the perfect compatibility of all smart technologies and interactions implemented in their smart buildings. They also bear the full responsibility and liability with respect to smart space's infrastructure in their properties. Case in point: if it is illegal, say, to install facial recognition cameras inside certain retail outlets in a smart shopping mall, should a tenant decide to go ahead and set up such devices in his rented space without informing the landlord, then the landlord bears the responsibility. Hence, owners will have to actively monitor all devices implemented by tenants in their properties.

Indeed, in the proposed structure for digital rights, it is the owners' duties to ensure that all technologies and interactions implemented in their properties comply with legal and regulatory requirements. Lest responsibilities are unclear or diluted, ownership of Digital Access Rights should exclusively remain with owners at all times. Conversely, Digital Usage Rights should be divided among owners and tenants. Tenants are the most qualified to leverage on smart space attributes so as to generate income. Use of smart space is a smart building's attribute which the owner does not retain. This attribute is bounded by physical space according to the lease terms agreed upon by landlords and tenants. Owners relinquish this subset of rights to tenants who remain rights holders as long as their leases are on-going. Once their leases expire, Digital Usage Rights should automatically revert to property owners.

During the life of their leases, tenants bear full responsibility for the way they use smart space (e.g. by using their own proprietary digital tools) and specific interactions they select to implement in their rented spaces. As their Digital Usage Rights are bounded by physical surfaces, they cannot overstep into other tenants' and owners' smart space, nor interfere with it. This would be equivalent to trespass. Digital Usage Rights of all common areas in a smart building belong to property owners who might decide to relinquish this subset of rights under special circumstances, e.g. for well-defined areas and/or interactions over limited periods of time. Out of fairness for all tenants, owners' ability to relinquish their Digital Usage Rights in a smart building's common areas would have to be strictly codified by contractual agreements between property owners and all tenants as a clause in ad hoc "smart space leases" that could be added to existing leases for physical space.

With digital rights' implementation comes the issue of data collected in smart buildings. Who should own these data? And, who should have the right to use analytics to leverage on these data?

One might argue that since data are collected in their properties, owners should own all rights related to data. As a matter of fact, if Digital Access Rights' ownership is the attribution criteria, all data collected in a smart building would belong to property owners. However, this seems sub-optimal inasmuch as tenants do play a role in data collection and would eventually benefit the most from an optimal use of data analytics in smart space. Tenants are the most qualified to create value from data collected in their rental spaces.

In the proposed structure of digital rights, the rule for attributing Digital Usage Rights is simple: data collected in a smart building's tenanted space belong to tenants while data collected in common areas and non-tenanted space belong to property owners.[13] This would provide a balanced and unquestionable yardstick for allocating rights related to data collection and use. As stated by Barzel (1997), "the value of multi-attribute assets is not necessarily maximized if these assets are owned by single individuals; it may be enhanced by allocating ownership over individual attributes according to comparative advantages". This point highlights another fundamental dimension of any successful smart space strategy for the real estate industry: it needs to be cooperative, possibly even more so than in physical space. Cooperation and value sharing will build trust among all stakeholders in smart space, and make smart buildings profitable assets for both landlords and tenants. As cost bearers for all technologies implemented in their properties, landlords will need to develop strong partnerships with their tenants to create as much value as possible from digital rights.

- **Digital rights and space users' digital surrounding worlds**

Through data collection and analytics applied in smart space, digital rights refer to the optimisation, or to put it more bluntly the control, of space users' experiences in smart real estate. The scope of this optimisation depends on smart space's objectives in a particular building, e.g. increasing sales in a smart shopping mall, productivity and well-being in a smart office building. Hence, digital rights are multiform and closely linked to the concept of Umwelt in smart space (see Appendix 2.1).

Digital Usage Rights enable rights owners to tap into space users' digital surrounding worlds and, in many ways, to shape them. In that respect, Digital Usage Rights carry with them the right to monetise space users' Umwelt. Umwelt captures digital rights' temporal dimension and ultimately a large chunk of their value for rights holders. Markedly, Digital Usage Rights without the corresponding data component would be significantly less valuable as they would lack the long memory built over time while Umwelt is being shaped at each point of pre-designed interactions in smart space.

- **Digital rights and the need for digital governance in the real estate sector**

The concept of digital rights is not devoid of potential controversies. Cynics might argue that smart buildings' technological apparatus is essentially about controlling space users' attention in smart environments in order to profit from digital rights. If one plays the devil's advocate, Weiser's pervasive computing which emphasises peripheral attention might just be a calm way to let things happening in the background eschew humans' attention. Who can reassure space users that nothing nefarious is actually going on? Digital rights would be the legal and economic expression of this opaque process which implies constant monitoring in smart real estate and the accumulation of as much data as technically feasible.

In response to this view, McCullough (2013) who pleads in favour of tangible information commons, what he calls 'ambient commons', proposes a vision of the world where "citizens have a right to engage one another and the built world they inhabit in ways that are unmediated, uninstructed, unscripted, and undocumented". Such technology-free idyllic information environment would wipe out digital rights in smart buildings, by irremediably destroying their value. Does it make sense? Is the absence of technology in the built environment the right answer to the challenges posed by pervasive computing and smart technologies?

Beyond the debate about the humanist implications of "cognitive assemblages" in the built environment (Hayles, 2017), it makes no doubt that without safeguards in place, digital rights may contribute to an Orwellian world of algorithmic control and cognitive manipulation in smart real estate insofar as they give rights holders the economic incentive to behave in such a way. Conversely, with proper rules and regulations upholding an ethics of smart space whose principles would have to be defined, probably under the stewardship of some official authorities (e.g. as part of broader digital governance principles for the real estate sector), digital rights may foster the emergence of ambient commons whereby space users' attention in smart environments is valued and protected, notwithstanding the underlying motives which might eventually turn out to be mercantile.

In sum, digital rights have to be accompanied by a clear set of rules pertaining to digital governance in the built environment. Digital rights' ability to generate value for the real estate sector hinges on this insofar as transparency and trust in smart space will condition space users' willingness to engage with smart buildings. Hence, digital rights are not only a way for real estate players to create and appropriate value in smart buildings, they also represent new sources of societal responsibilities and complex ethical issues which will realistically take a lot of efforts for all stakeholders to get a full grasp of (Lecomte, 2015).

BOX 2.1: What does it mean to own a smart building in a smart city?

- In smart cities, a new real estate space known as *smart space* sits at the intersect of physical space and digital space.
- As a result, there are four layers to smart space: two layers in physical space (land-smart grid, the building's physical structure) and two layers in digital space (ICT infrastructure, digital skin-cloud).
- Smart buildings can be valued by applying specific hedonic pricing models.
- Two hedonic pricing models are proposed in this book: (i) an hedonic model based on smart space's four layers. The model is built around a smart building score called the *Smart Index Matrix*; and (ii) an activity-based hedonic model which considers that a smart building is equivalent to the sum of human-building interactions taking place within the building. Each interaction per activity carried out in the building is individually valued and added up to determine a smart building's price.
- In addition to property rights for physical space, smart buildings come with rights attached to smart space.
- These new property rights known as *digital rights* cover all activities within a building pertaining to data collection and analytics, embedded technologies (e.g. sensors, actuators), and interactions between a building and its occupants in smart space.
- Digital rights can be broken down into two distinct subsets of rights: (i) *Digital Access Rights* (rights to create and control smart space) which belong to property owners; and (ii) *Digital Usage Rights* (rights to use smart space) whose ownership is divided between property owners (common areas and non-tenanted spaces) and tenants (tenanted spaces).
- Ownership of data collected in the building is defined according to Digital Usage Rights, allowing for a divided data ownership between property owners and tenants.

- Owning a smart building in a smart city means having ownership of: land (including access to and use of smart grid*), the building's physical structure and ICT infrastructure, property rights in physical space, and digital rights in smart space (i.e. Digital Access Rights in full and divided ownership of Digital Usage Rights and Data). The price of a smart building has to include all these smart real estate resources.

(*) In the proposed regime of digital rights, rights relative to smart grids are deemed to be part of property rights in physical space.

2.2 Economic foundations of digital rights in smart buildings

This section presents a theoretical approach to digital rights, by modelling smart space in economic terms. Its aim is to add the digital realm to the classic framework applied in real estate economics. To do so, it relies on Henri Lefebvre's (1974) analysis of urban space. Lefebvre views urban space, or "lived space", as either dominated space or appropriated space. The two categories of space experienced by people coexist in cities. In a capitalist economy, property rights signify the domination of physical space by property owners, which translates into digital rights for smart buildings in smart cities.

The book proposes twelve axioms to model smart space in smart buildings according to the Lefebvrian paradigm of space. These axioms capture the power struggle underlying smart space attribution as different stakeholders in a building (owners, tenants, occupants) might have diverging interests, in particular as far as control in and over space is concerned. Findings from this analysis can serve to inform the pricing of digital rights in smart buildings.

The fundamental principles for an economic analysis of digital rights are introduced after a brief presentation of Henri Lefebvre's theories on urban space and their relevance to smart space.

- **Lefebvre's paradigm of space domination and appropriation**

In his seminal opus on urban space, *The Production of Space* (1974), Henri Lefebvre asserts that in cities, there are two categories of space: dominated (dominant) space and appropriated space. Dominated space is "a space transformed and mediated- by technology, by practice". Dominant space is "invariably the realization of a master's project". For instance, military architecture, fortifications and ramparts, dams and irrigation systems are classic examples of dominated space.

The polar opposite to dominated space is appropriated space. An appropriated space is "a natural space modified in order to serve the needs and possibilities of a group that it has been appropriated by that group". A site, a structure, a square, or a street may exemplify appropriated space although "it is not always easy to decide in what respect, how and by whom and for whom they have been appropriated".

Lefebvre assesses that dominated spaces and appropriated spaces which are antagonistic should be combined. There is no appropriation without domination. Hence, appropriation is the result of a struggle with overpowering historical trends towards domination. Dominated space is a space of power. It is laden with "constraints and violence [which] are encountered at every turn".

Conversely, appropriation is a process that plays out over time, and cannot "be understood apart from the rhythms of time and of life". When it comes to the private sphere, Lefebvre propounds that "in the best of circumstances, the outside space of the community is dominated, while the indoor space of family life is appropriated". What people essentially buy when purchasing their house is time, i.e. the time to appropriate their own domestic spaces.

Technology does play a crucial role in enabling spaces to become dominated. More than any other elements in the built environment, commercial buildings condense the whole paradigm of space domination by technology, which is not devoid of consequences for space users' ability to appropriate smart space. "Thanks to technology, the domination of space is becoming, as it were, completely dominant. [...] In order to dominate space, technology introduces a new form into a pre-existing space". According to Lefebvre, the more a space is functionalised, the less susceptible it is to appropriation. A highly functionalised space is removed from the sphere of space users' lived time which is "diverse and complex".

Irrespective, Lefebvre acknowledges that things are never in black and white in the complex relationship between technology and space. Indeed, "there is no such thing as technology or technicity [...] bearing no trace of appropriation" even though technology systematically favours domination over appropriation[14]

Another way to look at dominated and appropriated spaces is to think in terms of quantitative and qualitative spaces. Dominant space is quantitative, i.e. it relies on objective measurements, whereas appropriated space is qualitative. Interestingly, the space of consumption, the quintessential productive space, is quantitative whereas the consumption of space out of any productive activities (e.g. leisure) is qualitative. Lefebvre assesses that "the dominant tendency [...] is towards the disappearance of the qualitative, towards its assimilation subsequent upon [...] brutal or seductive treatment".

At the more extreme end of the spectrum, a space which is rendered totally functional and dominated becomes abstract. Abstract space is measurable not only as geometrical space, but also as "social space [which] is subject to quantitative manipulations: statistics, programming, projections". As a tool of domination, abstract space is lethal by "[asphyxiating] whatever is conceived within it".

Lefebvre, who analyses the dichotomy between domination and appropriation from space users' perspective, is firmly against property rights regimes which, in his views, foster urban space domination by land owners[15]. Lefebvre's vision supports the right to the city for all city dwellers (Purcell, 2013). Property rights are supposedly hindering this fundamental right to the city which should belong to people who inhabit it. Space users should be entitled to their own "appropriated space-time" so that their use value comes to replace the market's exchange value of properties. In the context of digital rights, one could argue that digital rights should not exist in the first place as they 'rob' space users of their legitimate right to smart space. The analysis of digital rights presented here approaches this aspect of the Lefebvrian paradigm in a very pragmatic and non-partisan manner. It does not question the existence of digital rights. Rather, it focuses on their optimal attribution among the different stakeholders involved in a smart building.

- **Space appropriation in smart buildings**

The Lefebvrian paradigm of dominated/appropriated space provides a useful framework to analyse smart space through the prism of control. Digital rights are the tools enabling economic control over smart buildings as income-, or rather value-, generating properties. The phrase "value-generating property" embodies the multidimensional real estate resources at work in a smart building (physical, embedded ICT infrastructure, digital skin/cloud, data). Digital rights offer control over these multiple resources.

Digital rights are therefore a marker for space domination and appropriation[16]. Digital Access Rights (DARs) epitomise space domination in the space-time realm of commercial real estate while Digital Usage Rights (DURs) symbolise space appropriation in the digital-time realm (as introduced in Lecomte, 2020). Markedly, there are no Digital Usage Rights without pre-existing Digital Access Rights. That is, there is no appropriation of smart space without technology-powered domination of pre-existing space. In a simplistic vision of spatial domination, smart buildings' technological apparatus allows for the domination of physical space and the emergence of smart space.[17]

Hence, smart space's genesis supposes at its very core the domination of physical space by technology. Without this fundamental process, smart space would not emerge. All smart space is therefore dominated space. This originally dominated space acts as the intrinsic building block of a smart building and gives rise to Digital Access Rights, i.e. rights to dominate physical space with pervasive technology and create smart space. The value of these rights should somehow reflect the scope of spatial domination, e.g. the number of human-technology interactions in a smart building.

Once smart space is being dominated (i.e. a functioning smart building), it can only create value for owners and tenants by being appropriated. Appropriation in smart space implies the ability to use smart space as the driver or background of value-creating economic processes in real estate. Digital Usage Rights allocate this value between owners and tenants, including potentially the most valuable smart real estate resource of all: data. Digital Usage Rights embody space appropriation in a smart building. By renting out spaces, tenants appropriate both physical space and smart space.

In addition to tenants as space appropriators, building occupants' situation can also be analysed in light of Lefebvre's paradigm. Space users' interactions in smart space generate a long-term memory process captured and powered by data and conceptually known as Umwelt. Umwelt is a space user's own digital surrounding world which takes shape over time as she/he interacts in smart space. A myriad of questions arise when the notion of Umwelt collides with digital rights. Is Umwelt truly a form of spatial appropriation, or simply domination in disguise? Who should own space users' Umwelts? In particular, should the rights to collect data in smart space (as part of DURs) come with the rights to own space users' digital surrounding worlds? And, ultimately, is space appropriation possible at all for smart buildings' occupants given the technology involved and/or the proposed regime of digital rights?

To identify the rightful ownership of space users' Umwelts in smart space, let's focus on data. Data is the raw material of these personalised digital surrounding worlds. According to the digital rights regime presented in this book, data ownership is divided between property owners and tenants based on Digital Usage Rights (DURs). Hence, the right to shape building occupants' digital surroundings belongs to tenants for their tenanted spaces and property owners for all other spaces. Nevertheless, should space users be granted rights to their Umwelts in parallel to what DURs prescribe?

The answer to this question can be unequivocally positive provided specific rights unbundled from DURs are granted to space users:

- right to access one's Umwelt and/or modify it in part or in full;
- right to control use of one's Umwelt for some or all activities/ interactions in smart space and related data collection;
- and as an extreme case of the above, the right to prevent use of one's Umwelt in smart space altogether (without any authorised data collection).

Unless some or all of the above-mentioned rights emerge, building occupants have no abilities whatsoever to control their Umwelts[18] (i.e. to appropriate smart space). Granting building occupants rights over their Umwelts would represent a dilution of DURs potentially at the expenses of both property owners and tenants. Equivalent monetary value to that extracted from DURs' full ownership might not directly materialise with building occupants. Nonetheless, one can expect these rights to trigger an increase in space users' welfare, and consequently to lead to accrued experienced utilities. Tenants might benefit reputationally but also economically through increased traffic and sales. In turn, property owners might benefit through increased valuation. How much net value is thus created would eventually determine owners' and tenants' willingness to unbundle and share their DURs.

Hence, the decision to grant building occupants' rights to Umwelt represents a trade-off between direct and indirect value creation in a smart building. Owners and tenants would have to decide on their digital strategy as part of what amounts to an optimal digital ecosystem within a smart building. All stakeholders would have to agree on a 'digital charter' defining the dos and don'ts in a smart building. In the future, regulators can be expected to intervene in digital rights' attribution, e.g. by giving some level of control to space users over their own Umwelt. Controlling DURs could be part of regulators' agenda as well as limitations on DARs' full ownership whereby property owners are requested to turn off specific interactions/ data collection according to space users' own idiosyncratic, albeit legally binding, requests. Over time, the share of building occupants' Umwelts in the overall value of a building's DURs will keep growing to the point of dominating all DURs. As mentioned in Lecomte (2020), smart space is different from physical space because it continuously grows over time, each time a space user steps into a smart building.

Implied in the analysis of digital rights presented in this chapter is the view that without proper safeguards, control over building occupants' Umwelt is an extreme form of spatial domination for the exclusive benefit of digital rights owners. It is extreme insofar as attempts to appropriate smart space by space users are doomed to fail without space users being aware of it, or worse with space users being under the illusion fuelled by calm technology that they are in control over smart space. In smart urban environments, domination is so ubiquitous and pervasive that it becomes invisible.

In theory, data analytics powering smart buildings make it possible for space users to appropriate smart space much faster than they can appropriate physical space in non-smart buildings. However, can quantitative space ever be qualitative? Lefebvre (1974) explains:

> Domination by technology tends towards non-appropriation- i.e. towards destruction. [...] Appropriation itself implies time (or times), rhythm (or rhythms), symbols and a practice. The more space is functionalised – the more completely it falls under the sway of those 'agents' that have manipulated it so as to render it unifunctional- the less susceptible it becomes to appropriation.

Space users' Umwelt which combines time, rhythm, and practice in smart space could be the answer to this fundamental dilemma, provided it can ever set itself free from the grasp of technology. To achieve that, it might need to be granted a legal identity with rights of its own (e.g. as a legally defined digital-self with rights to privacy among others).

As mentioned before, without safeguards such as full public disclosure and rights granted to space users, the seemingly perfect space appropriation which translates into smart space's remarkable user-centricity could easily result in even greater control through code as evoked by Lessig (2006). Indeed, in smart space as in cyberspace, code can be the de-facto law with the consequence to institutionalise algorithmic control in space. To refer to Lefebvre's terminology, smart space has a natural tendency to become abstract. That's why pressures towards space users' control in smart buildings would be very difficult to contain in a 'laisser-faire' environment.

Furthermore, smart space's overpowering quest for value means it is essentially a productive space. Contrary to the 'old' physical space analysed by Lefebvre in the 1970s when the consumption of space (out of the 'space of consumption') could be unproductive, there are no unproductive spaces in smart buildings unless they are designed to be so. By definition, every inch of smart space is dominated, ready for appropriation in exchange for DURs. The odd exception might be spaces designed to be unproductive although they might be concomitantly contributing to smart buildings' value creation in other synergetic ways. Hence, all forms of spatial consumption in smart buildings are intrinsically productive, either directly (e.g. generating sales in a retail outlet) or indirectly (e.g. data collection feeding the buildings' analytics).

Faced with this new economic reality, commercial real estate players should acknowledge the dichotomy between smart space domination and smart space appropriation in their business models and aim, under what can be expected to be a growing number of exogenous constraints (e.g. cybersecurity, challenge to their digital rights) to optimise smart space's value-generating potential for their properties in the interest of all stakeholders.

- **Axioms**

Twelve axioms are proposed to model digital rights and smart space in economic terms. The objective is to incorporate the digital realm into existing models developed in real estate economics. These models were designed for the space-time and money-time realms of real estate only, before pervasive computing even existed. The twelve axioms presented here propose an economic analysis of digital rights that encompass all three realms. By highlighting the rationale behind the regime of digital rights proposed in this book, they ultimately lay out the foundations for much broader and in-depth studies that the digitalisation of real estate will undoubtedly trigger in the field of real estate economics.

The twelve axioms cover four broad topics: the creation of digital rights (axioms 1–3), utilities in smart space (axioms 4–7), the supply of smart space (axioms 8–10), and profit maximisation in smart space (axioms 11–12). Appendix 2.2 which refers to the water rights model of property rights to shed light on the digital rights regime introduced in this book provides the legal background to axioms #1 and #2 listed below.

Axiom #1: Primacy of physical space over digital rights

Property rights supersede any digital rights. Digital rights are attached to property rights. They are derivative of building owners' property rights. Digital rights are bounded by physical space which delineates their reach in a smart building. Thus, digital rights cannot emerge ex-nihilo out of property rights. As a result, property rights and digital rights are inseparable.

Only property rights holders are entitled to create smart space (Digital Access Rights) and to use smart space (Digital Usage Rights). The latter rights are transferrable to tenants for clearly delineated physical space and duration according to contractual agreements between landlords and tenants (e.g. smart space leases).

The inseparability of property rights and digital rights asserts the dominance of the physical realm over the digital realm in smart real estate. The opposite rule (i.e. separability of property rights and digital rights) would overlook the fact that smart buildings are first and foremost physical structures, which serve as platforms to digital and not the reverse. This axiom potentially limits third parties' involvement in digital rights (e.g. technology companies which might be purveyors of smart space solutions) in a parallel market for smart space as there is no possible ownership in the digital realm without underlying tenures in the space realm.

The primacy of property rights over digital rights underscores the importance of physical space for digital rights which would be worthless without it. Dominated physical spaces are the raw material from which digital rights emerge. By the same token, smart space does not create value for property owners and tenants unless they are 'activated' by space users. In that sense, digital rights embody the fact that smart buildings are akin to a series of pre-set value creating processes with consequences in three realms of real estate: space-time, money-time and digital-time. For the legal background to this axiom, one may refer to the riparian doctrine of property rights introduced in Appendix 2.2.

Axiom #2: Transferability of digital rights

Digital rights are transferrable within the limits of Axiom #1 and in accordance with rules which differ between the two categories of digital rights: Digital Access Rights and Digital Usage Rights.

Digital Access Rights (DARs) cannot be transferred to tenants or third parties. They must remain under property owners' full and exclusive control at all times. Conversely, Digital Usage Rights (DURs) can be transferred. Landlords automatically transfer DURs attached to tenanted physical spaces as part of lease agreements. They may also transfer to third parties DURs on non-tenanted spaces. These transfers are strictly limited in space, time, and scope. In the event of a building's sale, digital rights along with property rights are transferred to the new owners. This includes all DARs, and DURs on non-tenanted spaces (e.g. public areas) which automatically revert to the new owners. Meanwhile, DURs on tenanted spaces follow the terms and conditions of ongoing lease agreements signed for these spaces.

By the same token, tenants have the ability to transfer to third parties part of all of their DURs according to terms and conditions stipulated in their smart space leases. In the event of lease termination or expiration on the physical space (space realm), all underlying DURs automatically revert to landlords, irrespective of who the digital rights holders are at the time. Fundamentally, all transfers of DURs to third parties are leaseholds with a break clause for the initial digital rights holders. In accordance with the principle of physical space's primacy, the only freehold in smart space stems from the ownership of property rights linked to the building's physical structure. The limited transferability of Digital Usage Rights represents a risk for third parties as they would have to relinquish their use of smart space upon a building's sale or lease termination, which might occur before their agreements' initial maturity.

Axiom #3: The production of smart space and the concept of digital vacancy in smart buildings

AXIOM 3.1: APPROPRIATED SPACE AS DOMINATED SPACE

All appropriated spaces in a smart building are dominated spaces. However, not all dominated spaces are appropriated. Hence, at any point in time, in the space realm, the total amount of dominated space (D) in a smart building is equal to, or larger than, the amount of appropriated space (A). D and A are measured in units of physical space (e.g. sq.m2, sq. ft) with $D \geq A$.

V_1 = D-A is a smart building's potential for immediate appropriation. V_1 is a measure of the building's digital vacancy in units of physical space (i.e. in the space realm). V_1 is a short-term vacancy indicator of appropriation. The appropriation ratio given by D/A is a variation of V_1. The larger the ratio, the more dominated spaces are available for appropriation in a building. The ratio is by definition greater than or equal to 1.

If the total amount of physical space in the building, P, is larger than D, then V_2 = P-D is another measure of digital vacancy in units of physical space, but contrary to V_1, V_2 is a long-term vacancy indicator since it would require for physical space to be dominated and turned into appropriable smart space for vacancy to decrease. This process bears a cost for the DAR holders (cost of domination).

AXIOM 3.2: THE PRODUCTION OF APPROPRIATED SPACE

Producing appropriated space from dominated space carries a cost for tenants equal to the price paid for Digital Usage Rights (DURs) bought from landlords.[19] In a classic landlord/ tenant framework, the price at which a landlord is willing to sell DURs should at least capitalise all rental incomes paid by the tenant for usage of smart space according to the terms of the lease:

Price of DURs ≥ Rents paid by tenant for usage of smart space (digital realm)

By the same token, the price that a tenant is willing to pay for DURs does not exceed the value he/she will be able to create by having the right to use smart space. For tenants, value created in smart space comes from two sources: their operations in smart space (e.g. incomes generated in retail outlets owing to the use of smart space) and value stemming from data collected in their rented spaces, keeping in mind that the long-term value of appropriation for a tenant lies in his/her ability to leverage on space users' Umwelts through data. Thus, for a dominated space to be appropriated by a tenant, it requires that within that space: Price of DURs ≤ Value created in smart space by the tenant.

Therefore, the price of DURs is bounded by rents paid by the tenant to the landlord for usage of smart space (floor) and the value created by the tenant in smart space (cap). Besides, for new supply of dominated spaces to be created by the landlord (if P-D > 0), it requires that the cost involved in dominating physical space – which is equivalent to the cost of Digital Access Rights (DAR) – be smaller than, or equal to, the price of DURs charged by the landlord to the tenant. Thus, for a given smart building with P physical space and D smart space, there will be new supply of dominated spaces ready for appropriation, provided V_2 is positive and price of DURs ≥ cost of DARs.

The issue of vacancy in smart buildings has to be assessed in light of landlords' ability to collect data in non-tenanted smart spaces. Vacant dominated spaces do not generate direct incomes for owners until they are appropriated by tenants (i.e. physically rented). But, although physical space is vacant in the space realm, the landlord who owns DURs on smart space has the ability to generate income through data collection and analytics in the digital realm. For vacancy in dominated smart spaces, there is thus a disconnect between the space realm and the digital realm. Concretely, the landlord is faced with the following trade-off: either to maintain smart space as dominated space only (without collecting any data), or to aim to appropriate it in order to create value through data. The landlord will opt to appropriate non-tenanted smart spaces (thus potentially reducing the supply of D available for tenants) if the cost of appropriation is such that: cost of appropriation of vacant dominated smart spaces ≤ value of data collected in these spaces. The same rule would apply to public areas in a smart building.

Therefore, there are three types of vacant space in a smart building: (i) physically vacant and non-dominated spaces, (ii) physically vacant and dominated smart spaces, (iii) physically vacant and appropriated smart spaces. The second type can satisfy the demand for D in the short term while the first type can be dominated to meet demand for D with a lag (time to domination) and at a cost (cost of domination). For a landlord to agree to rent the third type of space, it requires that full rents paid by tenants (rents on physical space plus DURs on smart space) more than compensate him/her for the loss of forgoing data collection and analytics in these spaces (opportunity cost), which is the case if: value of data collected by landlord – rents on physical space ≤ price of DURs.

Thus, the amount of smart space available for tenants' appropriation in a smart building is a function of the value attached to data collection and analytics carried out by landlords in smart spaces. If, as mentioned previously in the presentation of the digital rights regime, the value that a tenant can create in smart space outweighs the landlord's, then the amount of dominated space will tend towards P and a smart building's physical space will eventually be fully dominated by smart technologies (which might be de facto the way smart buildings are built in the future as fully integrated sets of processes in physical and digital spaces).

Axiom #4: Utilities of dominated and appropriated smart spaces

For all spaces in a smart building, the utility of appropriated smart space is always superior or equal to the utility of dominated smart space prior to appropriation so that $U(A) \geq U(D)$. If $U(A) < U(D)$, then appropriation destroys utility in smart space and should be reverted unless it is part of tenants' deliberate strategy (e.g. abstract space in Lefebvre's terminology).

Axiom #5: Utility of user centricity in smart space

Physical space is dominated by owners. Dominated space is appropriated by tenants in order to cater to space users' experiences. Hence, the quality of appropriation can be measured from space users' perspective as the additional utility derived from appropriated space versus dominated space.

For a given space s, the difference between space users' experienced utilities after and prior to appropriation assesses the additional utility created through appropriation: $\Delta U_s = U(A_s) - U(D_s)$.

Experienced utility in appropriated smart spaces is derived from features fostering smart space's user centricity. Therefore, ΔU_s is the additional utility of smart space's user centricity (UC) as experienced by space users so that $U(UC_s) = U(A_s) - U(D_s)$ or $U(A_s) = U(D_s) + U(UC_s)$. The same applies to all smart spaces in a building so that in any smart building, $U(UC) = U(A) - U(D)$ where D is the sum of all dominated spaces in a building and A the sum of all appropriated spaces in the same building.

Axiom #6: Time to spatial appropriation and user-centric utility as key value drivers in smart buildings

For an interaction i in smart space requiring Di dominated smart space and Ai appropriated smart space: $U(Di) \leq U(Ai)$ and $U(Ai) = U(Di) + U(UCi)$ where U(UCi) is space users' user-centric utility derived from interaction i.

The first derivative di = $\partial U(Ai)/\partial t$ is the time sensitivity of appropriated space Ai's utility. di is the slope of interaction i's utility curve over time. An alternative definition of di is to consider the time sensitivity of space users' user-centric utility: $\partial U(UCi)/\partial t$. di can be expected to be positive and then to plateau after a while as interaction obsolescence kicks in (see axiom #7).

The conversion time from dominated physical space to fully appropriated smart space for all interactions carried out in a building is key for property owners and tenants. To illustrate this point, let's consider interaction j carried out in the same physical space as interaction i and in competition with interaction i for smart space. Interaction j requires Dj dominated space and Aj appropriated space such that Dj = Di and Aj = Ai. Interactions i and j are mutually exclusive.

The graphs below show the evolution of U(Ai) and U(Aj) over time. At the inception of an interaction's operation, both utilities are at U(D), dominated physical space's utility such that U(D) = U(Di) = U(Dj). U(D) is (artificially) supposed to be fixed over time and common to all appropriated spaces in the building. Smart space needs to be appropriated in order to generate U(Ai) and U(Aj) for interactions i and j, respectively.

By comparing the Figures 2.3 and 2.4, it is obvious that U(Ai) picks up faster than U(Aj). Thus, interaction i's time to appropriation ti is shorter than

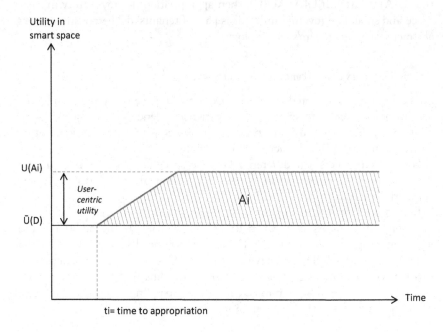

Figure 2.3 Axiom #5 – Utility of interaction i over time.

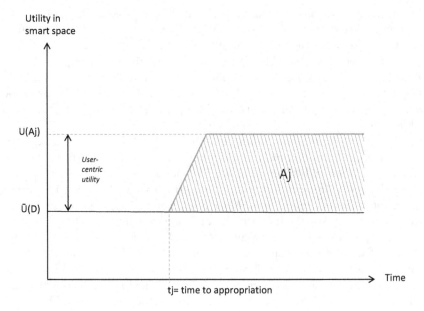

Figure 2.4 Axiom #5 – Utility of interaction j over time.

interaction j's tj. Based on time to appropriation only, interaction i is preferred to interaction j. However, time to appropriation is not sufficient to decide between the two interactions. In addition to time to appropriation, each interaction's cumulated user-centric utility measures the actual value created by an interaction in smart space over time. This is represented by the shaded area Ai and Aj on the graphs. In mathematical terms, the two areas are given by:

$$Ai = \int_0^\infty U(Ai)dt - \int_0^\infty U(Di)dt = \sum_{t=0}^\infty U(UCi)$$

$$Aj = \int_0^\infty U(Aj)dt - \int_0^\infty U(Dj)dt = \sum_{t=0}^\infty U(UCj)$$

To inform the choice between two interactions in the same smart space, the one with the largest value of A should be selected. The same rule can be generalised to n interactions in a smart building. Values determined over owners' investment horizon should be used in conjunction with time to appropriation to select interactions in smart space such that: $Max \sum_{i=1}^n Ai$. An interaction strategy based on user-centric utility maximisation obviously overlooks the role of profit in smart space decision making, a point covered thereafter in axiom #12.

Axiom #7: Interaction obsolescence in smart space

In a smart building, obsolescence is assessed one interaction at a time. Consider a smart building with appropriated smart spaces serving as the background to n interactions broken down into two types of interaction:

– Standard interactions (S) which are characteristic of a property type across the industry. Standard interactions are deemed as baseline interactions.
– Specific interactions (Sp) which define space specialisation and differentiation in smart space.

For one unit of smart space, the utility of specific interactions is always superior or equal to the utility of standard interactions: $U(S) \leq U(Sp)$. All interactions suffer from obsolescence. As smart space loses its appropriated characteristics (e.g. differentiation), its utility falls back to dominated spaces' utility $\bar{U}(D)$ (i.e. smart space prior to appropriation), thereby adding no extra value to owners and tenants, and no extra utilities to space users. Thus, $U(D)$ serves as a floor for all interactions' utilities in the building such that: $\forall i, \lim_{t \to \infty} U(\text{interaction } i) = \bar{U}(D)$.

In this context, specific interactions suffer more than standard interactions from obsolescence due to the speed at which technology enables competition among property owners and tenants. Specific interactions' obsolescence results in these interactions joining the rank of standard interactions over time. By shifting from Sp to S, a specific interaction becomes commoditised and loses its ability to generate additional user-centric utility for space users.

As the number of specific interactions dwindles over time so that standard interactions keep increasing, a building's total interactions in smart space end up generating less and less user-centric utility, resulting in decreased property value. If n is the total number of interactions in a building, then S + Sp = n with

$$\lim_{t \to \infty} S = n$$

$$\lim_{t \to \infty} U(Sp) = \bar{U}(S)$$

$$\text{And } \lim_{t \to \infty} U(S) = \bar{U}(D)$$

This has an impact on the value of digital rights. Due to interaction obsolescence, maintaining value in smart buildings requires a constant quest for owners to upgrade the set of interactions available in smart space. While DARs have no value beyond the cost of domination (which is expected to be stable, at least in the short term), DUR pricing is likely to be volatile over time and across tenants. In addition to market forces, DUR pricing will depend on assessments made by landlords of their tenants' ability to create value in smart space by leveraging on their DURs (see axiom #9). As the utilities of all interactions tend to converge to $\bar{U}(D)$ over time, the price of DURs would follow suit and decrease to the cost of domination C(DAR) if nothing is done to remedy interaction obsolescence: $\lim_{t \to \infty} P(DUR) = C(DAR)$.

Axiom #8: Inelastic supply of smart space

Because physical space is limited by land supply and construction, smart space is bounded by physical space. Notwithstanding the fact that technology might allow for higher interaction density in smart space, it cannot extend the quantity of physical space available in a building in both the short and long terms. Hence, supply of smart space is expected to be inelastic. This is a realistic assumption as one can assume that all physical spaces of newly constructed smart buildings will be dominated right from the start, i.e. D = P, and there is no supply of vacant non-dominated spaces available in the building.

Axiom #9: Appropriation multiplier of smart space

The simple model of smart space presented here considers that the supply of smart space is limited by an inelastic supply of physical space (axiom #8). That is, one unit of physical space combined with a fixed number of units of digital space, say one unit, creates one unit of smart space. The relationship between physical and digital spaces is deemed to be fixed over time. However, one can envision a more complex, and realistic, hypothesis where, owing to tenants' expertise in appropriating smart space, one unit of dominated physical space can be appropriated in such a way that it results in more than one unit of appropriated smart space. Therefore, there is a multiplier effect which should be modelled with an appropriation multiplier.

Let's call φ the appropriation multiplier:

- If φ = 1, one unit of physical space combined with one unit of digital space (i.e. one unit of dominated physical space) results in one unit of smart space (axiom #8);
- If φ > 1, one unit of physical space combined with one unit of digital space (i.e. one unit of dominated physical space) creates φ units of smart space, i.e. more demand for smart space can be satisfied with the same quantity of physical space;
- If φ < 1, appropriation destroys dominated smart space.

Figure 2.5 illustrates these three cases. The line φ = 1 delineates two areas:

- Above that line, smart space is being created in the building beyond physical space;
- Below that line, smart space is being destroyed in the building.

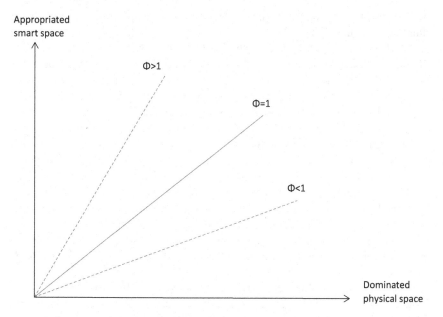

Figure 2.5 Axiom #8 – Appropriation multiplier Φ in smart space.

Changes in the appropriation multiplier can serve as an indicator for tenants' performances in supporting their activities in smart space as the appropriation multiplier enables tenants to increase physical space's yield. In the context of an inelastic supply of smart space due to physical space, φ can also serve as a density measure in smart space. The phenomenology of space users in smart space (Lecomte, 2020) is instrumental in determining smart spaces' optimal density.

To be implemented, the concept of multiplier supposes a consensus on what metrics to apply in smart space. Lecomte (2020) explores a range of potential measurements and suggests a phenomenological measure quantifying space users' experiences in smart space after Csikszentmihalyi's (1990) flow. Until a reliable metric for assessing smart space emerges, analyses based on appropriation are unlikely to be reliable.

A similar concept of multiplier could apply to the domination process of physical space in smart buildings. For the sake of simplicity, assumption is made in this chapter that smart space's domination is perfect. Hence, the value of DARs is the maximum it can be at all times. However, should a domination multiplier apply, this might not always be the case. If P is the physical space and λ the domination multiplier is such that: $D = \lambda * P$ with $\lambda > 0$.

Axiom #10: Physical space's inelasticity as source of loss for tenants in smart space

As supply of smart space is bounded by supply of physical space, demand for smart space might not be fully met. Smart space is a scarce resource. This unfulfilled demand for smart space results in a loss for tenants who are space appropriators as illustrated in Figure 2.6.

On the supply side: Sp is the supply of physical space. Sd is the supply of digital space. Contrary to Sp which is limited in the space realm, Sd is perfectly elastic in the digital realm. That is, as long as the price of Digital Usage Rights at which tenants are willing to buy usage of smart space from property owners is larger than the cost of dominating physical space, property owners will create smart space in the digital realm. However, due to the inelasticity of Sp, the supply of smart space Sss is limited to Sp: Sss = Sp. The appropriation multiplier φ is equal to 1, i.e. there is no multiplication effect in tenants' appropriation process.

On the demand side: demand for smart space Dss is a function of the cost incurred by tenants to appropriate smart space. This appropriation cost is equal to the price paid by tenants to landlords for DURs plus technology-related costs. For the sake of simplicity, the cost of appropriation above P(DURs) is ignored in this analysis. Demand for smart space decreases as the price of DURs increases.

If both Sp and Sd were perfectly elastic, Dss would be satisfied at (q*, p*). However, as Sp is inelastic, Dss can only be satisfied at point B such that (q', p'). (q*–q') is the unfulfilled demand for smart space due to physical constraint. At point B, the price for DUR is p', which is significantly larger than

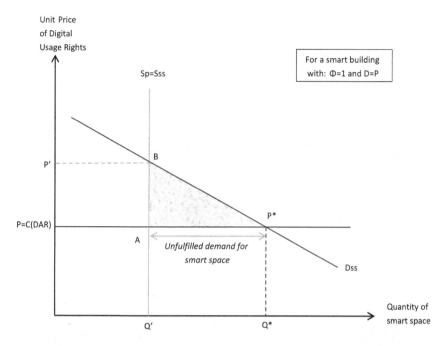

Figure 2.6 Axiom #9 – Inelasticity of physical space as source of loss for tenants.

p*. Hence, as a result of physical limitations constraining the creation of smart space, DAR holders can charge p' for DURs giving tenants usage of q' quantity of smart space. This generates a surplus for property owners equal to the area of the triangle (A, p*, B) on the diagram, which is also a loss for tenants who are overcharged for their usage of smart space. Physical constraints on smart space enable property owners to benefit from scarcity in DURs at tenants' expenses. For a given level of Sd, the smaller the supply of Sp, the larger the loss for tenants.

Let's consider the case where faced with this loss, tenants decide to sharpen their expertise in appropriating smart space so that their appropriation multiplier φ is larger than 1.

Figure 2.7 illustrates the new situation where D = P and φ > 1.

The loss incurred by tenants is reduced to area (C, p*, D) as the supply constraint on smart space is partly released owing to φ. Supply of smart space does not correspond to supply of physical space anymore since one unit of physical space can create φ units of smart space. As a result, more demand for smart space can be satisfied as shown by the quantity (q"–q') in Figure 2.7. In other words, for a given level of demand for smart space in a building Dss, less physical space is required in order to fulfil it. The multiplier effect may lead to a reduction in demand for physical space.

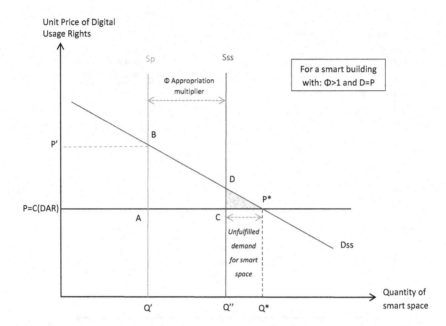

Figure 2.7 Axiom #9 – Price of Digital Usage Rights (DURs) per unit of smart space in a building ($\Phi > 1$ and $D = P$).

If φ is such that $q'' = q^*$ then φ is known as the equilibrium appropriation multiplier. At this level of φ, there are no losses for tenants nor surpluses for digital rights holders. If φ is such that $q'' > q^*$, then there is a surplus for tenants, which puts downwards pressures on the price of DUR at which property owners can transfer usage of smart space to tenants (i.e. the owners' price limit is the cost of domination, C(DAR)).

The appropriation multiplier is a way for tenants to release the pressure imposed on the price of DURs as a result of physical space's inelasticity. It also implies downward pressures on the demand for rented physical spaces in the space realm. The pressure on physical space depends on the relative value-creating potential of both physical and digital spaces inclusive of synergies between the two spaces.

In order to preserve the value of their property rights, owners of physical properties have to anchor smart space's value creation processes in physical space as much as they possibly can. Being able to correctly assess tenants' expertise in appropriating dominated physical space is also key in allowing landlords to fine-tune their pricing of DURs. As the cost of dominating physical space, C(DAR) can be expected to decrease due to technological progress over time, the optimal level of Dss will keep increasing with ever lower DUR prices. Thus, appropriation multipliers will have to increase faster than the speed at which the cost of domination decreases so that tenants do not lose out to DAR holders in the race for value in smart space. The bottom line of this modelling implies that: (1) the space with the most to lose from the competition for smart space's value between property owners and tenants is physical space in the space realm, and (2) technology becomes a tool for tenants to compete with property owners in the digital realm.

Axiom #11: Optimal level of space appropriation by tenants in a smart building

For tenants, the optimal level of smart space appropriation in a smart building is such that the marginal profit derived thanks to the usage of smart space is equal to the marginal cost necessary to appropriate smart space. That is: Marginal profit of smart space appropriation = Marginal cost of smart space appropriation, or Δ Profit from appropriation = Δ Cost of appropriation.

The cost of appropriation is equal to the sum of price paid for DURs and the technological cost of appropriating smart space. The latter component is deemed to be marginally negligible as progresses in technology allow for scale effects.[20] Hence, the optimal level of space appropriation in a smart building is such that: $\Delta \Pi(A) = \Delta P(DUR)$. It depends on the price charged by owners for DURs. If DURs are overpriced due to market inefficiencies (axiom #10), the quantity of smart space in a smart building is sub-optimal for tenants.

Axiom #12: Digital rights holders' search for profit maximisation as smart space's main objective

Whilst space users experience smart space through their own digital worlds (Umwelts), smart space is actually technology-dominated physical space with pre-defined engineered interactions. Thus, whereas space users are aiming to maximise experienced utilities in smart space, these interactions are designed to maximise profits for property owners and tenants. Profit and utility are obviously intertwined insofar as a smart building's ability to maximise its occupants' utilities in smart space is linked to property value as exemplified in the activity-based hedonic pricing model of smart buildings presented earlier in this chapter.

Therefore, owners' and tenants' profit maximisation always dominates space users' quest for utility maximisation in smart space since owners and tenants are the digital rights holders. At any point in time,

– Owners aim to maximise their net profits on smart buildings' entire spaces as defined by property rights and digital rights (i.e. non-dominated physical spaces, dominated physical spaces, tenanted and non-tenanted appropriated smart spaces). For them, DARs represent the cost necessary to dominate physical space and produce smart space. Owners' net profits from the entirety of spaces in the building are a function of: (1) net income on physical spaces, (2) DURs transferred to tenants for usage of smart spaces in dominated physical spaces, (3) value created through data collection and analytics in non-tenanted smart spaces (e.g. common areas), (4) cost of dominating physical spaces, and (5) capital gains in case of property sale. The optimisation problem facing property owners is as follows:

MAX net profits on all spaces in the building (sum of elements 1 to 5)
- Tenants aim to maximise net profits on their appropriated smart spaces. For them, DURs represent the cost necessary to use smart space. At the interaction level, two parameters identified in axiom #6 impact tenants' profits: (a) time to appropriation, (b) cumulated user-centric utilities over duration of operation. At the building level, shortages of dominated physical spaces to be appropriated might hinder their ability to generate profits in smart spaces, notwithstanding the presence of appropriation multipliers (axiom #9). Tenants' optimisation problem is as follows:

MAX net profits in tenanted appropriated smart spaces within a building
- Space users aim to maximise their experienced utility in smart space, which according to axiom #6 is given by:

$$\text{MAX } Ai = \sum_{j=1}^{n} A\,ij, \forall \text{ space user } i$$

where Aij is the cumulated user-centric utilities derived from interaction j by space user i, and n is the number of smart space interactions in the building.

By future proofing their properties' ICT infrastructures, upgrading existing interactions, and developing new ones, smart building owners will ensure that dominated physical spaces available for appropriation keep up with demand for smart spaces by tenants and space users, in terms of both quantity/functionality and utility. To achieve that, lease agreements for smart spaces should strive to promote cooperation between landlords and tenants, e.g. by establishing some degree of profit sharing for value created in smart space as part of standard terms in DUR transfers.

BOX 2.2: Economic foundations of digital rights in smart buildings (in twelve axioms)

The following twelve axioms rely on Lefebvre's (1974) paradigm of space domination and appropriation.

Axiom #1: Property rights and digital rights are inseparable. Digital rights are incidental to property rights.

Axiom #2: Digital rights are transferable within set limits. While Digital Access Rights (DARs) should remain under the exclusive control of property owners at all times, Digital Usage Rights (DURs) are transferable under smart space leasehold-type agreements with a break clause for the initial rights holders.

Axiom #3: All appropriated smart space in a building is dominated physical space.

Axiom #4: Utility of appropriated smart space is always superior or equal to utility of dominated physical space.

Axiom #5: Utility of appropriated smart space is equal to the sum of dominated space's utility and user-centric utility.

Axiom #6: Value created in appropriated smart space is a function of cumulative user-centric utility over time. The time necessary for an interaction to start generating user-centric utility is called *time to appropriation*.

Axiom #7: Ceteris paribus, all interactions' utilities tend to converge to dominated physical space's utility over time.

Axiom #8: The supply of smart space in a smart building is bounded due to physical space's inelasticity.

Axiom #9: Owing to technology, tenants can overcome physical space's inelasticity by appropriating more smart space from the same quantity of dominated physical space. This effect is captured by an *appropriation multiplier*.

Axiom #10: Constraints on the supply of smart space result in a loss for tenants. Appropriation multipliers enable them to reduce the loss.

Axiom #11: For tenants, the optimal quantity of appropriated smart space is such that marginal profit derived from smart space is equal to marginal cost of appropriation. At that point, tenants' profit in smart space is maximum.

Axiom #12: Smart space's underlying objective is to enable digital rights holders (i.e. property owners and tenants) to maximize profits derived from the ownership and operation of spaces in a smart building.

BOX 2.3: Digital rights and obsolescence in smart buildings

- Smart buildings' obsolescence can be measured at the level of interactions between a building and its occupants in smart space (axiom #7).
- Total interactions (T) encompass standard interactions (S) and specific interactions (Sp).
- Over time, Sp become commoditised, lessening smart space's differentiation value.
- As a result, specific interactions' utility U(Sp) tends to decrease to the level of utility U(S) experienced by space users with standard interactions only.
- Unless investments are made to upgrade interactions in smart space (e.g. by adding new Sp), the utility of all interactions tends to decrease to the average utility level of dominated physical spaces prior to appropriation so that $\lim_{S \to T} U(T) = \bar{U}(D)$
- This translates into a loss for digital rights holders as Digital Usage Rights' value may eventually fall to the cost of physical space domination, thereby wiping out any additional value created by appropriation of smart space.

2.3 Technologies empowering digital rights and their impact on the real estate sector's digital strategies

As water rights were instrumental in the first industrial revolution (Rose, 1990), digital rights are central in the so-called fourth industrial revolution. Digital strategies can be built around property owners' and tenants' entitlements in smart space. These entitlements are mediated by technologies implemented in buildings. So far in the analysis, the manner in which space is first dominated by technology, and then appropriated has been ignored. Assumption is made that digital rights holders control the full process as well as technologies at work.

In practice, smart space is not as abstract as it might appear in light of the twelve axioms presented here. There is a concrete, technical side to smart space which has been of keen interest to computer scientists for years. The digitalisation of real estate requires a myriad of technologies, each with potentially unique contractual arrangements involving external parties (e.g. cloud computing operators, software developers, IoT device providers, big data management experts).

The analysis presented in this book explicitly refers to state-of-the-art technologies centred on the cloud computing paradigm. As technologies embedded in the built environment keep progressing, computing paradigms might evolve, but irrespective of the dominant paradigm, digital rights attached to smart buildings should remain, exactly like property rights are not affected by construction technologies.[21] To bring some technological perspective to the analysis of digital rights, let's cover briefly the fundamentals of cloud computing. The objective is to highlight the interplay between technologies' service models, digital rights, and digital rights holders' strategies in smart space.

- **The cloud computing paradigm**

According to the definition of the US National Institute of Standards and Technology (Mell and Grance, 2011),

> cloud computing is a model for enabling ubiquitous, convenient, on-demand network access to a shared pool of configurable computing resources (e.g., networks, servers, storage, applications, and services) that can be rapidly provisioned and released with minimal management effort or service provider interaction.

Cloud computing's service models can materialise into three formats: SaaS (Software as a Service), PaaS (Platform as a Service), IaaS (infrastructure as a Service). Bayrak, Conley and Wilkie (2011) explain:

> Software as a Service is the service model in which the capability provided to the consumer is the ability to use the cloud provider's applications running on a cloud infrastructure. [...] Platform as a Service is the service model in

which the capability provided to the consumer is a development or runtime environment, programming languages and application programming interfaces (APIs) to design and deploy infrastructure consumer-created applications onto the cloud. [...] Infrastructure as a Service is the service model in which the capability provided to the consumer is processing, storage, networks, and other fundamental computing resources.

A variant of the cloud computing paradigm mentioned in the computer sciences literature is the CloudIoT paradigm which integrates cloud and IoT (Botta et al., 2016). The concept which seems especially relevant to the built environment has been dubbed "Everything as a Service", from Sensing as a Service (SaaS) to Database as a Service (DBaaS) and Video Surveillance as a Service (VSaaS). In essence, all technology-powered activities in smart buildings can be integrated with a cloud "whose capabilities in terms of storage and processing power [are] virtually unlimited".

The quality of service provided by clouds (QoS) is defined in Service Level Agreements (SLA) between operators and users. QoS measures "the levels of performance, reliability, and availability offered by an application and by the platform or infrastructure that hosts it" (Ardagna, Casale, Ciavotta, Perez, Wang, 2014). To allow for optimal and dynamic allocation of resources in clouds, negotiation of SLAs between participants should allow for "automatic allocation to multiple competing requests" (Buyya, Yeo and Venugopal, 2008).

- **Strategic dimensions of technological choices in smart buildings**

In any computing paradigm, the important features for the real estate sector will be the underlying service models and their strategic implications as assessed by digital rights. Specifically, how does the choice of a particular service model impact on property owners' Digital Access Rights and tenants' Digital Usage Rights? Digital rights are a yardstick for attributing value generated in smart space. If technologies' service models interfere with digital rights, there could be a shift, ever so slightly, in value allocation among contracting parties to the point that digital rights might ultimately become empty shells for their holders. This is especially the case for new real estate resources such as data.

The fact is that as of today, many real estate players do not have in-house technological expertise and capabilities enabling them to dominate and appropriate space without partnering with external parties who might be more attuned to value creation in non-physical space than, say, developers or classic brick-and-mortar property companies. Having an understanding of digital rights rooted in technology is essential to get a full picture of the power struggle that will inevitably take place over value created in smart buildings between commercial real estate's usual actors (i.e. property owners, tenants), on the one hand, and new entrant smart space solutions providers (e.g. technology giants), on the other hand.

A few key points should guide building owners and tenants when deciding on which service models to implement at different stages of smart space's life:

i   *Space domination*: Ownership of DARs entitles their holders to decide on the mode of domination for physical space. Poor quality of domination would affect Digital Usage Rights' value and eventually the value of physical space. High-quality domination, on the other hand, would underlie premium smart spaces. If the domination multiplier briefly mentioned before is less than 1, then domination wastes physical space in creating a less than maximum quantity of smart space, which would have an opportunity cost for owners. By the same token, the quality of physical space domination will be instrumental in fostering a building's future proofing abilities through its so-called smart readiness, i.e. a building's "full potential to deliver increased smart services [...] provided existing constraints are released over time" (Lecomte, 2019a). Nevertheless, owning technologies implemented for space domination is not crucial whereas leveraging on physical spaces to generate the best possible domination given demand for smart space by tenants is key. Technology partners' service models gearing towards "everything as a service" would provide flexibility to the real estate sector, and enable owners to easily adapt their buildings to a wide range of uses in the spirit of the 'omni-use' property type (Lecomte, 2019b). Markedly, since DARs carry significant legal responsibilities for their holders, building owners should be able to critically assess the domination process. This should give them a strong motivation to develop in-house expertise in order to keep control over dominated physical spaces, whether or not they actually own the ICT infrastructure embedded in their buildings.

ii   *Space appropriation*: Ownership of DURs entitles their holders to appropriate smart space, by adding user-centric utilities to tenanted dominated spaces. Due to the presence of an appropriation multiplier in the model, tenants are strongly incentivised to develop their own expertise in smart space appropriation and not to depend on landlords' expertise. Furthermore, as specific interactions play an instrumental role in the total user-centric utility generated in a smart building, DURs holders should be aware of the intellectual property value involved in spatial appropriation. Protecting intellectual property linked to smart space will lengthen the time it takes for specific interactions to become commoditised, thus guaranteeing the value of DURs for their holders for a prolonged period. By neglecting appropriated smart spaces' high IP content, DURs holders might unwillingly transfer value to third parties and deprive themselves of valuable real estate resources. Service models enabling space appropriators to nurture and protect their unique appropriation know-how, such as PaaS or IaaS, should be favoured.

iii   *Space operation and maintenance*: Service Level Agreements (SLAs) defining Quality of Service (QoS) will be central in the smooth functioning of smart space. As appropriated smart space is first and foremost dominated physical space, DAR holders (i.e. landlords) will play a big role in ensuring QoS for tenants' smart space. Experiences of the real estate sector in running long-term service partnerships (such as PPP) will be useful in that respect.

iv *Data management and analytics*: Once smart space is functional, the central issue becomes data. In the proposed digital rights regime, data ownership comes with Digital Usage Rights. Owners and tenants should be careful that collaborations with third parties do not jeopardise their full ownership of data. Full data ownership means the ability to collect, store, and use data. Because of the legal responsibilities attached to DURs, rights holders should be mindful of issues related to cyber security, data protection, and privacy, so much so that a thorough risk assessment should always inform the decision to outsource data management and analytics. Finally, owners and tenants should be careful when opting to give up (in full or in part) their rights on data collected in smart space as this would represent a long-term loss of real estate value. Only real estate actors with short-term investment horizons might justify the transfer of data ownership to third parties, knowing that in the event of property resale, the gap in data ownership would negatively affect property value.

BOX 2.4: Data collection yield in smart buildings

- The ability of appropriated smart space to collect valuable data for Digital Usage Rights holders is a crucial feature of smart real estate.
- To gauge smart buildings' data collection potential, an indicator can be defined as the data collection yield per unit of appropriated smart space in a building. If τ is the data collection yield, then total data collected in a building D_T is given by τ times total appropriated space A_T in the building, or $\tau = D_T/A_T$.
- The same concept can be applied at the interaction level where τi is the data collection yield of interaction i in smart space so that $\tau i = D i/A i$ where $D i$ is the quantity of data collected through interaction i and $A i$ is the quantity of appropriated space necessary for interaction i to take place.
- All three smart space indicators presented in this chapter are intertwined: the domination multiplier λ can impact the appropriation multiplier φ which, in turn, might affect the data collection yield in smart space τ.
- New indicators in real estate analysis are necessary to account for real estate's digital realm and capture the new processes of space production and value creation in smart buildings. As a prerequisite, these indicators require a consensus about the relevant metrics applicable for smart space.

3 Questions around space users' digital surrounding worlds (Umwelts)

This chapter concludes with a brief discussion about space users' digital surrounding worlds, especially their legal nature. One can expect numerous debates about this point as technology becomes increasingly pervasive in the built environment. It has been noted previously that in line with Lessig's (2006) second life in cyberspace, a digital self emerges in smart buildings. Lecomte (2019a, 2020) talks about Umwelt to describe the digital surrounding world of this second life taking shape in smart environments (see Appendix 2.1).

Umwelts will undoubtedly be the object of a fierce battle between those who are concerned with the technological domination of humans' surroundings, on the one hand, and those who aim to optimise control in real estate, on the other hand (e.g. optimisation in view of monitoring or policing space users, or in a more utilitarian perspective in view of maximising value generated in smart buildings). In any cases, it is more than likely that in most countries, regulators will not let the real estate sector decide on its own how building occupants' Umwelts should be dealt with in smart buildings. The concept of Umwelt epitomises the new set of social and ethical responsibilities facing the real estate sector with pervasive computing and embedded technologies.

It has been previously suggested that DUR holders should transfer to building occupants some level of control over their digital surroundings as part of a trade-off between direct and indirect value creation in smart real estate. The digital self would therefore be a by-product of smart space usage, an incidental right to digital rights whose ownership does not automatically belong to the actors of this second life (i.e. space users themselves), but to the owners of the physical and digital infrastructures where it occurs. The latter include the real estate sector, but also any parties involved in smart space (e.g. technology companies).

Going back to the property rights framework discussed in this chapter, there are many unanswered questions regarding Umwelt. Concretely, is Umwelt a space user's digital persona with a legal existence of its own, or just a series of data in ever bigger databases devoid of legal existence (apart from the relevant laws on data protection and privacy)? The view presented in this chapter is that Umwelt unquestionably gives rise to a digital persona, the afore-mentioned digital self.

However, this digital self who emerges out of algorithmic interactions under digital rights holders' full control only serves to feed the illusion of freedom in space. In that sense, Umwelt does not exemplify increased and better appropriation, but rather it is an indication of ever tighter domination of all spaces in smart buildings, including building occupants' most private sphere, their unique ontological perception of one's digital surrounding world (Lecomte, 2019a).

That's why axiom #5 posits that the utility derived from appropriation captures smart space's user-centricity in full. Smart space appropriation is first and foremost appropriation of space users' Umwelts so that DURs holders logically control space users' digital surrounding worlds. That's the reality transcribed in the proposed digital rights regime which can be seen as the product of natural order, unless regulators decide to step in and alter it.

The analysis presented here focuses on a series of twelve economic axioms to avoid being embroiled in what could be a very heated debate crystalising many fears about technological domination in human lives (a.k.a horizontal technology in Ihde, 1990). As new technologies start to materialise in the built environment, the real estate sector's best answer to these fears will come from a proactive approach to digital governance as well as clearly defined digital strategies in smart buildings.

Notes

1   The notion of Gibson's affordances powered by technology in physical space (i.e. technology affordances) was pioneered in research on media spaces for collaboration in the early 1990s (e.g. Gaver, 1992).
2   The number and definition of interactions in the activity-based hedonic model of smart buildings should be broad enough to encapsulate the full range of subtle variations in space users' experience for different activities. It should also be concise enough to be manageable. Contrary to quality variables in hedonic models anchored in physical structure and location, hedonic variables in this model are non-observable constructs. Understanding space users' phenomenology in smart buildings (Lecomte, 2020) will be instrumental in defining relevant quality variables that capture smart space's breadth and depth.
3   The dichotomy between standard and specific interactions in smart buildings will be useful in implementing the activity-based hedonic model of smart buildings as one would expect larger coefficients for specific interactions than for standard ones. Over time, there will be a natural trend for specific interactions to become standard. A building whose interactions are mostly standard has little competitive advantages. It is a generic building. Conversely, a building whose interactions in smart space are mostly specific shows little versatility and might be difficult to repurpose. In the latter case, one important factor to consider will be the potential synergies between physical and digital spaces for a different use insofar as both physical space and digital space can potentially get repurposed.
4   The concept of cyber-dasein is modelled after William Mitchell (2003)'s seminal Me++ Cyborg and Martin Heidegger's phenomenology (Lecomte, 2019a). This new type of space user comes with idiosyncratic phenomenological traits triggered by embedded technologies in the built environment, especially pervasive computing (Lecomte, 2020). Cyber-dasein's experiences in smart real estate are ambient, pervasive, fluid, and continuous. They occur at the periphery of building occupants' attention. However, contrary to Mitchell's smart city dwellers, the cyber-dasein is not a cyborg, but a non-augmented human "absorbed in fulfilling his daily concerns". Lecomte (2020) introduces in detail the principles for a phenomenology of smart real estate's occupants. These principles which condition humans' mode of engagement with real estate in smart environments are instrumental in modelling smart buildings' values.
5   In a classic OLS hedonic framework, spatial effects are analysed through the prism of locational and neighbourhood attributes. In smart urban environments, space's user centricity in smart buildings adds a new dimension to spatial heterogeneity, that of an existential real estate space defining familiar regions (known as "Gegend" in Lecomte, 2019a) where building occupants carry out their activities and where their own personal surrounding world ("Umwelt") takes shape. This highly personal environing world tends to expand as more and more data are collected each time they step into smart real estate. The terminology used to describe space users' experiences in smart space is borrowed from German philosopher Martin Heidegger's phenomenology. A glossary of the main terms used to analyse experiences in smart space is reproduced in Appendix 2.1.

6 The prospect of D, the difference between decision utility and experienced utility in smart buildings, being equal to zero questions the link between smart cities and control (as a direct reference to French philosopher Gilles Deleuze (1992)'s theory on "societies of control"). Space users' free will in space, notwithstanding its question-ability in any man-made architectural structures, would be irremediably jeopardised once technology manages to outperform space users themselves in maximising their utilities in smart real estate. The utility derived from the tied bundle of utility-bearing characteristics that is a smart building in the hedonic pricing model would no longer be a matter of decision but that of an optimised, albeit imposed and monitored, experience. Lancaster's (1966) theory does imply consumers' ability to make choices, which would be missing in a perfectly functional, arguably Orwellian, smart space. This is the paradox of smart real estate: it might foster utility at the expense of conscious choice. Ubicomp's focus on periphery and calm technology makes the process all the more invisible to space users. Undoubtedly, the trade-off between free will and utility will be a major dilemma facing the real estate sector when deciding on which technologies to implement in smart buildings and the best ways to do it (e.g. public disclosure in each individual space, possibility for building occupants to opt out).

7 The question of trust in context-aware environments has been tackled very early on by computer scientists researching the impact of ubiquitous and pervasive computing on users. For instance, Robinson and Beigi (2003) assert that to bridge "the divide between real world-oriented tasks and the interfacing of facilitating technology", in-teractions that mimic "the explicit parameters of physical human-human interaction" are more likely to build trust. Digital rights would be all the more valuable as smart buildings' occupants trust smart space. The latter point might be in itself a sufficient incentive for digital rights' owners to make sure that this is actually the case (e.g. respect of cyber privacy laws, data protection laws and any legal requirements that will necessarily appear in response to the implementation of smart technologies in the built environment). This point seems to support the view that digital rights should be owned by the longer-term stakeholders in a building, i.e. owners rather than ten-ants who might engage in short-term profit maximising practices with respect to smart space, which could have long-term negative consequences for the property.

8 As technology stands today, a high density of smart devices in the same physical space comes with massive drawbacks. Lobachev and Cretu (2016) explain that "in big con-crete buildings [...], the signal [of wireless sensors] faces a lot of interference, from both electronic equipment as well as due to signal bouncing off the walls, ceilings and floors of the rooms". As a result, it is very difficult to have "a high concentration of sensors in a single given area" so that more advanced technologies (e.g. smart sensors network utilising power over Ethernet) are required.

9 Another approach to determine scarcity of smart space would be to focus on space users' phenomenology in smart real estate (e.g. Lecomte (2020)'s reference to Csikscze-ntmihalyi's (1990) flow as a metric for smart space). As analysed by McCullough (2013), space users' attention in smart space is a scarce resource. Concerns about 'ambient commons' in smart environments precisely stem from the fact "some resources are inalienable, such as attention". Attention overload (akin to pollution in smart space) is a real threat in smart urban environments. In this framework, digital rights would embody smart space's optimal phenomenological capacity in parallel to its physical and technological components. Thus, the creation of digital rights would be linked to space users' ability to benefit from interactions in smart buildings so as to maximise, say, space users' flow in smart space. Like in the approach presented in this book, scarcity in smart space would give rise to privately owned digital rights. Noticeably, this phenomenological approach would deal with concerns about attention pollution in smart buildings.

10 The emergence of digital rights makes the need for digital governance all the more pressing. To deal with the regulatory requirements and potential legal liabilities at-tached to smart space, real estate companies should consider having an explicit

"digital governance policy" shared with all space users/ investors and implemented by a dedicated team of multidisciplinary specialists. Given the strategic dimension of this new activity for the real estate industry, a digital governance committee could be set up as part of the overall corporate governance. The team in charge at the building level should combine ICT skills, big data acumen, expertise in digital technologies (e.g. sensors), awareness of space users' psychology as well as the ability to cooperate with marketing team, IT team at the corporate level, and property managers at the property level.

11 In *The Role of Investment Real Estate in Portfolio Management* (1970), Graaskamp notes that the speed of change in property rights matters for corporate actors which might not be able to cope with drastic changes happening too fast. He writes:

> Property rights do change and exist in certain form only as long as society achieves its objectives in terms of encouraging development and husbandry. Nevertheless, change in property rights must be implemented at a rate which each enterprise can tolerate in terms of its cash cycle and the threshold of insolvency or there could be a taking of property without due process.

12 Lessig (2006) proposes an interesting definition of boundaries in cyberspace which is anchored in code instead of geography. Cyberspace which is "about making a different (or second) life [is] regulated primarily through the code of cyberspace [...]. [Code] defines the terms upon which cyberspace is offered". As "programming determines which people can access digital objects and which digital objects can interact with other digital objects", code is law in humans' second life in cyberspace. This second life regulated by code is what Lecomte (2020) calls the "being-there" in smart real estate.

13 In a more favourable regime for property owners, data related to specific interactions (as defined in leases) could belong to tenants only, whereas data linked to standard interactions belong to both tenants and owners. Data ownership will undoubtedly become an instrumental asset in smart real estate and lead to high stakes negotiations between owners and tenants.

14 Lefebvre (1974) wonders how abstract space's (i.e. the extreme form of dominated space) lethal powers are unleashed in a city, and ponders that "freewheeling technology" could be a reason.

15 Henri Lefebvre belongs to the tradition of Marxist philosophers. For him, property rights alienate urban space from its inhabitants, just as for Marx capital alienates workers from the means of production and the product of their labour (Purcell, 2013).

16 The impact of digital rights on urban landscapes will depend on the type of smart urban environments in which smart buildings are immersed. In ubiquitous cities where, in a nutshell, the digital skin is homogeneous (Anttiroiko, 2013), digital rights will play an important role in fostering space specialisation and the emergence of omni-use properties (Lecomte, 2019b). In augmented cities (Aurigi, 2009), digital rights will participate to what can be called 'smart space zoning' of enhanced locations, by imprinting standard or specific human-smart technology interactions to physical spaces (resulting in augmented places). In both cities, directives pertaining to smart space zoning might be necessary for city officials to achieve their goals. In addition to physical space, smart space might thereby fall under the purview of planning activities at the neighbourhood and city levels.

17 The intertwining of physical spaces and smart spaces will be an important feature of smart architecture. One can logically expect smart building's physical space to be conceived in view of achieving synergies with smart space's digital layer, and vice versa. These synergies could, for instance, materialise in an optimisation of smart space's affordances or a building's overall versatility.

18 The question of individual freedom in space is obviously at the core of any regime of property rights in smart buildings. This point which is only briefly mentioned in this book implies a thorough analysis in terms of necessary digital governance and ethical behaviours to be applied in the smart real estate sector.

19 For the sake of simplicity, the cost of appropriation beyond the price paid for Digital Usage Rights is ignored in this analysis.
20 Assumption is made that due to scalability inherent to smart technologies, the cost of appropriation is equal to the price paid by tenants for Digital Usage Rights. However, once 'appropriated', smart space is not free to operate. Operation of smart space is appropriation in action. This operating cost is assumed to be included in the cost of appropriation (and negligible).
21 The case of spectrum property licences built on proprietary claims on frequencies which were made obsolete as a result of technological progresses in digital processing and wireless communications (Benkler, 2012) should serve as a cautionary tale for digital rights holders about any forms of complacency with respect to technology's impact on their rights in smart buildings.

References

Adida B., Chang E., Fletcher L., Hong M., Sandon L., and Page K. (1998) The future of trespass and property in cyberspace, *MIT Internet Policy Initiative*.

Alchian A., and Demsetz H. (1973) The property rights paradigm, *The Journal of Economic History*, 33:1, pp. 16–27.

Anttiroiko A.V. (2013) U-cities reshaping our future: Reflections on ubiquitous infrastructure as an enabler of smart urban development, *AI and Society-25th Anniversary Volume: A Faustian Exchange: What is to Be Human in the Era of Ubiquitous Technology?* 28, pp. 491–507.

Ardagna D., Casale G., Ciavotta M., Perez J., and Wang W. (2014) Quality-of-service in cloud computing: Modelling techniques and their applications, *Journal of Internet Services and Applications*, 5:11, pp. 1–17.

Aurigi A. (2009) U-city: Keeping space and place in the picture, in *Ubiquitous City: Future of City, City of Future* (Lee S.H. ed), Daejeon: Hanbat National University Press, pp. 162–179.

Barzel Y. (1997) *Economic Analysis of Property Rights*, Cambridge: Cambridge University Press, second edition.

Batty M. (2002) Thinking about cities as spatial events, *Environment and Planning B: Planning and Design*, 29, pp. 1–2.

Bayrak E., Conley P., and Wilkie S. (2011) The economics of cloud computing, *The Korean Economic Review*, 27:2, pp. 203–230.

Benkler Y. (2012) Open wireless vs. licensed spectrum: Evidence from market adoption, *Harvard Journal of Law & Technology*, 26, pp. 71–162.

Berman M., Libert b., Beck M., and Yoram J. (2016) *Assets vs. Access: A Digital Reality for Commercial Real Estate*, Knowledge@Wharton, University of Pennsylvania (September 14).

Botta A., deDonato W., Persico V., and Pescape A. (2016) Integration of cloud computing and internet of things, *Future Generation Computer Systems*, 56, pp. 684–700.

Butler L. (1985) Allocating consumptive water rights in a riparian jurisdiction: Defining the relationship between public and private interests, *University of Pittsburgh Law Review*, 47, pp. 95–181.

Buyya R., Yeo C., and Venugopal S. (2008) Market-oriented cloud computing: Vision, hype, and reality for delivering IT services as computing utilities, *2008 10th IEEE International Conference on High Performance Computing and Communications*, pp. 5–13.

Calabrese F., Reades J., and Ratti C. (2010) Eigenplaces: Segmenting space through digital signatures, *Pervasive Computing*, 9:1, pp. 78–84.

Carvalho L. (2015) Smart cities from scratch? A socio-technical perspective, *Cambridge Journal of Regions, Economy and Society*, 8, pp. 43–60.

Csikszentmihalyi M. (1990) *Flow: The Psychology of Optimal Experience*, New York: HarperCollins.

Curry E., and Sheth A. (2018) Next-generation smart environments: From system of systems to data ecosystems, *IEEE Intelligent Systems*, 33:3, pp. 69–76.

Deleuze G. (1992) Postscript on the societies of control, *October*, 59 (winter), pp. 3–7.

Demsetz H. (1967) Towards a theory of property rights, *American Economic Review*, 57, pp. 347–359.

Dourish P., and Bell G. (2011) *Divining a Digital Future*, Cambridge: The MIT Press.

Edmonds R.C. (1984) A theoretical basis for hedonic regression: A research primer, *AREUEA Journal*, 12:1, pp. 72–85.

Evans G., and McCoy J. (1998) When buildings don't work: The role of architecture in human health, *Journal of Environmental Psychology*, 18:1, pp. 85–94.

Fisher E.M., and Fisher R.M. (1954) *Urban Real Estate*, New York: Henry Holt and Company.

Freyfogle E. (1989) Context and accommodation in modern property law, *Stanford Law Review*, 41:6, pp. 1529–1556.

Gaver W. (1992) The affordances of media spaces for collaboration, *CSCW 92 Proceedings*, pp. 17–24.

Gibson J. (1977) Chapter 8: The theory of affordances, in *The Ecological Approach to Visual Perception*, Boston: Houghton Mifflin, pp. 127–145.

Graaskamp J.A. (1970) The role of investment real estate in portfolio management, *Graaskamp on Real Estate*, The Urban Land Institute, 1991, pp. 310–371.

Graaskamp J.A. (1981) Fundamentals of real estate development, in *Graaskamp on Real Estate*, The Urban Land Institute, 1991, pp. 228–265.

Gross N. (1999) *The Earth Will Don an Electronic Skin*, Business Week.

Haar C., and Gordon B. (1958) *Riparian Water Rights vs. a Prior Appropriation System: A Comparison*, Boston University Law Review, 38, pp. 207–255.

Hayles N.K. (2014) Cognition everywhere: The rise of the cognitive nonconscious and the costs of consciousness, *New Literary History*, 45:2, pp. 199–220.

Hayles N.K. (2017) *Unthought*, Chicago and London: The University of Chicago Press.

Hunter D. (2003) Cyberspace as place and the tragedy of the digital anticommons, *California Law Review*, 91:2, pp. 442–518.

Ihde D. (1990) *Technology and the Lifeworld*, Bloomington: Indiana University Press.

Johnson D.R., and Post D. (1996) Law and borders – The rise of law in cyberspace, *Stanford Law Review*, 48, pp. 1367–1402.

Kahneman D. (1994) New challenges to the rationality assumption, *Journal of Institutional and Theoretical Economics*, 150:1, Symposium on the New Institutional Economics Bounded Rationality and the Analysis of State and Society, pp. 18–36.

Kahneman D., Wakker P., and Sarin R. (1997) Back to Bentham? Explorations of experienced utility, *The Quarterly Journal of Economics*, 112: 2, pp. 375–405.

Lancaster K.J. (1966) A new approach to consumer theory, *The Journal of Political Economy*, 74:2, pp. 132–157.

Lecomte P. (2015), Putting humans back at the centre: The impact of smart cities on real estate, *The Business Times* (Singapore), September 3, 2015.

Lecomte P. (2019a) New boundaries: Conceptual framework for the analysis of commercial real estate in smart cities, *The Journal of Property Investment and Finance*, 37:1, pp. 118–135.

Lecomte P. (2019b) What is smart? A real estate introduction to cities and buildings in the digital era, *Journal of General Management*, 44:3, pp. 128–137.

Lecomte P. (2020) iSpace: Principles for a phenomenology of space user in smart real estate, *The Journal of Property Investment and Finance*, 38:4, pp. 271–290.

Lefebvre H. (1974) *The Production of Space*, Oxford: Blackwell Publishing.

Lessig L. (2006) *Code: And Other Laws of Cyberspace, Version 2.0*, New York: Basic Books.

Liu K., and Gulliver S. (2013) Chapter 8: Designing intelligent pervasive spaces for living and working, in *Intelligent Buildings: Design, Management and Operation*, 2nd edition (Clements-Croome D., ed), London: ICE Publishing, pp. 119–132.

Lobachev I., and Cretu E. (2016) Smart sensor network for smart buildings, *2016 IEEE 7th Annual Information Technology, Electronics and Mobile Communication Conference*, Vancouver, pp. 1–7.

Ma J., Yang L., Apduhan B., Huang R., Barolli L., and Takizawa M. (2005) Towards a smart world and ubiquitous intelligence: A walkthrough from smart things to smart hyperspaces and UbicKids, *Journal of Pervasive Computing and Communications*, 1:1, pp. 53–68.

McCullough M. (2013) *Ambient Commons*, Cambridge: The MIT Press.

Mell P., and Grance T. (2011) The NIST definition of cloud computing, Computer Security Division, Information Technology Laboratory, *National Institute of Standards and Technology*, 53:1.

Mitchell W.J. (1995) *City of Bits: Space, Place and the Infobahn*, Cambridge: The MIT Press.

Mitchell W.J. (2003) Me++ *The Cyborg-Self and the Networked City*, Cambridge: The MIT Press.

Pejovich S. (1996) Property rights and technological innovation, *Social Philosophy and Policy*, 13:2, pp. 168–180.

Purcell M. (2013) Possible worlds: Henri Lefebvre and the right to the city, *Journal of Urban Affairs*, 36:1, pp. 141–154.

Rabari C., and Storper M. (2015) The digital skin of cities: Urban theory and research in the age of the sensored and metered city, ubiquitous computing and big data, *Cambridge Journal of Regions, Economy and Society*, 8, pp. 27–42.

Ratcliff R.U. (1949) *Urban Land Economics*, New York: McGraw-Hill Book Company Inc.

Ratcliff R.U. (1961) *Real Estate Analysis*, New York: McGraw-Hill Book Company Inc.

Ratti C., and Claudel M. (2014) The rise of the invisible detail: Ubiquitous computing and the 'minimum meaningful', *Architectural Design*, 84:4, pp. 86–91.

Ratti C., and Haw A. (2012) Living bits and bricks, *The Architectural Review*, Viewpoints (April 24).

Reeves H.S. (1996) Property in cyberspace, *The University of Chicago Law Review*, 63, pp. 761–799.

RICS (2017) *Artificial Intelligence: What it Means for the Built Environment*, Royal Institution of Chartered Surveyors, Insight Report, London.

Robinson P., and Beigi M. (2003) Trust context spaces: An infrastructure for pervasive security in context-aware environments, *Security in Pervasive Computing in Lecture Notes in Computer Science*, 2802, pp. 157–172.

Robson A., and Samuelson I. (2011) The evolution of decision and experienced utilities, *Theoretical Economics*, 6, pp. 311–339.

Rose C. (1990) Energy and efficiency in the realignment of common-law water rights, *Journal of Legal Studies*, XIX, pp. 261–296.

Rosen S. (1974) Hedonic prices and implicit markets: Product differentiation in pure competition, *The Journal of Political Economy*, 82:1, pp. 34–55.

Schmidtz D. (1994) The institution of property, *Social Philosophy and Policy*, 11:2, pp. 42–62.

Schwab K. (2016) *The Fourth Industrial Revolution*, New York: Crown Business.

Stigler G. (1950) The development of utility theory I, *Journal of Political Economy*, 58:4, pp. 307–327.

Trelease F. (1954) Coordination of riparian and appropriative rights to the use of water, *Texas Law Review*, 33, pp. 24–69.

Umbeck J. (1981) Might makes rights: A theory of the formation and initial distribution of property rights, *Economic Inquiry*, 19, pp. 38–59.

Warwick K. (2013) Conscious buildings? *Intelligent Buildings International*, 5:4, pp. 199–203.

Watts M. (2011) The philosophy of Heidegger, *Continental European Philosophy*, New York: Routledge.

Weimer A., and Hoyt H. (1966) *Real Estate*, 5th edition, New York: The Ronald Press Company.

Weiser M. (1991) The computer for the 21st century, *Scientific American*, 265:3, pp. 94–105.

Weiser M., and Brown J.S. (1996) The coming of age of calm technology, in *Beyond Calculation* (Peter J. Denning and Robert M. Metcalfe., eds), pp. 75–85, New York: Springer.

3   The tokenisation of commercial real estate

Tokens as a new tool in financial engineering applied to real assets

Introduction: behind the hype

This chapter deals with real estate tokens and tokenisation, a process involving Digital Ledger Technologies and blockchains. Tokenisation has garnered a lot of attention in recent years to the point of being hailed as the most important innovation in the real estate industry since the introduction of REITS in 1960s America. The self-proclaimed 'revolution' triggered by real estate tokenisation has become somewhat of a buzzword. As a matter of fact, with all the hype surrounding tokenisation, it is easy to feel a little dizzy when looking at claims made by promoters and supporters of real estate tokens. Pitchbooks seem to have replaced textbooks.

However, behind the undeniable technological breakthroughs encapsulated by blockchains and smart contracts, is tokenisation as innovative a concept in real estate finance as it is claimed to be? Is tokenisation a radical financial innovation that will truly "unlock the value of real world assets" (IBV, 2018) and, in the process, revolutionise real estate finance by "allowing the creation of a new financial system" (Laurent et al., 2018)? And more generally, do tokens represent the ultimate embodiment of micro markets and a clean break with aggregate thinking in real estate finance, by opening up a "new era of much greater personalisation and customisation" (Laurent et al., 2018)?

To answer these questions, the analysis presented in this chapter aims to be as neutral as possible by separating tokenisation's actual potential as a concept that might (or might not) push the boundaries of real estate finance from the noises caused by the entrepreneurial excitement surrounding tokens and their underlying blockchain technology. To do so, this chapter starts by defining tokenisation and assessing its proposed application to single real estate assets in light of well-established concepts in financial economics and findings in the real estate finance academic literature. Based on this analysis, tokenisation does not appear as a full-blown revolution but as a tool in financial engineering that can be applied to real assets. Two applications of blockchain-based tokenisation are introduced: index tokenisation and data tokens which could, respectively, offer new underlying assets for real estate derivatives (Chapter 1), and complement digital rights in enabling a finer allocation of value created in smart buildings (Chapter 2).

1 Basic principles of tokenisation

1.1 *Tokenisation 101*

1.1.1 *Definition*

The concept of tokenisation has first emerged as an application of distributed ledger technology more than as a financial concept. In recent years, in view of tokenisation's growing importance in the international financial system, intergovernmental organisations and international bodies in charge of monitoring the global financial system have aimed to shed light on tokenisation. For instance, the Financial Stability Board (FSB) in a study on *Decentralised Financial Technologies* (2019) defines tokenisation as "the representation of traditional assets – e.g. financial instruments, a basket of collateral or real assets – on distributed ledger technology". Pre-exiting real assets are represented on the ledger "by linking or embedding by convention the economic value and rights from these assets into digital tokens created on the Blockchain" (OECD, 2020). Tokenisation is therefore the generic term used to describe "the process of moving traditional non-digital securities to a digital form using blockchain technology" (Pang et al., 2020). Importantly, the digital form is understood to bring about the fractionalisation of real estate assets into smaller component parts.

In the context of commercial real estate, tokenisation is a broad term which can materialise under many forms by using tokens to represent a range of ownership interests, e.g. equity in legal structures such as real estate investment trusts or private equity real estate funds, shares in debt secured against a portfolio of properties, cash flow stream from a single property (Won, 2019; Baum, 2020). As mentioned by Freedman and Fetner (2019), "to tokenize real estate is to fractionalize the ownership of real world assets digitally". In line with our discussion on micro markets for direct commercial real estate, the analysis presented in this chapter focuses on digital fractionalisation of equity real estate assets (i.e. buildings, funds, real estate companies, and indices) powered by Blockchain applications.

1.1.2 *Fractionalisation*

Fractionalisation of real estate assets, the process of splitting real estate assets into small compartment parts, is not a new concept in real estate finance (e.g. Davis, Harris and McCormick, 1983; Davidson, 1992). Different ways to split a property's freehold ownership among several parties have been customarily implemented. These include "joint ownership, physical sub-divisions with strata title, time shares, leaseholds, tranching and syndication" (Baum, 2020). Noticeably, the ease of fractionalising real estate assets hinges on each country's set of laws as national jurisdictions around the world have very different legal requirements with respect to fractionalised ownership of real properties. For instance, regarding joint ownership, Baum points out that in the UK, the maximum number of legal owners to a property is limited to four whereas in France and other

Southern European countries, assets can be jointly owned. By the same token, strata title which makes it possible to implement physical sub-division of properties by creating several new legal titles has been implemented in a limited range of countries only, e.g. Australia, Canada, India, Malaysia, New Zealand, Singapore, and the UAE.

Over the years, the concept of fractionalisation has led to several attempts to create markets for fractional ownership of properties. In the 1980s, the process of fractionalising single properties called 'unitisation' was applied to create a few investment vehicles, e.g. Single Property Ownership Trusts (SPOTs), Single Asset Property Companies (SAPCOs), and Property Income Certificates (PINCs)[1] (Baum, 2020). All three investment vehicles failed to pick up and were eventually dropped. One issue raised by Roche (1995) which might have led to their early demises stems from "technical concerns about the relationship of property valuations and market prices for the divided units" (Baum, 2020).

Tokenisation's situation is no different from the one encountered with unitisation in the past. The emergence of digital fractionalisation supposes a market microstructure characterised by a dual market, i.e. a market for physical properties in the real world (off-chain market) trading in parallel to a market for digital real estate tokens on the Blockchain (on-chain market). If proponents of real estate tokenisation are right, tokens would attract a myriad of small investors. International bodies worry that should it be the case, a dual market could lead to liquidity bifurcation between off-chain and on-chain markets (OECD, 2020), resulting in liquidity mismatch between tokens and the underlying asset (FSB, 2019).

Irrespective, benefits of real estate assets fractionalisation are supposed to include, among others, wider appeal through fast and affordable access to 'quasi-direct commercial property' leading to a democratisation of the real estate asset class, and accrued liquidity enabling tokenisation to unlock value by releasing the so-called liquidity premium embedded in real estate prices (Laurent et al., 2018, Ferreira, 2020).[2]

1.1.3 Role of blockchains and smart contracts in real estate tokenisation

There is no arguing that Distributed Ledger Technologies (DLTs) and blockchains which are powering tokenisation are innovative technologies. Blockchains, which is one particular form of DLTs applied in areas such as cryptocurrency and real estate, allow for permanent and tamper-proof records of all transactions ever made (RICS, 2020). Blockchains also foster transparency: all transactions occurring on a public blockchain can be accessed by anyone while private blockchains are accessible to authorised participants. In the process, they implement a "model of decentralised consensus and information" (Cong and He, 2019), which "remoulds the landscape of competition". Owing to their immutability and transparency, blockchains provide a secure and efficient environment for asset fractionalisation.

In addition to fractionalisation, blockchain technology also promises to "shake up and revolutionize the real estate sector", by automating the entire transaction process (Garcia-Teruel, 2020). In that sense, Distributed Ledger Technologies

(DLTs) are the glamorous aspect of real estate tokenisation. They are complex enough to capture people's imagination, simple enough to have direct practical applications that everybody can understand, and full of feel-good promises for the future of commercial real estate by being associated with such positive concepts as democratisation, value unlocking, and transparency.

However, the litmus test for tokenisation is not the technology but the financial process it empowers. In particular, do blockchains allow for the creation of sustainable markets for fractionalised real estate securities? After all, past experiences show that financial innovation is only as good as it can sustain new liquid markets. Poor liquidity has been a major hurdle for new innovative instruments in real estate finance, e.g. Shiller (2008)'s assessment of CME housing futures.

By definition, blockchains are static. Once fractionalisation is completed, blockchains as a stand-alone technology do not enable the creation of a market for fractionalised real estate securities inasmuch as blockchains are inherently databases. Mik (2019) explains that "ledgers and databases are collections of data, reflections of transactions occurring outside them". Because of their "limited computational capabilities", blockchains are not transactional platforms, "just as a ledger cannot by itself transact". To develop a marketplace, smart contracts have to be added to a blockchain ecosystem as a top layer, which comes with security challenges (Delmolino et al, 2016).

Markedly, the nature of direct commercial real estate and blockchain could not be more different. Properties are located in the physical world, known as off-chain in a blockchain ecosystem. Their physicality and constant interactions with the outside world stand in stark contradiction with blockchains' digital and self-contained nature. In contrast to on-chain events, off-chain events (i.e. occurring in the real world) have to be controlled with one's own eyes. Blockchains and smart contracts which are not directly connected to these off-chain events have to develop interfaces. This can be achieved thanks to "third-party service providers [known as oracles] that provide information about the external world" (Mik, 2019). For instance, whenever a payment is made based on some contractual performance, "the smart contract must contact an oracle to verify that the performance has in fact taken place". The oracle herself has to rely on external sources of information. Off-chain events affecting commercial buildings are numerous and diverse, especially in times of crisis. Therefore, blockchain-based tokenisation of physical commercial buildings is neither obvious nor straightforward.[3]

1.2 Token taxonomy: security, utility, and hybrid tokens

1.2.1 Security tokens versus tokenised securities

Blockchain-based fractionalisation of direct real estate can take two forms: (i) fractionalisation of ownership in the assets themselves (e.g. single buildings or portfolios of properties) and (ii) fractionalisation of securities based on claims over the assets' property rights and cash flows. Akin to traditional securities, the resulting fractional shares of value are asset-backed tokens "tied to an underlying physical asset" (Hargrave, Sahdev and Feldmeier, 2019). The two processes yield very different representations of securities: security tokens and tokenised securities, respectively (MIT, 2019). Security tokens are securities that do not exist out of the blockchain (on-chain), whereas tokenised securities are blockchain-embedded representations of real world securities (off-chain). The former are similar to "bearer assets" while the latter are akin to "depository receipts" (MIT, 2019). These two routes to commercial property fractionalisation are represented in Figure 3.1.

An asset fractionalised through security tokens (route 1 on Figure 3.1) is directly issued on the distributed ledger (Hileman and Rauchs, 2017). Since this asset exists on-chain, it is known as a native asset. Security tokens derive their values from tokenised assets' future cash flows like any other securities (Cong, Li and Wang, 2018). Therefore, the value of a security token increases with the underlying on-chain assets' cash flows, and vice versa. Conversely, an existing off-chain asset can be fractionalised through tokenised securities (route 2 on Figure 3.1). It is "digitised and represented by tokens on the distributed ledger network" (Hileman and Rauchs, 2017). The value of tokenised securities depends on the value of the underlying off-chain assets' cash flows, given an intermediate structure, such as a special purpose vehicle (SPV), a partnership, or a trust, usually required by law (Baum, 2020).

There are significant operational differences between the two routes. While native assets issued on the blockchain can be efficiently settled on-chain in a

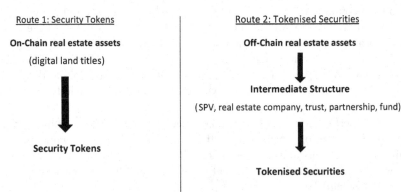

Figure 3.1 The two routes of real estate tokenisation – From real estate assets to on-chain tokens.

decentralised market setting, tokenising real world assets (route 2) cannot be fully on-chain and decentralised. As noted before, physical asset tokenisation will always require off-chain processes as the distributed ledger itself cannot manage real world events such as disputes. Furthermore, the question of tokens' collaterals remains murky. Should tokens be fully backed by existing off-chain assets being held in custody? The latter point is important as security tokens have the potential to disrupt global financial markets (OECD, 2020). In any case, there will be a need for "trusted parties that are responsible for guaranteeing these claims and [...] held legally accountable" (Hileman and Rauchs, 2017). Hence, no matter how much tokenisation might thrive by disconnecting real estate assets from the so-called real world, the reality of real estate will always remain primarily spatial.

Baum (2020) propounds that even though route 1 has become something of a poster child for asset tokenisation, route 2 which makes it possible to develop tokenised securities (from a real estate company, trust, partnership, or fund) seems more feasible in practice than creating a security token out of physical assets (route 1). The latter wrongly carries "the idea of a tokenised Nirvana" which is misleading considering that "the asset itself cannot easily be tokenised without digitalised land title and (in most cases) a change in property law". Case in point: to date, there are no examples of successful land title digitalisation or title tokens (Konashevych, 2020).

1.2.2 Utility tokens and hybrid tokens

Depending on the features implemented in them, tokens can give access to different combinations of assets' ownership and usage. Thus, in addition to security tokens, tokenisation can result in several other types of tokens. A token which gives access to the use of a product and service without any transfer of property rights is known as a *utility token*. Montaz, Rennertseder and Schroder (2019) define utility tokens as "a promise that the investor can redeem the token like a voucher for the company's products or services". In that respect, utility tokens are akin to "corporate coupons" (Cong, Li and Wang, 2018). Their value derives from their utility (Ferreira, 2020).

Utility tokens are intended for use within a specific blockchain platform. They might be successfully applied to a range of uses in commercial real estate (Baum, 2020), e.g. the use of space by controlling the right to occupy designated areas in a building, the use of energy in a prosumer building, or more generally the use of any resources attached to a smart building such as cloud computing capacities.

In parallel to utility tokens, hybrid tokens can also be designed by combining utility and return, i.e. features of utility tokens and security tokens. Such "semi-utility semi-return" tokens could find their best use for hospitality and F&B properties, such as hotels, pubs, restaurants, and coffee shops (Baum, 2020). Box 3.1 presents a glossary of the main technical terms used in the context of real estate tokenisation.

BOX 3.1: Glossary of tokenisation's main technical terms

The following glossary is a compilation of definitions gathered from published references listed for Chapter 3.

Blockchain: a particular application of Distributed Ledger Technology (DLT) adopted in cryptocurrency and many areas such as supply chain, insurance, and real estate (RICS, 2020). Blockchains can be public or private. A private blockchain only allows authorised parties to take part in a closed network, whereas in a public blockchain, information is shared by all, monitored by everyone though owned and controlled by no one (RICS, 2020).

DLT (Distributed Ledger Technology): DLT refers to a novel and fast-evolving approach to recording and sharing data across multiple data stores (or ledgers). This technology allows for transactions and data to be recorded, shared, and synchronised across a distributed network of different network participants (World Bank, 2017).

Off-chain: occurring in the real world.

On-chain: occurring on the blockchain.

Security tokens: blockchain-native tokens, i.e. securities that do not exist outside of the blockchain. The categorisation of security tokens as "investment contract" depends on each country's jurisdiction. In the USA, the Howey test's four conditions are applied (MIT, 2019).

Smart contract: a computerised transaction protocol that executes the terms of a contract (Szabo, 1994).

Token: a blockchain-based digital representation of an asset (MIT, 2019). Tokens are representations of claims on issuers' cash flows, or rights to redeem issuers' products and services (Cong, Li and Wang, 2018). Akin to a traditional security, they can be understood as a fractional share of value in an underlying asset or enterprise (Hargrave, Sahdev and Feldmeier, 2019).

Tokenisation: the process of creating a fractional ownership interest on an asset (utility or security) with a token that is blockchain-based (Won, 2019).

Tokenised securities: blockchain-embedded representations of real world securities (MIT, 2019).

Utility tokens: tokens intended to provide digital access to an application or service. Utility tokens are used solely in the functioning of a network and are not investment contracts (MIT, 2019).

---

2 Single real estate asset tokenisation: a critical analysis

The tokenisation of single properties which is a special case of real estate asset tokenisation has gained a lot of attention. A few transactions have taken place in recent years, whereby tokenised securities, rather than security tokens, were issued following route 2 mentioned above.[4]

This section looks at the digital fractionalisation of single properties and analyse how the concept of single asset tokens fits within concepts in financial economics and findings in real estate finance.

2.1 Potential benefits and challenges of single asset tokenisation

The MIT Digital Currency Initiative (MIT, 2019) identifies a series of potential benefits attached to commercial real estate tokenisation, especially single asset tokenisation. They insist that these benefits are 'potential' only insofar as "some benefits [...] may not apply to commercial real estate or may not be achieved immediately". Among these benefits are:

– The democratisation of commercial property investment,
– The customisation of real estate portfolios through exposure to single buildings instead of whole sector,
– Additional liquidity thanks to the unlocking of a global investor base and secondary markets,
– Automation of trading, compliance, verification, and escrow,
– Cost efficiency "by removing intermediaries and increasing efficiency of processes",
– Faster clearing and settlement in minutes or hours instead of days, thereby freeing capital tied in the market,
– Increased data transparency.

These potential benefits are customarily heralded by tokenisation proponents with very sweeping claims. We review below three claims pertaining to liquidity, transparency, and tokenisation as the new securitisation method of choice for private real estate.

Claim #1: Will single asset tokenisation unlock the liquidity premium for all investors?

One potential benefit of tokenisation is the so-called "unlocking of liquidity" enabled by single property digital fractionalisation. The rationale behind this claim boils down to a simple idea: "liquid assets command a premium"; therefore tokenisation which is supposed to increase liquidity "can increase asset value" (MIT, 2019). The OECD (2020) provides a more nuanced view of this claim:

> As investors expect higher yields from typically illiquid assets [...], tokenised assets may carry lower illiquidity premia allowing for the asset to trade closer to its fair value. This, however, may be a difficult proposition to test as liquidity/illiquidity premia are difficult to isolate, quantify, and dissociate from systemic or market risk.

Following Amihud and Mendelson (1986)'s seminal paper exploring the relations between the value of equity and its underlying liquidity, numerous past research in real estate finance have clearly shown the implications of illiquidity on private commercial real estate valuations and markets. Liquidity is a multidimensional concept in real estate finance which is all the more complex as it fluctuates throughout the property cycle. Liquidity is "positively correlated with the asset market cycle, [i.e.] liquidity is typically greater when the market is up, [...] and vice versa" (Fisher et al., 2003). In the UK, it is estimated that the liquidity premium for commercial properties ranges between 3% and 3.5% on average over time, although it can fall to 1.5% during rising markets and increase up to 10% in the event of liquidity dry-out (Investment Property Forum: IPF, 2015).

Financial theory supports the claim that tokens foster liquidity. Duffie, Garleanu and Pedersen (2007) identify that "illiquidity discounts are higher when counterparties are harder to find, [... and] when the fraction of qualified owners is smaller [...]". Security tokens meet these two conditions. On paper, security tokens can attract a large number of investors on a global scale as mentioned by the MIT researchers. Pragmatically, they can also reduce the costs of searching for properties and matching between buyers and sellers.[5] Search efficiency resulting in shorter negotiated transaction processes translates into less trading frictions in commercial property markets (Liu and Qian, 2013).

Past research also supports the claim that tokenisation impacts commercial property's illiquidity discount. Benveniste, Capozza and Seguin (2001) find that "creating liquid equity claims on pools of relatively illiquid property assets increases value by 12%–22%". For individual properties, liquidity "adds 16% to their value relative to a notional nontradable property asset". The only caveat identified by Benveniste et al. is the fixed costs associated with creating such claims. The issue of operational cost mostly disappears when considering a blockchain-powered market (Pang et al., 2020). Therefore, ceteris paribus, security tokens' illiquidity discounts should be significantly lower than those of non-tokenised comparable properties (keeping in mind that prices are not returns).[6]

In practice, however, the danger is to replace one source of illiquidity with another, i.e. the private commercial property market's well-researched illiquidity with public tokens markets' illiquidity. Research shows that there is cross-market liquidity between public and private commercial real estate markets (e.g. Bond and Chang, 2012). This implies that tokens are not immune from the underlying asset liquidity (or lack of liquidity thereof), which is itself associated with the value of financial claims on this asset (Downs and Zhu, 2019). Noticeably, most Security Token Offerings (STO) will result in small cap, if not microcap, markets. Moss and Lux (2014) explain that among UK and European listed real estate companies, the valuation premium of larger liquid companies versus small illiquid ones with similar assets increased significantly by 20%–40% post Global Financial Crisis due to the increased value placed by investors on liquidity since 2008. Single asset tokens could end up trading in a collection of small, illiquid markets in contrast to the liquid exchange traded markets (i.e. REITS) described by Case (2017).

Now, supposing that single asset tokens markets are liquid, tokenisation can indeed unlock the liquidity premium. But, for whom? To benefit from this un-locking, one needs to be in a situation of arbitrage between illiquid (private[7]) and liquid (tokens) markets for the same asset. Given the way the tokenisation process is structured (Ernst and Young, 2020), only the asset's owners at the time of STO are ever in that position. Since a lower illiquidity discount commands a higher valuation, property owners would be able to raise more funds from the sales of their buildings during a STO than they would by selling the building on the open real estate market. Thus, tokenisation can act as an additional tool in prop-erty owners' funding toolkit, e.g. by offering developers a new way to refinance their balance sheets. STO's appeal as a funding strategy for the real estate sector logically varies with the liquidity premia prevalent at different stages of the asset market cycle. This alternative source of financing is particularly relevant in the event of illiquid underlying asset markets, i.e. when tokenising an asset poten-tially unlocks high liquidity premium.

By emphasising liquidity, tokenisation seems to be targeted at short-term inves-tors who are willing to sacrifice returns for cash convertibility. In contrast, long-term investors who opt for tokens receive lower returns in exchange of a liquidity feature they don't truly value nor need. For them, a better alternative is to invest in real estate investment trusts (REITs) or private equity real estate funds. In sum, even if commercial property liquidity premia were to materialise in full into larger valuations for tokenised properties, this is not the pot of gold heralded in tokeni-sation pitchbooks. Hence, as pointed out by ING research (ING, 2019), "although fractional ownership could unlock more liquidity, it will not necessarily generate higher demand for those assets".

Claim #2: Will single asset tokenisation promote transparency in commercial real estate markets?

Bringing transparency to the commercial real estate markets is reportedly one of the fundamental benefits expected from tokens (Laurent et al., 2018). The tokeni-sation process itself is supposed to foster transparency of commercial real estate's "underlying data" (MIT, 2019). There are two dimensions at work here: first the institutional connection between transparency and agency in token markets, and second the role that data transparency can play in reducing asymmetric informa-tion in commercial property markets.

Interestingly, the concept of transparency which is omnipresent in tokenisa-tion pitchbooks is rarely mentioned in relation to corporate governance. Agency problems inherent to tokenisation, and single asset tokens for that matter, are mostly overlooked. However, Baum (2020) asserts that "even where [single asset tokenisation] is possible, control issues will need to be negotiated. Existing mech-anisms like General Partners/ Limited Partners structures and companies deal with this well enough". Thus, route 2 (tokenised securities) with its intermediate corporate structure addresses these issues better than route 1 (security tokens) where agency problems are taking investors into totally unchartered territories.

Cong and He (2019) shed some light on this question in the context of block-chains. As a by-product of blockchain technology, transparency's role goes beyond access to underlying data. It is about 'truth'. Decentralised consensus enabled by decentralised markets provides the closest there is to the truth. They write:

> Consensus enables agents with divergent perspectives and incentives to interact as if it is provided the "truth" which has profound implications on the functioning of society, including ethics, contracting, and legal enforcements among others. [...] Compared to traditional contracting, blockchains have the potential to produce a consensus that better reflects the "truth" of contingencies that are highly relevant for business operations.

Implied in this view of a blockchain-powered economy is the wider idea that participants in a blockchain network do collectively have enough knowledge or intelligence to expertly assess what the 'truth' is.[8] The notion of consensus as truth did not originate with blockchains. It derives from the consensus theory of trust, a sociological approach defended by such thinkers as American philosopher C.S Peirce (1839–1914) and, more recently German critical theorist Jürgen Habermas. Habermas contends that there is "an operational character of truth through identifying the property methodologically by reference to the procedure of verification" (Pettit, 1982),[9] a procedure enabled by blockchain and off-chain processes (such as oracles) in real estate tokenisation.

A decentralised and dynamic consensus yields a pragmatic version of truth which does not require trust and make blockchain a "trustless technology" (Scott, 2015). De Filippi (2019) notes that "trust in people is replaced by trust in the underlying technological framework". In that sense, whatever agency problems might arise with tokens would be automatically ironed out, not because token holders trust one another, but because together as a collectively intelligent body, they can achieve the truth. This "trustless dream" is obviously questionable in the case of single asset tokens whose underlying markets are likely to be quite narrow, and as a result, liable to manipulations.

More generally, in listed companies, truth is achieved through a set of corporate governance rules which go way beyond data transparency and involve business ethics (e.g. Donaldson and Dunfee, 1999). These rules lay out trust-building practices defining social contracts between managers and shareholders. Corporate governance in securitised real estate has long been a concern for real estate researchers, especially in the case of externally managed REITs (e.g. Lecomte and Ooi, 2013). Real estate tokens are not immune from agency problems. What if some token holders meddle with events underlying data, let alone the token market itself, to create the conditions for other token holders to adhere to a flawed consensus? Cong and He (2019) highlight that "blockchain technology, while holding great potential in mitigating information asymmetry and encouraging entry, can also lead to greater collusive behaviour".[10] Issues of control do not magically go away because the scope has shrunk from a portfolio of properties (REITs) to a fraction of a single property (single asset tokens).

Arguably, the focus on single assets makes agency problems even more relevant to token holders than they are to REITs' unitholders who enjoy property portfolios' risk-alleviating benefits. Whoever has physical control over depreciating, income-producing assets which have to be regularly valued does matter to real estate token investors.

Furthermore, blockchains make sweeping assumptions about the way real estate markets work and economic agents behave. Tokenisation-driven transparency may not be desirable for all participants in commercial real estate markets (Freedman and Fetner, 2019). Most commercial real estate players do not thrive on transparency (OECD, 2020), especially at the property level where confidentiality and asymmetry of information are matters of strategic significance.[11] In spite of transparency's ability to change the balance of power in their relations with landlords, will tenants in a tokenised property welcome real-time public disclosure of their commercial real estate dealings?

Strikingly, tenants are ignored in the analysis of real estate tokenisation even though single asset tokenisation involves the most granular level of information possible in commercial real estate. There is a paradox with blockchain-based fractionalisation of commercial real estate: one should not trust others on-chain, but be fully trustful off-chain once private information have been made public. Renting space in a tokenised commercial building has non-trivial implications in terms of confidentiality that tenants have to consider with care.

Claim #3: Will single asset fractionalisation of commercial real estate replace publicly listed REITs?

Single asset tokens offer an alternative to publicly listed real estate investment trusts (REITs). The MIT Digital Currency Initiative (MIT, 2019) notes that US REITs account for only 7% of the total commercial real estate market value, leaving

> a huge piece of possibly higher returning commercial real estate assets […] beyond retail investors' reach. Tokenising these private deals and providing them to a broader set of investors bridges this gap. It gives retail investors access to these previously exclusive deals.

Additionally, MIT researchers explain that retail investors are "at the mercy of REIT managers and do not have the option of customizing their real estate exposure". Tokens "allow [them] the flexibility to tweak their exposure to the underlying" and build a diversified global portfolio of tokenised properties with minimum capital requirements.

The double benefits of flexibility and granularity which give small investors control over their real estate investments would outweigh the REIT regime's advantages, e.g. access to a portfolio of institutional grade properties, high and stable dividend pay-out, tax pass-through entity status, professional management, transparency compared to direct private commercial real estate, and the liquidity of listed securities. Let's review some of these points and see how tokens compare to REITs.

First, in most regimes around the globe, REITs tend to be focused on one property type only, thereby offering investors 'pure play' vehicles. Although investing in REITs does not allow the granularity of single asset tokens, it still gives access to investments whose scopes are usually contained within clearly delineated geographic boundaries (e.g. regional, national).[12] Second, whether they are internally or externally managed, REITs are expected to comply with corporate governance principles which are, in part, embedded into the REIT regime itself (e.g. pay-out ratio, leverage limit). Third, in addition to their pass-through entity status, some REIT regimes offer unique tax benefits: for instance the umbrella partnership structure in the USA (UPREIT), enabling property owners to defer capital gain taxes on the sales of their properties to a REIT. What will be the tax impact of tokenising a property with latent capital gain? ANREV (2019) notes that "it is doubtful regulator would view [tokens] any different to a private equity investment at best".

More fundamentally, the key difference between REITS and singe asset tokens stems from the nature of real estate resources encapsulated in each investment vehicle. Specifically, tokenisation neglects the value created by property management in buildings, the so-called 'franchise value' part of warranted premiums to NAV in REITs' pricing models. Green Street Advisors (2014) talk about "real estate plus". While the real estate sector moves from asset provision to service provision (RICS, 2017), ignoring this dimension is a major shortcoming of tokenisation. As explained in Chapter 2 of this book, digitalisation changes the nature of real estate resources. In smart buildings, property managers' digital know-how is instrumental in creating value for investors. Furthermore, there is a scale effect attached to this digital know-how: fractionalised single assets without a dedicated team of expert managers are at a clear disadvantage compared to portfolios of properties benefitting from synergies in such crucial areas as data collection and analytics (e.g. a retail REIT leveraging on data collected in several shopping malls). Markedly, there is a mismatch between tokenisation's innovative underlying technology (blockchain) and its reliance on a dated conception of what buildings are and where value is created in commercial real estate.

When REITS were first created by US President Eisenhower in 1960, they addressed a need in capital markets, i.e. "to give all investors the opportunity to invest in large scale portfolios of income-producing real estate" (source: NAREIT). With single asset tokens, "there is a risk that this is an elegant technology solution to a very small problem, or a solution which a majority of market participants do not wish for" (Baum, 2020).

2.2 Conceptual contribution of single asset tokenisation to real estate finance

Dealing with property heterogeneity, managing risk in real estate investments, and coming up with radical innovation that can create sustainable markets have been constant challenges for real estate finance. The following section discusses tokenisation's contributions to these challenges.

• *Does single asset tokenisation address the issue of property heterogeneity?*

One important hurdle in commercial real estate pricing models stems from heterogeneity at the property level. Each property is unique in the way it interacts with the environment. This issue has motivated the development of the genetics-based model described in Chapter 1 of this book. Single asset tokenisation fractionalises property rights and cash flows into smaller tradable units. In doing so, it lowers the entry point of commercial real estate investing. But, it does not fundamentally alter the nature of the underlying fractionalised asset. Whether considering a property in its entirety or in parts (tokens), heterogeneity remains the same. Reducing the scope of the asset does not alter the scale of analysis. Tokens are about promoting accessibility, not dealing with heterogeneity.

• *Does single asset tokenisation contribute to risk management in commercial real estate?*

The model of Arrow-Debreu securities is a classic framework used in financial economics to assess an asset's contribution to risk management. In "Nuclear Financial Economics", Sharpe (1995) explains that "to deal with risk, Arrow and Debreu introduced the concept of a contingent contract – a contract 'for delivery of goods or many contingent on the occurrence of [a] state of affairs'. Arrow-Debreu securities are akin to pure securities (also known as primitive securities) 'where a unit security [...] is a claim paying one monetary unit if state s occurs and nothing otherwise. Any security whatever may be regarded as a bundle of the elementary types' [...]" (Arrow, 1964). Are single asset tokens pure securities? Single asset tokens encapsulate a myriad of time-state claims. They are not pure securities. In fact, there is no attempt with tokenisation to break down claims on single properties into a series of pure securities.[13]

Blockchain is intrinsically a data management technology, not a financial technology. Sharpe (1995) notes that financial engineering is "the development and the creative application of financial technology to solve problems in finance and to exploit financial opportunities". With single asset tokens, financial engineering is limited to basic fractionalisation. Single asset tokenisation does not contribute by itself to real estate risk management.

• *Does single asset tokenisation represent a radical financial innovation in real estate finance?*

The concept of asset fractionalisation is not new in real estate finance (Baum, 2020). What is new with tokenisation is the use of sophisticated technology to implement and manage the fractionalisation process. It is fractionalisation with a technological twist. Is it enough for tokenisation to qualify as a radical financial innovation in real estate finance and justify a revolution? Shiller (2004) defines radical financial innovation as "a form of innovation that requires changes in society that reach far beyond one firm, and most likely require changes in an array of institutions, and depends for its success on substantial public education as well". In the context of risk management, "a radical financial innovation should [permit] risk management to be extended far beyond its former realm, covering important new classes of risks". In view of this definition, single asset tokenisation is not a radical financial innovation in real estate finance nor in real estate risk management. Single asset tokenisation does not radically change investors' thinking about commercial real estate assets. Specifically, it does nothing to enlighten them about the true nature of real estate risk and how to best hedge it (e.g. by providing a risk model of commercial real estate).

3 Suggested applications of tokenisation in real estate finance

Of the three concepts analysed in this book (factorisation, digitalisation, and tokenisation), tokenisation is the least innovative conceptually even though it relies on a cutting-edge technological apparatus. Nonetheless, provided the right applications, tokens might play an important role in the future of real estate finance by offering a tool that financial engineers can apply to real assets. Baum (2020) underscores that "if real estate tokenisation were to become popular, several innovations become conceivable, including structured finance, hybrid real estate tokens and digital future exchanges". The following section introduces two such innovations: first, index tokenisation which is the application of blockchain-based tokenisation to indices of private commercial real estate used as underlying to real estate derivatives, and second, data tokens which are utility tokens on data collected in smart buildings. The objective in introducing these innovations is to explore how tokens can be used to address two of the real estate sector's needs:

- the long-standing need for better risk management instruments given index-based real estate derivatives' shortcomings mentioned in Chapter 1,
- and the emerging need to optimally allocate and safely monetise real estate resources in smart buildings, such as data, as explained in Chapter 2.

3.1 Index tokenisation

Establishing a successful market for index-based real estate derivatives has been hindered by issues that real estate researchers have found challenging to overcome, including:

- The lack of granularity in the spot commercial real estate market which "may restrain the trading of commercial real estate derivatives [...]" (Tunaru and Fabozzi, 2017),

- The lack of replicability of the underlying index inhibiting "banks from launching derivative product and simply replicating it by buying the properties contained in the underlying index" (Syz, 2008),
- The numerous frictions in the real estate derivatives market "because the index and its components cannot be traded continuously and instantly at the prevailing spot price without transaction costs" (Syz, 2008),
- The impossibility to implement dynamic hedging strategies using real estate derivatives since "it is hardly possible to trade the constituents of a property index [which] are usually indivisible and not traded in small units" (Syz, 2008).

Considering these shortcomings, Syz (2008) explains that "if a property index can be decomposed into factors, some of which are traded assets, then the index can at least in part be mimicked". This is where, in addition to factorisation analysed in chapter 1, tokenisation can add value to real estate derivatives, by contributing to establish a more liquid market for real estate derivatives. Several alternative formats can be envisioned. The following paragraph reviews three alternatives.

Real estate derivatives on single asset tokens: the first alternative is to design real estate derivatives on single asset tokens. However, given the expected narrowness of single asset tokens' spot markets, it is highly unlikely that the regulatory authorities (e.g. Securities Exchange Commission and Commodity Futures Trading Commission under the 1982 Shad-Johnson accord in the USA) will easily approve such instruments. As pointed out by Shiller (1993), the risk of manipulation in the cash market is high and challenging to curtail for commercial real estate. Notwithstanding their intrinsic challenges, real estate derivatives on single asset tokens can make sense as part of combinative hedges alongside other tradable assets and/or factors.

Real estate derivatives on index of tokens: Won (2019) mentions the creation of indices of tokens as a possible future application of tokenisation. Indices of tokens, i.e. indices made up of single asset tokens, could be used as underlying to real estate derivatives in lieu of existing indices of institutionally owned commercial real estate (e.g. MSCI-IPD indices). In principle, this alternative could solve the above-mentioned issues of granularity, replicability, and frictions of property indices. In practice, it supposes that large and liquid markets for single asset tokens operate. Even if it were the case, tokenised properties available for constructing indices of tokens may not be of institutional grade and comparable to properties included in valuation-based indices of commercial real estate, therefore limiting indices of tokens' representativeness and contribution to investors' hedging strategies. Interestingly, indices of tokens can open the door to index customisation. With n tokens, n! customised valuation-based indices can be created. Issues of governance, especially as far as periodic valuations of the underlying properties are concerned, have to be ironed out before such a model can be implemented. Customised indices of tokens may best serve as constituents in combinative hedges as mentioned previously for single asset tokens.

Real estate derivatives on tokenised indices: both real estate token-based deriv-atives models presented before suppose a functioning market for single asset to-kens. This is clearly a limitation. The third alternative presented hereafter does not rely on existing single asset tokens. Instead, it relies on a process defined as *index tokenisation*. While indices of tokens pool single asset tokens into an index, index tokenisation creates security tokens from off-chain properties included in an index (e.g. NCREIF Property Index). These security tokens known as *index tokens* are designed to mimic off-chain properties' returns. Returns on private commercial real estate indices are thus fractionalised into a series of index tokens, each token replicating the individual return(s) of one actual off-chain property in the index. Hence, index tokenisation does not involve fractionalisation of off-chain properties nor the on-chain transfer of off-chain assets. Only index returns are fractionalised into property-level returns through the creation of on-chain derivative securities, i.e. index tokens which are blockchain-native and whose values derive from off-chain returns. Figure 3.2 illustrates the concept of index tokenisation.

Index tokenisation can be implemented on a perpetual basis (one token per off-chain property for all periods) or on a periodic basis (one token per period for each off-chain property). Assuming that several blockchains can be opened in parallel,

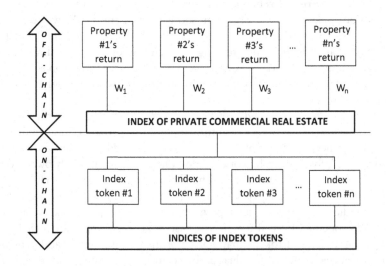

Notes: (i) Property returns (e.g., total returns, market values) are periodically computed by the index provider according to the index' methodology (e.g., Young, Fisher and D'Alessandro, 2017 for the NCREIF Property Index). These returns are then weighted (e.g., W_i for property i might be an equal weight or a valuation-based weight) and released as an aggregate periodic return in % for the index. (ii) Index tokens are security tokens based on fractionalised index returns rather than fractionalised properties. For properties in the index of private commercial real estate, there are n! possible indices of index tokens.

Figure 3.2 Index tokenisation for private commercial real estate indices.

the latter format enables more flexibility and trading opportunities, by opening up a range of periodic maturities (e.g. quarterly returns tokens) to market participants. The index tokens market involves blockchains for easy order matching and position clearing, as well as smart contracts for transacting. For starters, private blockchains are made available to accredited investors only. Both long and short positions can be allowed provided transactions find counterparties on the chain. The risk of insufficient liquidity obviously looms large on such a market, which may eventually justify the opening of the market to both hedgers and speculators on public blockchains.[14]

3.2 Utility tokens for smart real estate: data tokens

Chapter 2 underscores the emergence of new resources in smart buildings in smart cities. Among these resources, data are expected to play a paramount role in creating value for property owners. According to the model of digital rights, ownership of data collected in a smart building is based on Digital Usage Rights. Data collected in tenanted spaces belong to tenants whereas data collected in common areas and non-tenanted spaces belong to property owners.

Property owners who wish to monetise their share of collected data can 'rent out' some data to a third party, e.g. one of their tenants. One way to do so is to set up a private blockchain allowing property owners to sell utility tokens on data or *data tokens*. Data tokens are attached to a specific use of data during a limited period of time, e.g. selling to a tenant the right to use data collected in a shopping mall's common areas during a week or at certain times of the day. The same model of data tokens can apply for tenants looking for ways to monetise data collected within their rented spaces. Any innovation involving data collected in space is sensitive and obviously has to abide by data protection and privacy laws.

In sum, utility tokens can complement the concept of digital rights and help establish a transparent and frictionless rental market for smart real estate's resources, thereby allowing for a finer allocation of value created in smart buildings.[15]

Notes

1 Roche (1995) defines Single Property Ownership Trust (SPOT) as

> a securitisation arrangement which would have provided the investor with a specific share of a single property's income flow and capital value via a trust mechanism. Strictly an investor would have held units in the trust rather than securities in a company.

> A Property Income Certificate, or PINC, is "a tradable equity security in a tax transparent single property company which entitles the holder to a direct share of the property's income flow and capital value. A PINC company could be geared, [but] never traded".

2 The notion of democratising access to property markets owing to tokenisation is often associated with a range of sociological goals defining a lifestyle where property ownership does not matter as much as before, e.g. shared ownership of properties. Ernst and Young (2020) talks about inclusive finance and highlights that fractioning assets

allows "multiple people [to] buy together an asset and use it, which is key to a society where usage is more and more supplementing ownership". These objectives are commendable but hardly new. In real estate, the concept of having partial use commensurate with partial ownership is called timeshare. More generally, what people actually pay for when they buy or rent properties is time to appropriate space as pointed by Lefebvre (1974) in his analysis of real estate tenures: eternity in case of freehold and shorter periods (leaseholds) with possibly idiosyncratic periodicity (timeshare arrangements) for other tenures . Tokens are simply encapsulating time in a digital format.

3 In that respect, asset classes such as fine art, wines, and other collectibles whose off-chain lives are a lot less eventful than buildings' (no cash flows, no depreciation and limited interactions, if any, with their environments under optimal conservation conditions) would be potentially more suitable for tokenisation than commercial real estate assets. Baum (2020) notes that "artwork does not suffer depreciation or obsolescence, or need refurbishment, or deliver income, making it somewhat less complex as a fractionalised asset than real estate". Despite tokenisation's promise of a fully decentralised market, the tokenisation of fine art still requires custodianship by a central authority or trusted third party. Custodianship is an essential characteristic of real asset tokenisation as highlighted in OECD (2020).

4 A regulated exchange called IPSX (The Property Stock Exchange) has been set up in London in 2019 in order to trade single real estate asset companies, albeit not security tokens nor tokenised securities, insofar as IPSX does not use blockchain or DLTs.

5 The application of blockchains in commercial real estate should contribute to improve the property search process (Deloitte, 2017), by aggregating on-chain fragmented listings data from multiple listings services.

6 In theory, provided their markets are liquid and efficient enough, security tokens are expected to generate lower expected returns for their holders than private commercial real estate since they hold less risk (ceteris paribus).

7 A privately owned asset can be off-chain (physical) or on-chain.

8 The view that blockchains through consensus can bring out a dimension larger than individual agents' contributions is in line with Pierre Lévy (1994) who describes collective intelligence powered by digital technologies (e.g. the internet) as a trigger to a "real time democracy".

9 In a seminal text, Habermas (1973) explains the concept of consensus-based truth as follows:

> I may ascribe a predicate to an object if and only if every other individual who could enter into discussion with me would ascribe the same predicate to the same object. In order to distinguish true from false statements, I refer to the judgement of others- in fact the judgement of all others with whom I could ever undertake a discussion […] The condition for the truth of statements is the potential agreement of all others […] Truth means the promise of achieving a rational consensus.

10 Specifically designed governance principles should regulate tokens at every stage of their investment cycle, from offering to redemption. For instance, regulators should define the rules governing investors' exit strategies, e.g. "en-bloc" sale of all tokens to a third party based on a quorum system.

11 In the real estate tokenisation discourse, the mitigation of asymmetric information and the democratisation of commercial real estate markets are usually closely intertwined. The lack of transparency supposedly benefits large investors who appropriate most of the value created in commercial real estate, whilst small investors are left out. This argument seems ideological rather than economic unless blockchains are actually meant to trigger a shift out of the Western capitalist model to a new type of model which remains to be properly defined.

12 In terms of risks, single asset tokens are potentially riskier than REITs due to their narrower focus on one property only. In contrast to securitisation (e.g. MBS), tokenisation does not strive to restructure assets' cash flows. Tokens' returns directly reflect, without

filter, the underlying property's life cycle. As the building ages, secondary tokens offerings might be required to finance capital expenditures, thus diluting existing tokens holders' interests. Due to the importance of property management in the real world, security tokens may end up being externally managed vehicles, an eventuality which underscores the key role that governance must play in real estate tokenisation.

13 In practice, a strict application of the Arrow-Debreu model is unrealistic, a point mentioned in the introduction of this book (after Shiller, 2004). However, a tokens market which involves no financial engineering does not suffice to manage risk for property hedgers.

14 As a prerequisite condition to index tokenisation, index sponsors should be willing to share some granular, albeit anonymised, data with the public, which may be way more than the level of disclosure agreed upon with their data contributing property owners.

15 Depending on use "which can evolve toward or away from a security" (Token Alliance, 2018), utility tokens are sometimes deemed as securities by market authorities. One important characteristic for data tokens to qualify as tokens and not securities would be that there is no secondary market for them: once purchased, they have to be immediately used rather than stored and resold.

References

Amihud Y., and Mendelson H. (1986) Asset pricing and the bid-ask spread, *Journal of Financial Economics*, 17, pp. 223–249.

ANREV (2019) Tokenising real estate – What it means and why it is important, ANREV Technology and Innovation Working Group, Asian Association for Investors in Non-Listed Real Estate Vehicles, Hong Kong.

Arrow K.J. (1964) The role of securities in the optimal allocation of risk-bearing, *The Review of Economic Studies*, 31:2, pp. 91–96.

Baum A. (2020) Tokenisation – The future of real estate investment? Oxford Future of Real Estate Initiative, University of Oxford Research, Saïd Business School.

Benveniste L., Capozza D., and Seguin P.J. (2001) The value of liquidity, *Real Estate Economics*, 29:4, pp. 633–660.

Bond S., and Chang Q. (2012) Liquidity dynamics across public and private markets, *Journal of International Money and Finance*, 31:7, pp. 1890–1910.

Case B. (2017) Comparing real estate values in the liquid and illiquid markets, NAREIT Market Commentary blog, www.REIT.com (February 2, 2017).

Cong L.W., and He Z. (2019) Blockchain disruption and smart contracts, *The Review of Financial Studies*, 32:5, pp. 1754–1797.

Cong L.W., Li Y., and Wang N. (2018) *Tokenomics: Dynamic Adoption and Valuation*, Becker Friedman Institute, Working Paper No. 2018–49, University of Chicago.

Davidson B. (1992) Valuation of fractional interests in real estate limited partnerships – Another approach, *The Appraisal Journal*, 60:2, pp. 184–194.

Davis W.D. Sr, Harris D.L., and McCormick P.A. (1983) The valuation of partial interests in real estate, *Journal of ASFMRA*, 47:2, pp. 17–21.

De Filippi P. (2019) Blockchain technology and decentralized governance: The pitfalls of a trustless dream, Decentralized thriving: Governance and Community on the Web 3.0, hal-02445179.

Delmolino K., Arnett M., Kosba A., Miller A., and Shi E. (2016) Step by step towards creating a safe smart contract: Lessons and insights from a cryptocurrency lab, in *Financial Cryptocurrency and Data Security* (Rohloff K., Clark J., Meiklejohn S., Wallach D., Brenner M. and Ryan P., eds), Lecture Notes in Computer Science, vol. 9604, Berlin and Heidelberg: Springer-Verlaf, pp. 79–94.

Deloitte (2017) *Blockchain in commercial real estate: the future is here!*, Deloitte Center for Financial Services, Deloitte Development LLC.

Donaldson T., and Dunfee T.W. (1999) *Ties that bind: A social contracts approach to business ethics*, Cambridge: Harvard Business School Press.

Downs D., and Zhu B. (2019) REITs, underlying property markets and liquidity: A firm level analysis, 2019 European Real Estate Society annual meeting, ESSEC Business School, Cergy-Pontoise, France.

Duffie D., Garleanu N., and Pedersen L.H. (2007) Valuation in over-the-counter markets, *The Review of Financial Studies*, 20:6, pp. 1865–1900.

Ernst and Young (2020) Tokenisation of assets: Decentralized finance (DeFi), vol. 1, Spot on: Fundraising and StableCoins in Switzerland.

Ferreira A. (2020) Emerging approaches to blockchain-based token economy, *The Journal of the British Blockchain Association*, 3:1, pp. 1–9.

Financial Stability Board (2019) *Decentralised Financial Technologies*, Report on financial stability, regulatory and governance implications.

Fisher J., Gatzlaff D., Geltner D., and Haurin D. (2003) Controlling for the impact of variable liquidity in commercial real estate price indices, *Real Estate Economics*, 31:2, pp. 269–303.

Freedman R., and Fetner D. (2019) Waking up to the dream of real estate tokenisation, Metatrends, www.propmodo.com (February 19, 2019).

Garcia-Teruel R.M. (2020) Legal challenges and opportunities of blockchain technology in the real estate sector, *Journal of Property, Planning and Environmental Law*, 12:2, pp. 129–145.

Green Street Advisors (2014) Reit valuation: The NAV-based pricing model, REIT valuation: Version 3.0, Green Street Advisors, Newport Beach.

Habermas J. (1973) Wahrheitstheorien in *Wirklichkeit und Reflexion* (Fahrenbach H., ed), Pfüllingen: Neske, pp. 211–265.

Hargrave J., Sahdev N., and Feldmeier O. (2019) Chapter 7: How value is created in tokenized assets, in *Blockchain Economics: Implications of Distributed Ledgers: Markets, Communications Networks, and Algorithmic Reality* (Swan M., Potts J., Takagi S., Witte F. and Tasca P., eds), Between Science and Economics, vol. 1, Singapore: World Scientific Publishing, pp. 125–143.

Hileman G., and Rauchs M. (2017) Global blockchain benchmarking study, Cambridge Centre for Alternative Finance, University of Cambridge Judge Business School.

IBV (2018) Moving to a token-driven economy: Enabling the digitalization of real-world assets, IBM Institute for Business Value, ExpertInsights@IBV.

ING (2019) New money VI: Asset tokenization – A new chapter for the capital markets industry? Economic and Financial Analysis.

IPF (2015) *Liquidity in Commercial Property Markets*, Summary Report, IPF Research Programme 2011–2015, Investment Property Forum, London.

Konashevych O. (2020) Constraints and benefits of the blockchain use for real estate and property rights, *Journal of Property, Planning and Environmental Law*, 12:2, pp. 109–127.

Laurent P., Chollet T., Burke M., and Seers T. (2018) The tokenisation of assets is disrupting the financial industry. Are you ready? *Deloitte Inside Magazine*, Issue 19, pp. 62–67.

Lecomte P., and Ooi J. (2013) Corporate governance and performance of externally managed Singapore REITs, *The Journal of Real Estate Finance and Economics*, 46, pp. 664–684.

Lefebvre H. (1974) *The Production of Space*, Oxford: Blackwell Publishing.

Lévy P. (1994), *L'intelligence collective: pour une anthropologie du cyberspace*, Editions La Découverte, Paris : France.

Liu P., and Qian W (2013) *Illiquidity measures and the pricing implications in commercial real estate*, Real Estate Research Institute, Published working paper.

Mik E. (2019) Chapter 9: Blockchains: A technology for decentralized marketplaces, in *The Cambridge Handbook of Smart Contracts, Blockchain Technology and Digital Platforms* (DiMatteo L., Cannarsa M. and Poncibo C., eds), Cambridge: Cambridge University Press, pp. 160–182.

MIT (2019) *Tokenized Securities & Commercial Real Estate*, MIT Digital Currency Initiative, Working Group Research Paper, MIT Management Sloan School, MIT Media Lab.

Montaz P., Rennertseder K., and Schroder H. (2019) Token offerings: A revolution in corporate finance? *The Capco Institute Journal of Financial Transformation*, 49, pp. 32–41.

Moss A., and Lux N. (2014) The impact of liquidity of the valuation of European real estate securities, *Journal of European Real Estate Research*, 7:2, pp. 139–157.

OECD (2020) The tokenisation of assets and potential implications for financial markets, OECD Blockchain Policy Series.

Pang P., Tang H.F., Lam J., Chan J., Hobler N., Kan K.K., Jeong H., and Lau R. (2020) *Real Estate Tokenisation: Hong Kong, Singapore*, Report by Liquefy, Sidley Austin, KPMG, and Colliers International.

Pettit P. (1982) Habermas on truth and justice, in *Marx and Marxisms* (Parkinson G.H.R., ed), Cambridge: Cambridge University Press, pp. 207–228.

RICS (2017) Artificial Intelligence: What it means for the built environment, RICS Research 2017, RICS Research Trust, Royal Institution of Chartered Surveyors, London.

RICS (2020) A critical review of distributed ledger technology and its applications in real estate, RICS Research 2020, RICS Research Trust, Royal Institution of Chartered Surveyors, London.

Roche J. (1995) *Property Futures and Securitisation: The Way Ahead*, Cambridge: Woodhead Publishing Ltd.

Scott B. (2015) Visions of a techno-Leviathan: The politics of the Bitcoin blockchain, E-International Relations, ISSN 2053-8626.

Sharpe W. (1995) Nuclear financial economics, in *Risk Management: Problems and Solutions* (Beaver W. and Parke G., eds), New York: MacGaw-Hill, 1995.

Shiller R. (1993) *Macro Markets: Creating Institutions for Managing Society's Largest Economic Risks*, Oxford: Oxford University Press.

Shiller R. (2004) *Radical Financial Innovation*, Cowles Foundation Discussion Papers 1461, Cowles Foundation for Research in Economics, Yale University, New Haven.

Shiller R. (2008) *Derivatives Markets for Home Prices*, NBER Working Paper 13962, Cambridge, MA: USA.

Syz J. (2008) *Property Derivatives: Pricing, Hedging and Applications*, Wiley Finance, Chichester: John Wiley & Sons.

Szabo N. (1994) Smart contracts, unpublished manuscript.

Token Alliance (2018) Understanding digital tokens: Market overviews and proposed guidelines for policymakers and practitioners, The Chamber of Digital Commerce.

Tunaru R., and Fabozzi F.J. (2017) Commercial real estate derivatives: The end or the beginning? *Journal of Portfolio Management*, Special Real Estate Issue, 43:6, pp. 179–186.

Young M., Fisher J., and d'Alessandro J. (2017) New NCREIF Value Index and operations measures, *Journal of Real Estate Literature*, 25:1, pp. 221–235.

Won J. (2019) Tokenized real estate: Creating new investing and financing channels through blockchain, blog.realestate.cornell.edu (April 30, 2019).

World Bank (2017) Distributed Ledger Technology (DLT) and Blockchain, FinTech Note 1, World Bank Group, Washington.

Final remarks

This book introduces three concepts: the factorisation, the digitalisation and the tokenisation of commercial real estate. These concepts promote a micro-scale perspective on commercial real estate assets, thereby paving the way for micro markets in real estate finance.

Contrary to factorisation and tokenisation, digitalisation is not a financial engineering process but a far-reaching and revolutionary phenomenon. Its paradigm-shifting impact on space, the actual commodity of real estate, means that real estate models have to accommodate new resources in smart real estate while pervasive computing and the large-scale implementation of non-conscious cognitive devices in smart buildings alter humans' interactions with the built environment in what social scientists describe as a "tectonic shift" (Hayles, 2014). This shift translates into the emergence of digital-time, the third realm of commercial real estate. Digital rights propose an effective way to allocate value created in smart buildings among the various stakeholders operating in the digital realm.

Smart buildings' positioning as platforms to digital opens the door to a myriad of ethical issues pertaining to data collection and use. The dogma of an omnipotent technology whose advances are unquestionably constitutive of progresses has the potential to jeopardise the very essence of human life in space (e.g. Lefebvre, 1974). Safeguards are required. The book mentions the need for the real estate sector to come up with digital governance principles in smart space. Moreover, technologies like blockchain are not agnostic. Their implementation supposes a certain set of assumptions about the way markets work and real estate players behave, which may not be fully compatible with the modus operandi of real estate markets in practice. Building consensus around new instruments and their associated markets will be instrumental in the success of real estate finance's innovations.

Pioneer real estate thinkers knew a few things about commercial real estate's idiosyncrasies. Factorisation, digitalisation and tokenisation underscore how important their contributions are to the future directions of real estate finance. Markowitz (1993) advised real estate researchers "to start from scratch [and] use whatever methodology the problem calls for" in order to "develop [their] own real estate theory which addresses itself very much to the illiquidities of the problem".[1] Setting free from normalities of well-established financial theories is a challenge.

It requires imagination coupled with scientific rigour as well as multidisciplinary endeavours. This book suggests that researchers start by developing a "map of the cat", i.e. a risk model of commercial real estate at the most granular level. Meanwhile, advancements in data analytics and Artificial Intelligence should be leveraged to gain deeper insights into commercial property's heterogeneity.

Acknowledging seemingly insurmountable idiosyncrasies at the property level does not mean entering into a world of single assets markets, in contrast to what single asset tokenisation has in store for commercial real estate. Instead, positioning property heterogeneity at the core of real estate finance ensures that instruments and markets are intrinsically compatible with the underlying assets while aiming for large and liquid markets. That said, any future innovations in real estate finance will have to be compatible with smart real estate's new environment embodied in the above-mentioned three realms of real estate: physical, financial, and digital. In particular, the potentially dominating technological dimension of smart real estate should not disconnect real estate finance from the underlying assets' fundamental spatiality, even if the way that pricing models, such as the hedonic pricing method, account for value in space has to be overhauled with the emergence of smart space.

MacKenzie (2006) after Friedman (1966) talks about modern economic theories of finance as an engine not a camera of financial markets. Real estate finance needs to find an engine that will contribute to the success of innovative instruments and markets. But, this engine should also be a camera that faithfully reproduces commercial properties in all their empirical dimensions at every scale in every realm. Micro markets are an attempt to achieve just that.

Note

1 Markowitz, H. (1993) Unpublished quotes drawn verbatim from transcribed comments of Modern Portfolio Theory Roundtable, *Buildings Magazine* sponsor. Quoted in DeLisle (2000), pp. 55–56.

References

Friedman M. (1966) The methodology of positive economics, in *Essays in Positive Economics* (Friedman M., ed), Chicago: University of Chicago Press, pp. 3–16, 30–43.
Hayles N.K. (2014) Cognition everywhere: The rise of the cognitive nonconscious and the costs of consciousness, *New Literary History*, 45:2, pp. 199–220.
Lefebvre H. (1974) *The Production of Space*, Oxford: Blackwell Publishing.
MacKenzie D. (2006) *An Engine Not a Camera*, Boston: The MIT Press.

Appendix 1.1

Macrovariables in commercial real estate: a selection of academic literature

Research Paper: Author (date)	Type of Commercial Real Estate Markets Under Study	Study Period	Macro-Factors	Main Findings
J.S. Hekman (1985)	Office construction markets in fourteen US cities	1979–1983	Rents: – Vacancy rate in class A existing office buildings – Constant dollar Gross National Product ("a measure of national demand forces") – Total employment in the SMSA (Standard Metropolitan Statistical Area- "to control for the effect of city size on rent") – Local unemployment rate ("a local market demand measure") Investments: – Ratio of finance-insurance-real estate, service and government employment in 1980 to that in 1970 – Construction cost per square foot divided by GNP deflator – Nominal interest rate on ten-year government bonds less three-month T-bill rate.	
T. Grissom, D. Hartzell and C. Liu (1987)	78 industrial properties in four US regions	1973–1983	Based on APT (FLM) framework: Five-factor models Ten-factor models	Evidence of regional markets for industrial real estate. Risk premiums associated with common systematic risk attribute(s) as well as the number of priced risk factors differ across regions.

(Continued)

Research Paper: Author (date)	Type of Commercial Real Estate Markets Under Study	Study Period	Macro-Factors	Main Findings
J. Kling and T. McCue (1987)	US Office building market	1972–1985	– National office construction – National output – Interest rate – Aggregate price – Money supply data	Nominal interest rates explain a majority of the variation in office construction. The impact of nominal rates is mainly through its predictive influence on anticipated output.
D. Geltner (1989)	Indices of US unsecuritised investment grade real estate properties (FRC and PRISA indices)	1971–1987	Based on consumption CAPM framework: national per capita consumption	Consumption betas are higher than the real stock market betas.
K. Chan, P. Hendershott and A. Sanders (1990)	US equity REITs	1973–1987	Based on a multifactor APT (MVM) model: Prespecified "set of macroeconomic innovations that capture the pervasive forces in the economy": same five factors as in Chen, Roll and Ross (1986)	REITs' returns are positively related to the risk and term structure returns and negatively related to unexpected inflation
T. McCue and J. Kling (1994)	US equity REITs	1972–1991	Multifactor model after Lawrence and Siow (1985): – consumer price index – three-month T-bill rate – industrial production index – construction contract index	Macroeconomic variables explain approximately 60% of the variation in real estate returns. Nominal interest rates alone account for more than 36% of the variation.
Chen, Hsieh and Jordan (1997)	US equity REITs	1974–1991	Five-factor MVM and FLM framework: – Change in term structure – Change in risk premium – Expected inflation – Change in expected inflation – Unexpected inflation	MVM is superior in explaining EREIT returns. Unanticipated inflation, unanticipated change in the term structure and/or a market factor are priced over different sample periods.
D. Ling and A. Naranjo (1997)	US commercial real estate markets (listed and direct): – REIT and non-REIT listed real estate indices,	1978–1994	Based on a Multifactor Asset Pricing Model (nine economic risk factors): – Market portfolio – Term structure premium – Bond default premium – Real three-month T. Bill return	The growth rate in real per capita consumption and the real T-Bill rate are consistently priced across all real estate markets: real estate returns are

	Sample / Data	Period	Factors / Variables	Findings
	– NCREIF return data disaggregated by region and property type.		– Real per capita growth rate of nondurable goods and services – growth rate of industrial production – Unexpected inflation – Expected inflation – Change in expected inflation.	exposed to consumption risk. The term structure of interest rates and unexpected inflation do not carry significant risk premiums.
Y. Liang and W. McIntosh (1998)	US commercial real estate markets in forty-six major MSAs (NCREIF Property Index).	1983–1997	Employment growth	Employment growth contributes to real estate returns in the short-term, but it has no impact over long-term expected return (e.g., ten years)
G. Karolyi and A. Sanders (1998)	US equity REITs	1983–1995	– Monthly growth rate of seasonally adjusted, real, industrial production, – Value-weighted NYSE, Amex and Nasdaq index less one-month T-Bill – One month T-bill return less CPI rate – Intermediate-term government bonds less one-month T-bill return – Yield spread on Baa corporate bonds less Aaa corporate bonds – Monthly dividend yield on S&P500 – One month T-bill return	Both the stock and bond market risk premiums capture a small portion of the predictable variation in returns. Changes in the prices of the economic risks are more important than changes in betas themselves in explaining the predictable variation in REIT returns.
D. Ling and A. Naranjo (1999)	US commercial real estate markets : listed (equity REITs and publicly traded real estate companies) and privately held (NCREIF indices)	1978–1994	Multifactor asset pricing model: – real per capita growth rate of personal consumption expenditures for non-durable goods plus services – Market portfolio – Term structure premium – Real three-month T-Bill – Unanticipated inflation – Default premium – Growth rate of industrial production	The growth rate in real per capita consumption is consistently priced in commercial real estate markets. Models of commercial real estate returns that exclude consumption are misspecified.

(Continued)

Research Paper: Author (date)	Type of Commercial Real Estate Markets Under Study	Study Period	Macro-Factors	Main Findings
C. Brooks and S. Tsolacos (1999)	UK listed real estate market: FTSE Property Total Return index	1985–1998	– Rate of unemployment – Three month T-bill rate – Interest rate spread – Unanticipated inflation rate – Dividend Yield	Interest rate term structure and unexpected inflation have a contemporaneous effect on property returns.
I. De Wit and R. Van Dijk (2003)	46 major office districts in Asia, Europe, and the United States: quarterly data (capital value, net rent, vacancy, office stock in sq. meters)	1986–1999	Static panel-data model and dynamic panel-data model: – four variables related to supply and demand for office space or to economic growth: percentage change in the stock, percentage change in vacancy rate, percentage change in GDP/GMP (country or MSA specific), percentage change in unemployment rate – two variables to pick up effects of shifts in value of money: level of inflation, change in inflation (country specific).	GDP/GMP and inflation positively influence real estate prices, while changes in unemployment and vacancy rate negatively affect rents. Total returns are inversely related to the vacancy rate. The stronger the growth in GDP/GMP, the higher total return.
K. Liow (2004)	Singapore office and retail real estate markets: URA quarterly office and retail property price indexes.	1979–2000	Five-factor model: – GDP growth – Growth rate in industrial output – Unexpected inflation – Short-term interest rate – Stock market portfolio	Expected risk premiums on office and retail markets are time-varying. They are impacted by unexpected inflation and short-term interest rates.

A. Plazzi, W. Torous, and R. Valkanov (2008)	Commercial real estate returns and rental growth rates across US metropolitan areas (Global Real Analytics): apartment, office, retail, industrial properties	1986–2002	– Term spread – Credit spread – Inflation – Three-month T-bill rate	Commercial real estate's risk characteristics vary with the state of the economy. Cross-sectional dispersions in returns and rental growth rates are forecasted by the term and credit spreads. They are countercyclical, increasing in recessions and decreasing in expansions.
L. Peng (2016)	Capital appreciation returns from 14,115 US institutional grade commercial properties in the NCREIF database (of which 3,633 properties with total returns). Four property types (apartment, industrial, office, retail)	1977–2012	Multifactor models including: – Fama & French (1993) factors: stock market risk factors – Pastor & Stambaugh (2003) factor: liquidity factor – Two bond market factors	Positive loadings for all property types on the stock market factor, the size factor, the liquidity factor and credit spread. Negative loadings: book-to-market factor, term spread.

Appendix 1.2

Combinative and factor-based hedges in interest rate risk management

Yield curve risk management exemplifies how hedges can be designed around well-identified risk factors even if they are not directly observable. It makes no doubt that yield curve risk and commercial real estate risk are fundamentally different. The former is easily amenable to modelling by researchers whereas the latter has been refractory to this type of abstraction. Nonetheless, innovations in interest rate hedging are rich in teachings for commercial real estate as far as alternative formats of derivatives could be applied to real estate derivatives.

The factorial nature of interest rate risk has been identified by researchers for a long time. For instance, Gay and Kolb (1983) identify five key factors impacting the choice of optimal hedges for a bond or a bond portfolio: (1) maturity of the hedged and hedging instruments, (2) the coupon structure of the hedged and hedging instruments, (3) the length of time the hedge will be in effect, (4) the risk structure of interest rates, (5) the term structure of interest rates. At inception of the hedge, the hedger knows the first three factors. Factors 4 and 5 which are susceptible to changes over time are sources of risk.

Various non-index-based hedges exist in order to allow fixed income investors to hedge their risk. The most common versions are combination hedges where several derivatives instruments are combined to replicate the duration of the bond(s) to be hedged. Morgan (2008) who studies the US markets over the period 1998–2005 explains that combination hedges systematically outperform single hedges.

Three-factor hedges of Treasury bond market (Litterman and Scheinkman, 1991)

One of the main problems facing bond investors stems from non-parallel shifts in the yield curve. Litterman and Scheinkman (1991) propose a sophisticated approach centred on three factors selected to best describe the yield curve of US Treasury zero coupon bonds and model factors 4 and 5 mentioned in Gay and Kolb (1983) above.

None of the three factors are directly observable. The price sensitivity which depends on the three factors is determined thanks to a matrix of interest rates historic covariances. Litterman and Scheinkman explain:

> The impact of Factor 1 on yield levels leads us to name it the level factor. We call the second factor steepness, even though it does not correspond to any of the steepness measures commonly used. [...] The third factor, which we call curvature, increases the curvature of the yield curve in the range of maturities below twenty years; the effect on yields tails off above twenty years.

Interestingly, variance decomposition, a technique mentioned in Chapter 1 as a way to identify commercial real estate risk factors, is used by the authors to assess the relative importance of the three factors. Total variance can be overwhelmingly explained thanks to the three factors (98.4% on average). Three mimicking factor portfolios, i.e. portfolios sensitive only to the movements of a particular factor, are constructed. The level factor explains over 80% of total variance across all maturities (from 6 months to 18 years). Thus, the authors suggest applying a methodology called 'first factor hedging' in which only the most important factor is hedged, thereby taking care of most of the return risk. A similar approach is applied to hedging City office building returns in Lecomte (2014).

A bond portfolio may be hedged by a mix of the three mimicking portfolios having the same sensitivities to the three factors as the original portfolio. A single bond can be hedged with two standard hedging instruments mimicking the exposure to the three factors.

Yield curve risk management with combination hedges (Leschhorn, 2001)

Leschhorn (2001) proposes a hedging methodology that combines two standard hedging instruments. A single bond can be hedged with a linear combination of these two instruments. The only requirement is that the bond's maturity should be in-between the maturities of two neighbouring standard hedging instruments.

This approach does not rely on historical data. Instead, it uses "a simple model of yield curve movements". This allows for "non-parallel yield-curve changes that are triggered by the yield changes of standard hedging instruments". Beyond its combinative format which makes it relevant to real estate derivatives, the method proposed by Leschhorn is interesting insofar as it relies on a parametric model rather than historical data for identifying the optimal hedge.

Teachings of yield curve hedging methodologies for real estate derivatives

Combination hedges applied for managing yield curve risk in fixed income port-folios/ single bond highlights a few important points:

Teaching #1: In order to develop a simple and relevant model of risk, it is nec-essary to identify and standardise common risk factors. A taxonomy of risk factors is a first step in the quest for optimal hedges.

Teaching #2: A combination of ad-hoc hedging instruments whose selection re-lies on risk factors (both observable and unobservable) impacting the asset to be hedged makes it possible to achieve a customised hedge whose hedging efficiency is better than that of a single instrument. Lecomte (2007) had such intuition for commercial real estate. Past research on combinative hedges applied to interest rate risk management show that this is systematically the case. Both conceptual and empirical analyses are required to validate such alternative derivatives format for commercial real estate.

Teaching #3: A model-based approach can be a workable way to design optimal hedges, provided the variables resulting in the unobservable risk factor(s) are clearly identified and measured.

Teaching #4: First factor hedging can be selected as the optimal hedging strategy when a myriad of factors have a limited impact on the overall risk. For in-terest rate risk management, the choice of first factor is relatively straightfor-ward insofar as there is an obvious dominating factor. Noticeably, in case of atomised risk structure, there is a significant risk of blind spots (after Jorion, 2007). The answer to this question hinges on researchers' ability to qualify commercial real estate's risk structure and its stability over time.

Appendix 1.3

Hedonic variables from a selection of hedonic models applied to commercial real estate

Clapp J. (1980) Office market in Los Angeles MSA (California, USA)

- Total rentable square feet of floor space in the building
- Age of the building
- Number of office floors
- Internal parking
- Beverly Hills address
- Annual amount of property taxes
- Smog levels in the immediate area
- Square feet of office space within a two-block radius
- Distance by road from the building to the nearest freeway entrance and by freeway to CBD
- Average commuting time for employees from home to the building by car.

Hough D. and Kratz C. (1983): Chicago CBD office buildings (Illinois, USA)

- Radial distance from the building to the center of the CBD
- Proximity to commuter transportation: radial distance to the nearest commuter train station and availability of public parking near the building
- Measures of building responsiveness to tenant needs: age of the building, its total gross floor area, average rental per floor
- Building amenities: number of floors, presence of a restaurant, availability of a conference room
- Building disamenities: age of the building, presence of snack shop, elevated train tracks next to building
- Measures of architectural quality: national or Chicago landmark, architectural award.

T. Brennan, R. Cannaday, and P. Colwell (1984): Chicago CBD office rents (Illinois USA)

- Lease features: rental rate in dollars per square foot per year, square feet included in a particular lease transaction, amount of 'stop' in dollars per sq ft per year, CPI escalation in the lease, base year escalation;

- Physical characteristics of the building: total square feet;
- Physical characteristics of the unit: percent area paid not usable, such as hall-ways and lobby (loss factor), vertical location of the building;
- Location of the building in terms of a north-south and east-west grid: distance in blocks from LaSalle Street along east-west axis, distance in blocks from Madison Street along north-south axis, office building located east/west of LaSalle Street;
- Any other variables.

E. Mills (1992): Office rents in the Chicago metropolitan area in 1990 (Illinois, USA)

- Year building was built
- Number of rentable square feet in the building
- Parking, shops, restaurant, bank, daycare, health club
- Minimum and maximum square feet on a floor
- Historic landmark
- Escalation factor in the asking rent
- Net offered lease with/ without stop clause
- Location: loop, N Michigan, R North, Evanston, Northbrook, O'Hare, Schaumburg, Oakbrook.

Shilton L. and A. Zaccaria (1994): Office buildings sale prices in Manhattan over 1980–1990 (New York, USA)

- Time of Sale
- Age
- Gross Footage
- Number of Floors
- Footprint
- Development Potential
- Number of Landmarks within two blocks
- Distance (Blocks) to Central Park
- Distance (Blocks) to Grand Central Station

Wheaton W. and R. Torto (1994): Office rents in 50 metropolitan areas over 1979–1991 (USA)

- Square feet of lease
- Term of lease in years
- High stories (5+)
- New building
- New building built for tenant
- Lease in gross rent
- Lease gross with taxes passed through
- Year
- Submarkets

Munneke H., and B. Slade (2000): Office property market in Phoenix over 1991–1996 (Arizona, USA)

- Physical characteristics:
  - Total Building area (in sq, ft) based on the rental data: TOTALSF
  - Building footprint (TOTALSF/HEIGHT)
  - Total building area (in sq. ft.) based on the transaction data: SQFT
  - Building footprint (SQFT/HEIGHT)
  - Number of stories
  - Lot area measured in sq. ft
  - Age of property measured in years
  - Number of buildings in complex
- Lease characteristics:
  - Load factor
  - Occupancy rate at time t
  - Full service: no expense stop
  - Full service: base-year expense stop
  - Full service: $ amount expenses stop
- Location characteristics:
  - Distance to central business district (miles)
  - Property located in the Central Phoenix area
  - Property located in East Valley area
  - Property located in the North/Northwest Phoenix area
  - Property located in Scottsdale area
- Financial characteristics:
  - Cash
  - Bank financing
  - Seller carryback
  - Private financing
- Sales characteristics:
  - Transaction sold out of bank portfolio of foreclosed properties
  - Exchange
- Time/market characteristics:
  - t equals 1991, 1992, 1993, 1994, or 1995
  - Current mortgage interest rate
  - Change in the number of building permits issued over the last year
  - Change in population over the last year.

Tu, Yu, Sun (2004): Office property market in Singapore (Singapore)

- Area: Floor area of the transacted office unit
- Age: Age of the transacted office unit, derived from the difference between the contract date and the construction date (years)
- Level: the floor level where the office unit locates (number)
- Tenure: dummy variable capturing the nature of the lease (leasehold/freehold)

Appendix 1.4

Case study – Combinative and factor-based hedging of non-listed office buildings in the City of London

The following case study is an abridged version of the analysis presented in Lecomte (2014): *Testing Alternative Models of Property Derivatives: The Case of the City of London's Office Market*, Journal of Property Investment and Finance, 32:2. This version was published as a Red Paper by the Asian Association for investors in Non-listed Real Estate Vehicles (ANREV) in March 2014. The Investment Property Forum's support was instrumental in securing access to the Investment Property Databank's time series at the property level. Their contribution is kindly acknowledged. All errors and omissions are mine.

IPD indices as potential underlying to property derivatives

The Investment Property Databank (IPD) proposes a large series of indices related to the London and City property markets covering 5 levels of granularity (from National/All Property to Local/Office). Among these indices, the following 9 total return indices are selected for the analysis:

- UK Annual All Property (level 1),
- UK Annual All Office (level 2),
- London Office Properties Annual index (level 3),
- City Office Properties – Local Authority Annual Index (level 4),[1]
- City Office Properties – Region Annual Index (level 4),
- EC1 Office Properties Annual index (level 5),
- EC2 Office Properties Annual Index (level 5),
- EC3 Office Properties Annual Index (level 5),
- EC4 Office Properties Annual Index (level 5).

IPD indices are customarily used as underlying to existing property derivatives in the UK. As of December 2013, GBP 1.54 billion worth of Total Return Swaps (TRS) traded on UK National Annual indices were outstanding, with the bulk of the TRS linked to the UK All Property index.

---

1 IPD proposes two indices for the City office market with two different definitions of the City's geography: an index based on the *Region* (London)'s definition and one based on the *Local Authority* (City of London Corporation)'s.

Besides, the IPD UK All Property Total Return index is used as underlying to futures contracts traded on EUREX. These annual contracts which were introduced in February 2009 have been met with limited success so far. In July 2011, EUREX introduced three additional contracts based on IPD UK sector indices, i.e. UK Annual All Retail, UK Annual All Office, and UK Annual All Industrial. Hence, the UK Annual All Property index (level 1) and the UK Annual All Office index (level 2) are two important benchmarks that will define the comparative benefits of index-based hedges using more granular indices as underlying.

IPD database of City office properties

IPD kindly agreed to share historical total returns of 224 City office properties in their database (out of 405 City office overall). The database covers the following information for each building:

- Annual total returns over the holding period (which can be any period from 1981 to 2007),[2]
- Construction date or latest renovation date as defined in IPD ground rules,
- Truncated postal code limited to the EC area and broad indication of neighbourhood,
- Available floor space for each year of the holding period.

Of the 224 buildings, only 37 have a holding period equal to or longer than 15 years. For the sake of statistical significance, the analysis focuses on these 37 buildings.

Factors

Historical data are analysed in order to identify exogenous (macro) and endogenous (micro) factors impacting returns in the selected sample of London-based office properties. Seventeen macro-factors and two micro-factors are included in the analysis as reported in Table A.1.

Four different types of hedges are tested:

- Single index-based derivatives (including EUREX futures contracts) over full holding period (37 individual buildings)
- EUREX futures contracts over full holding period (4 portfolios)
- Pure factor hedges over full holding period (37 individual buildings and 4 portfolios)
- Combinative hedges over full holding period (37 individual buildings and 4 portfolios)

---

2 Due to data availability at the property level, the period covered in the database ends in 2007 before the Global Financial Crisis.

Table A.1 List of 17 macro-factors and 2 micro-factors

17 Macro-Factors	Independent Variables
New Supply of City office buildings	YoY%
City Employment	YoY%
Inflation Rate	Annual Inflation Rate
Household Consumption	YoY%
Productivity Rate	YoY%
Gross Domestic Product	YoY%
UK Bank Base Rate	Average Monthly Rate over the year
10 Year Gilt	10 Year Gilt
10 Year Spread	Average Annual Spread %
6 month LIBOR	6 month LIBOR
FTSE 100 Index	YoY%
Annual Transaction Volume (LSE)	YoY%
Gold Price (London)	YoY%
S&P 500 Index	YoY%
CBOE VXO Index	CBOE VXO Index
Total Assets owned by London and Scottish Banks	YoY%
British Pension Funds' Real Estate Assets	YoY%

2 Micro-Factors	Independent Variables
Property Age	Actual Age in years
Construction Type	Category 1 to 5 (Age group)

Simulation 1: Single index-based derivatives over full holding periods (individual buildings)

We first identify for each property in the sample the index yielding the best level of hedging effectiveness. There are 9 IPD indices to choose from, embodying 9 potential derivatives including the 2 EUREX contracts. The simulations which are conducted over full holding periods enable us to characterise different risk profiles among the 37 buildings, and to determine the levels of hedging effectiveness that alternative models of property derivatives should achieve in order to add value. Table A.2 presents the results.

On average, hedging effectiveness across all properties and all indices amounts to 0.3774. The range is very large: the highest hedging effectiveness tops 0.8378 (building 28/ underlying: City Office Region), while the lowest is close to 0 (building 33/ underlying: EC4 Office). Twenty-three properties achieve their best hedges with the EC Office index series. Interestingly, the best EC Office index is not necessarily the one corresponding to the building's location. For instance, building 15 which is located in EC3 gets his best hedge with EC2 Office index as underlying. The two EUREX contracts only provide the best hedge for 3 buildings. Their average hedging effectiveness is equal to 0.2878 and 0.3392 respectively, i.e. basis risk remains superior to 50%.

Table A.2 Simulation 1: Single index-based derivatives over full holding periods (individual buildings)

Building #	Construction Date	Holding Period	Postal Code	Floor (M2)	Eurex Contracts R2		Summary: 9 IPD Indices R2			Best Underlying Index
					UK – All Property	UK – All Office	Max	Min	Average	
1	1991	1989–2007	EC2	3,680	0.4664	0.5485	0.7011	0.4664	0.6143	City Office (local)
2	1939	1981–1995	EC2	660	0.3205	0.3289	0.5483	0.2475	0.4174	EC3 Office
3	1933	1981–2007	EC4	1,766	0.1871	0.3265	0.5041	0.1871	0.3881	EC2 Office
4	1966	1981–1999	EC3	790	0.2271	0.2537	0.3415	0.2271	0.2898	EC4 Office
5	1960	1981–1997	EC4	17,206	0.5592	0.5856	0.7845	0.5592	0.6930	City Office (region)
6	1973	1981–1997	EC3	3,540	0.4342	0.4450	0.6937	0.4226	0.5718	EC3 Office
7	1890	1981–1998	EC2	4,222	0.2296	0.2224	0.2650	0.2024	0.2365	EC2 Office
8	1900	1981–2004	EC2	601	0.1977	0.1751	0.2997	0.1751	0.2444	EC2 Office
9	1950	1981–2007	EC4	9,799	0.5337	0.6697	0.7478	0.5337	0.6875	City Office (region)
10	1960	1981–2000	EC3	2,189	0.2823	0.3176	0.5171	0.2823	0.4243	EC2 Office
11	1930	1981–2007	EC2	953	0.5851	0.5351	0.6194	0.4528	0.5682	EC3 Office
12	1958	1993–2007	EC4	2,663	0.0003	0.0258	0.0585	0.0003	0.0305	London Office
13	1995	1981–2000	EC2	8,835	0.2751	0.2918	0.4435	0.2444	0.3394	EC2 Office
14	2004	1986–2007	EC4	10,609	0.2784	0.4168	0.5080	0.2784	0.4152	EC3 Office
15	1930	1981–2002	EC3	9,077	0.2864	0.3516	0.5724	0.2864	0.4287	EC2 Office
16	1976	1981–1997	EC3	13,861	0.4546	0.5148	0.5716	0.4546	0.5093	EC1 Office
17	1975	1981–2007	EC2	28,252	0.2074	0.2699	0.4977	0.2074	0.3917	EC3 Office
18	1992	1958–2007	EC2	NC	0.3140	0.4549	0.5306	0.3140	0.4374	EC1 Office
19	1925	1981–1995	EC1	1,450	0.2381	0.2876	0.3745	0.2381	0.3254	EC3 Office
20	1959	1981–1995	EC2	4,729	0.1844	0.2340	0.3295	0.1823	0.2326	EC1 Office

Building #	Construction Date	Holding Period	Postal Code	Floor (M2)	Eurex Contracts R2		Summary: 9 IPD Indices R2			Best Underlying Index
					UK – All Property	UK – All Office	Max	Min	Average	
21	1958	1981–1999	EC3	734	0.5434	0.5779	0.6906	0.4949	0.5883	EC4 Office
22	1992	1991–2007	EC3	71,403	0.5033	0.7225	0.7765	0.5033	0.7166	London Office
23	1920	1981–2002	EC3	15,970	0.3233	0.3869	0.6126	0.3233	0.4965	EC2 Office
24	NC	1981–2007	EC2	16,657	0.1522	0.2941	0.4472	0.1522	0.3562	EC3 Office
25	1939	1981–2003	EC2	697	0.2701	0.3166	0.4726	0.2625	0.3899	City Office (region)
26	1912	1981–2007	EC3	1,504	0.0255	0.0391	0.0391	0.0076	0.0199	UK – All Office
27	1956	1981–2007	EC3	4,161	0.1651	0.2947	0.3259	0.1651	0.2721	London Office
28	1928	1981–2001	EC3	4,756	0.5532	0.5961	0.8378	0.5532	0.7316	City Office (region)
29	1900	1981–2007	EC2	7,941	0.0246	0.0017	0.0246	0.0001	0.0036	UK – All Property
30	1982	1984–1999	EC4	11,993	0.1415	0.1497	0.2919	0.1415	0.2081	EC3 Office
31	1928	1981–2001	EC3	4,041	0.5067	0.6364	0.7004	0.5067	0.6487	EC1 Office
32	1964	1981–1997	EC4	8,036	0.2768	0.2972	0.4196	0.1860	0.3263	EC3 Office
33	1954	1981–2007	EC2	1,049	0.0000	0.0124	0.0140	0.0000	0.0059	London Office
34	1939	1981–2007	E1	2,877	0.1810	0.1603	0.1810	0.1023	0.1322	UK – All Property
35	1936	1981–1997	EC2	167	0.6190	0.6809	0.7243	0.5702	0.6425	London Office
36	1997	1981–2007	EC2	4,157	0.0063	0.0370	0.1302	0.0063	0.0827	EC2 Office
37	1984	1981–1995	EC3	3,647	0.0954	0.0927	0.1192	0.0723	0.0964	EC3 Office
Max	2004	NA	NA	71,403	0.6190	0.7225	0.8378	0.6190	0.7316	NA
Min	1890	NA	NA	167	0.0000	0.0017	0.0017	0.0000	0.0036	NA
Average	1953	NA	NA	7,908	0.2878	0.3392	0.4160	0.2878	0.3774	NA

Table A.3 Summarises simulation 1's main findings

IPD Index Used as Underlying	CD / Sample	Comments
UK All Property	0.2878 (average 37 buildings)	These two indices are used as
UK All Office	0.3392 (average 37 buildings)	underlying to EUREX contracts
EC3 Office	0.4160 (average 37 buildings)	Best hedging effectiveness over the sample on average.
City Office-Region	0.8378 (building 28)	Largest hedging effectiveness achieved for a single building (#28).
UK All Property	0 (building 33)	Lowest hedging effectiveness achieved by a single building (#33).

The best hedges' average effectiveness for all properties is equal to 0.4518. Again, the range is extremely large: from 0.8378 to 0.0140 (for building 28 and 33 respectively). The underlying index yielding the best hedging effectiveness across all properties is EC3 Office with an average effectiveness equal to 0.4160. That leaves basis risk at almost 60%, which is hardly satisfactory for a hedger. Interestingly, some buildings cannot be hedged at all with index-based instruments. Their returns are non-correlated with IPD indices, so much so that basis risk can reach 99%.

If we limit the range of available derivatives to the two EUREX futures contracts, the UK All Office unsurprisingly dominates the UK All Property contract, coming first for 30 properties out of 37. However, the UK All Office contract's average hedging effectiveness is only 0.3392, which is significantly lower than that of the best underlying indices chosen from the full range of 9 indices (0.4518 on average). Hence, the implied cost of non-availability of a wider range of futures contracts (i.e. underlying basis risk) is significant. In the case of our 37 properties, it amounts to over 10 basis points on average.

Simulation 2: EUREX Futures contracts over full holding periods (4 portfolios)

We now use Simulation 1's findings to construct 4 portfolios:

- Portfolio 1 made up of 7 buildings representative of the sample (4, 8, 10, 15, 26, 28, 37).
- Portfolio 2 made up of the full sample (i.e. 37 buildings minus building 18 for which information are not sufficient).
- Portfolio 3 made up of 3 properties (among those selected for Portfolio 1) selected for their lowest hedging effectiveness as individual property (8, 26, 37)
- Portfolio 4 made up of 3 properties (among those selected in Portfolio 1) selected for their largest hedging effectiveness as individual property (10, 15, 28).

Table A.4 Simulation 2 – EUREX Futures contracts over full holding periods (4 portfolios)

	Holding Period[a]	Average Annual Return	Standard Deviation	Sharpe Ratio[b]	Optimal EUREX Contracts R2	Underlying Index
Portfolio 1	1981–2007	11.8759	15.8794	0.2024	0.4407	UK All Office
Portfolio 2	1981–2007	11.3395	14.0641	0.2272	0.6830	UK All Office
Portfolio 3	1981–2007	11.5917	15.5385	0.1850	0.2069	UK All Office
Portfolio 4	1981–2002	11.9740	21.4966	0.1390	0.5013	UK All Office

a　All portfolios are held for 26 years, except portfolio 4 (21 years).
b　Risk-free rate is equal to the 10 year Gilt.

In the absence of information on the properties' annual estimated values, the annual weights of each building in the 4 portfolios are based on the floor areas as reported yearly in the IPD database. Table A.4 summarises our findings.

Over the 4 portfolios, the largest levels of hedging effectiveness are achieved with the UK All Office contract. In the case of Portfolio 2 (i.e. a well-diversified portfolio), basis risk falls to slightly over 30%. Unsurprisingly, the larger the portfolios, the more EUREX contracts are able to capture systematic risk. For portfolios which are not well diversified (e.g. Portfolio 3), hedges based on EUREX futures contracts are still substantially more effective than those achieved when hedging individual properties with the same contracts. Hence, although EUREX futures contracts are not well suited to hedge individual properties' returns, they are effective in case of portfolios, even under-diversified ones.

Simulation 3: Pure Factor hedges over full holding periods (37 individual buildings and 4 portfolios)

We now construct hedges by optimally combining the 19 factors listed in Table A.1. The nature and number of factors selected in the optimal hedges are determined by applying a stepwise regression methodology in order to limit multicollinearity among factors. Results for individual properties are reported in Table A.5 panel A.

Over the 37 properties, hedging effectiveness improves by 36% (compared to the best index-based hedges determined in Simulation 1), reaching 0.6146. Optimal hedges contain 3.54 factors on average, with the maximum number of factors in a single hedge being equal to 7. In terms of absolute gains, properties which register weak to average hedging effectiveness with single IPD indices as underlying do benefit the most from the use of factors. Conversely, properties whose returns are strongly hedged by using index-based instruments benefit very little from the use of factors, and in some cases suffer from it. Optimal factor hedges are dominated by three factors: new supply of City office properties, FTSE 100 transaction volume, and household consumption.

The same methodology is then applied to the 4 portfolios. Results are reported in Table A.5 panel B. For Portfolios 1, 2 and 4 whose risk is properly hedged by

Table A.5 Simulation 3 – Pure Factor hedges over full holding periods (37 individual buildings and 4 portfolio)

Panel A Buildings	Best Underlying Index (Simulation 1)	Optimal Pure Factor Hedge		% diff/ IPD Index
	R2	R2	# of Factors	
1	0.7011	0.8060	4	14.96%
2	0.5483	0.7900	3	44.08%
3	0.5041	0.7530	5	49.38%
4	0.3415	0.4170	1	22.11%
5	0.7845	0.8480	4	8.09%
6	0.6937	0.8410	5	21.23%
7	0.2650	0.5660	2	113.58%
8	0.2997	0.3460	3	15.45%
9	0.7478	0.7810	6	4.44%
10	0.5171	0.7840	5	51.61%
11	0.6194	0.4540	3	−26.70%
12	0.0585	0.3860	2	559.83%
13	0.4435	0.6830	4	54.00%
14	0.5080	0.7340	5	44.49%
15	0.5724	0.5900	4	3.07%
16	0.5716	0.5380	3	−5.88%
17	0.4977	0.6900	7	38.64%
18	0.5306	0.8620	5	62.46%
19	0.3745	0.2460	1	−34.31%
20	0.3295	0.6860	3	108.19%
21	0.6906	0.6880	3	−0.38%
22	0.7765	0.8680	4	11.78%
23	0.6126	0.6690	4	9.21%
24	0.4472	0.6650	5	48.70%
25	0.4726	0.8160	5	72.66%
26	0.0391	0.1920	1	391.05%
27	0.3259	0.5330	4	63.55%
28	0.8378	0.7560	4	−9.76%
29	0.0246	0.0950	1	286.18%
30	0.2919	0.8420	4	188.45%
31	0.7004	0.6860	3	−2.06%
32	0.4196	0.7720	3	83.98%
33	0.0140	0.1620	2	1056.69%
34	0.1810	0.5330	5	194.48%
35	0.7243	0.8270	3	14.18%
36	0.1302	0.4280	3	228.73%
37	0.1192	0.4080	2	242.28%
Average	**0.4518**	**0.6146**	**3.54**	**36.04%**

Panel B Portfolios	Best Underlying Index (Simulation 1)	Optimal Pure Factor Hedge		% diff/ IPD Index
	R2	R2	# of Factors	
Portfolio 1	0.6708	0.6380	4	−4.9%
Portfolio 2	0.9111	0.8800	5	−3.4%
Portfolio 3	0.2240	0.4410	4	96.9%
Portfolio 4	0.7776	0.7180	4	−7.7%

an index-based instrument, the use of factor hedge does not add any value. Conversely, for Portfolio 3 whose risk is not effectively hedged with an index-based instrument, the factor hedge almost doubles hedging effectiveness. This finding is consistent with results at the individual property level, i.e. factor hedges only add value in case of properties/portfolios whose risk is not effectively hedged with a single index instrument. For other properties/portfolios, the use of factors adds no value, and in some cases, turns out to be detrimental to the hedge's effectiveness.

Simulation 4: Combinative hedges over full holding periods (37 individual buildings and 4 portfolios)

Finally, a simulation is run to test the combinative template of property derivatives (i.e. a combination of index and factors). Stepwise regressions are applied in a similar way to those used to determine optimal factor hedges in Simulation 3. The only difference is that the best underlying IPD index for each property/portfolio over full holding period determined in Simulation 1 is added to the pool of macro/micro factors. Hence, optimal models are selected from 20 variables instead of 19 previously. Table A.6 summarises our results for the 37 properties (panel A) and 4 portfolios (panel B).

For individual properties, combinative hedges improve hedging effectiveness by 43.74% on average over single index-based hedges (Simulation 1) and 5.66% over pure factor hedges (Simulation 3). Hedging effectiveness reaches 0.6494, effectively reducing basis risk to less than 30%. Of the 37 properties, 21 achieve their most effective hedges with a combination of IPD index and factors whereas only 15 are best hedged with factors alone. Only one property (#11) registers its best hedge when using a single IPD index as underlying. For the 21 properties for which combinative hedges dominate, hedging effectiveness increases by 133% on average over single index hedges and by 123% over factor hedges. Notwithstanding some outliers (buildings 33 and 34), such significant improvements embody the potential benefits combinative hedges can represent for investors. Interestingly, a similar analysis applied to Chinese Office properties in 3 first-tier cities (Beijing, Shanghai, and Guangzhou) identifies the dominance of combinative hedges (encompassing macro-factors) over single and combined hedges made up of cross-hedging underlyings (Lecomte, 2013).

On average, combinative hedges contain 2.4 factors. Among the factors most frequently selected in the optimal models are City employment, inflation rate, and productivity. Noticeably, these factors differ from those listed in optimal factor models, e.g. new supply which is prevalent in factor hedges only plays a minor role in combinative hedges. It might already be encapsulated in IPD indices. As before, property age is marginal in the optimal models. Seven properties in the sample are not amenable to the combinative framework (4, 7, 12, 20, 26, 29, 37), with combinative hedges resulting in factor hedges without any IPD indices selected in the optimal models.

With respect to the 4 portfolios, the improvement is very significant for Portfolio 3 (+148% over Simulation 1, +26% over Simulation 3). It is less marked for portfolios whose returns are effectively hedged with IPD index-based instruments, e.g. Portfolio 2.

Table A.6 Simulation 4 – Combinative hedges over full holding periods (37 individual buildings and 4 portfolios)

Panel A Buildings	Combinative Hedge			% diff/ IPD Index	% diff /Factor Hedge	Best Hedge over Full Holding Period
	R2	*Index Rank*	*# of Factors*			
1	0.9100	1	4	29.80%	12.90%	IPD index + Factors
2	0.8680	1	3	58.31%	9.87%	IPD index + Factors
3	0.8000	1	5	58.70%	−0.25%	Factors
4	0.4170	none	1	22.11%	0.00%	Factors
5	0.8700	1	2	10.90%	2.59%	IPD index + Factors
6	0.7930	1	2	14.31%	−5.71%	Factors
7	0.5660	none	2	113.58%	0.00%	Factors
8	0.4530	1	2	51.15%	30.92%	IPD index + Factors
9	0.8000	1	2	6.98%	2.43%	IPD index + Factors
10	0.6510	1	3	25.89%	−16.96%	Factors
11	0.6190	1	none	−0.06%	36.34%	IPD index
12	0.3860	none	2	559.83%	0.00%	Factors
13	0.6980	1	3	57.38%	2.20%	IPD index + Factors
14	0.6500	1	3	27.95%	−11.44%	Factors
15	0.6730	1	2	17.58%	14.07%	IPD index + Factors
16	0.6810	1	1	19.14%	26.58%	IPD index + Factors
17	0.8250	1	3	65.76%	19.57%	IPD index + Factors
18	0.8670	1	3	63.40%	0.58%	IPD index + Factors
19	0.5850	1	1	56.21%	137.80%	IPD index + Factors
20	0.6860	none	3	108.19%	0.00%	Factors
21	0.7640	1	1	10.63%	11.05%	IPD index + Factors
22	0.9620	1	3	23.89%	10.83%	IPD index + Factors
23	0.7930	1	3	29.45%	18.54%	IPD index + Factors
24	0.5180	1	1	15.83%	−22.11%	Factors
25	0.8250	1	3	74.57%	1.10%	IPD index + Factors
26	0.1920	none	1	391.05%	0.00%	Factors
27	0.4100	1	1	25.81%	−23.08%	Factors
28	0.9200	1	3	9.81%	14.29%	IPD index + Factors
29	0.0950	none	1	286.18%	0.00%	Factors
30	0.5360	1	1	83.62%	−36.34%	Factors
31	0.7970	1	2	13.79%	16.18%	IPD index + Factors
32	0.8510	1	4	102.81%	10.23%	IPD index + Factors
33	0.2240	3	2	1499.38%	38.27%	IPD index + Factors
34	0.6060	1	4	234.81%	13.70%	IPD index + Factors
35	0.7243	1	none	0.00%	−12.42%	Factors
36	0.6040	4	5	363.90%	41.12%	IPD index + Factors
37	0.4080	none	2	242.28%	0.00%	Factors
Average	**0.6494**		**2.40**	**43.73%**	**5.66%**	

Panel B Portfolios	Combinative Hedge			% diff/IPD Index	% diff / Factor Hedge	Best Hedge over Full Holding Period
	R2	*Index Rank*	*# of Factors*			
Portfolio 1	0.765	1	2	14.04%	19.91%	IPD index + Factors
Portfolio 2	0.933	1	2	2.40%	6.02%	IPD index + Factors
Portfolio 3	0.556	1	3	148.21%	26.08%	IPD index + Factors
Portfolio 4	0.798	1	1	2.63%	11.14%	IPD index + Factors

Main findings

An empirical study of City office properties over the period 1981–2007 shows that standardised property derivatives, i.e. EUREX futures contracts and IPD index-based over the counter derivatives (swaps), do not address the hedging needs of individual property owners. Alternative models are significantly more effective than index-based derivatives overall.

Although it seems that a carefully selected set of macro/micro-factors does provide effective hedges for individual buildings, factors cannot replace indices. They complement them but don't substitute for them as exemplified by the out-performance of combinative hedges. Making selected indices and macro-factors simultaneously available to investors while keeping in sight the danger of artificially inflating the number of possible underlyings would enhance hedging effectiveness across the board.

The analysis highlights a typology of optimal hedges for individual City office buildings. The differentiating criterion is the ex post hedging effectiveness of IPD index-based instruments:

–   For properties whose returns are not effectively captured by a single IPD index, periodically rebalanced index-based hedges do not significantly add value. Instead, factor hedges should be selected as well as combinative hedges.
–   Conversely, for properties whose returns are effectively captured by a single IPD index, periodically rebalanced index-based hedges as well as combinative hedges are to be chosen in priority over factor hedges.

Besides, for portfolios of City office buildings, another typology appears:

–   For portfolios whose returns are properly captured ex-post by a single IPD index, EUREX contracts should be favoured over combinative hedges, given the large number of underlying rebalancing required by the latter. Factor hedges should be avoided.
–   Conversely, for portfolios whose returns are not effectively captured by a single IPD index, EUREX contracts should be avoided. In this case, combinative hedges should be favoured.

Lecomte (2014) who presents a more extensive study with the same dataset also identifies indices and factors that market authorities dealing with property derivatives might consider as underlying to derivatives instruments.

–   New EUREX contracts aimed at City office investors should focus on EC2 office and EC3 office indices targeting portfolio holders and owners of individual buildings, respectively.
–   Macro-factors which would benefit investors the most are household consumption, FTSE 100 transaction volume and new supply of City office buildings. In case of combinative hedges, City employment dominates all other factors and, thus would be a good complement to IPD indices, for instance, if made available to investors as underlying to listed options.

Appendix 1.5

Path analysis in commercial real estate risk analysis

The path analysis methodology developed by pioneer geneticist Sewall Wright in the 1920s is customarily used in genetic epidemiology of complex phenotypes. Roa and Rice (2005) explain that path analysis is "a form of structural linear regression analysis of standardized variables whose purpose is twofold: to explain the interrelationships among a given set of variables, and to evaluate the relative importance of varying causes influencing a variable of interest". According to Wright (1983), the purpose of path analysis is "the evaluation of the relative importance of the various causes of variation in a particular population". Path analysis has been applied in social sciences, e.g. econometric modelling in lieu of structural equation models.

Whilst variance partitioning focuses on variance analysis, path analysis centres on correlations and aims to decipher "interacting, uncontrollable and often obscure causes" by dealing with "a group of characteristics or conditions which are correlated" (Wright, 1921). Path analysis can be applied to both measurable causes which have to be standardised for comparability and unmeasurable variable causes.

Path diagrams describing the proposed structural relationships in a model are drawn up. Correlations between the variables are then computed. Rao and Rice (2005) explain:

> The gist of the method of path analysis consists of a comparison of these model-based correlations, which are algebraic function of unknown parameters, with the corresponding estimates based on actual data.

Over the years, Wright's method has been improved with the use of maximum likelihood as done in structured equation modelling (e.g. structural equation models, LISREL models, covariance structure models). As such, modern path analysis is a special case of structural equation models which "concentrate [...] on the pattern of covariation between the variables and minimize the difference between the observed and predicted pattern of covariation among them" (Shipley, 2016).

Path analysis models are very flexible. They make it possible to distinguish between primary and secondary causes and can accommodate temporal variations. However, several assumptions in the method question its applicability to the genetics-based model of real estate presented in this book. In the simplest models, gene effects on the phenotype are supposed to be small, equal, and additive, even though some more sophisticated models accommodate interactions at the polygenic level (Rao and Rice, 2005). Linearity and additivity among variables assumed in multivariate path analysis for the sake of solvability pose a challenge for the genetics-based model, which relies on variable interactions to qualify observable variables' impact on total return. Karlin et al. (1983) emphasise that this is a major inherent problem of path analysis which damages modelling assumptions' plausibility.

By the same token, assumption is made that phenotype does not influence the environment, which might actually be the case if a new building generating high levels of total return attracts more development of similar properties in a given urban area. Karlin et al. (1983) underscore that path analysis distinguishes between exogenous and endogenous variables. Exogenous variables are "pure causes and never effects" whereas endogenous variables are "always effects but may never be causes". As a result, reciprocal causations are not taken into account in the methodology, which may blur the distinction between causes and effects in a model.

A detailed discussion of concepts underpinning the path analysis is beyond the scope of this appendix. It can be found in biostatistics textbooks. The goal here is to illustrate how path analysis can add value to the application of the genetics-based model of real estate. The example below focuses on the occupancy gene presented in Figure 1.5 (Hypothetical Gene Regulatory Network) in Chapter 1.

Steps in implementing the path analysis methodology

The first step is to translate the hypothetical causal system into a path diagram. A causal model involving four variables can be set up. Variables which are observable (manifest) are represented in squares. Variables supposed to have a causal role in the model, albeit not directly observable (latent), are enclosed in circles. Manifest and latent variables are complemented by residual error term variables.[3] The simplistic model captures the hypothetical relationships between three genes on the physical structure chromosome (C_1G_2 size, C_1G_3 grade, C_1G_4 immaterial factors) and one gene on the lease structure chromosome (C_2G_2 occupancy) for a given property type (C_1G_1). Variables may also be broken down into their exogenous and endogenous dimensions as mentioned before. Exogenous variables have no causal parents in the model, whereas endogenous ones are caused by other variables in the model. Endogenous variables are assumed to be multivariate normal.

Physical structure genes tend to be exogenous contrary to lease structure genes which are more likely to endogenous. Location is both endogenous and exogenous. Although exogenous at the less granular levels of genes in the model (C_3G_1 global, C_3G_2 country, C_3G_3 region), it might have some endogeneity at the most

---

3 Shipley (2016) notes that by convention, a path model is deemed to include only manifest variables. If there are latent variables in the hypothetical causal model, then the path model is equivalent to a structural equation model.

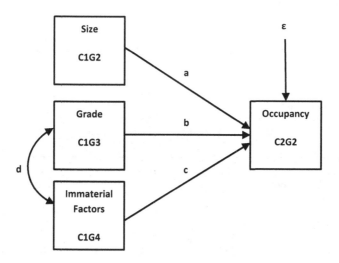

Figure A.1 Hypothetical causal model of occupancy in terms of physical structure for a given property type.

granular levels (C_3G_4 MSA, C_3G_5 neighbourhood) owing to reciprocal effects between a property and its environment.

Grade (C_1G_3) and Immaterial Factors (C_1G_4) are modelled as being correlated (double arrow in the causal model).

The second step is to translate the causal model into an observational model in the form of a set of structural equations. The causal model is turned into mathematical equations to form a statistical model. It is a less than perfect translation of the causal model. If the causal model comes with enough detail, the parameters can be directly specified (path coefficients, variances, and covariances). The mean value of the variables is of no interest to the statistical model which exclusively focuses on the relationships between the variables. All variables are centred by deducting the mean value for each variable. Parameters a, b, and c are derived from maximum likelihood estimators based on centred variables. ε is the residual error term of occupancy C_2G_2.

$C_1G_2 = N\ (0, \delta_{C1G2})$
$C_1G_3 = N\ (0, \delta_{C1G3})$
$C_1G_4 = N\ (0, \delta_{C1G4})$
$C_2G_2 = aC_1G_2 + bC_1G_3 + cC_1G_4$
$\mathrm{Cov}(C_1G_2,\ C_1G_3) = \mathrm{Cov}(C_1G_2,\ C_1G_4) = \mathrm{Cov}(C_1G_2,\ \varepsilon) = \mathrm{Cov}(C_1G_3,\ \varepsilon)$
    $= \mathrm{Cov}(C_1G_4,\ \varepsilon) = 0$
$\mathrm{Cov}(C_1G_3,\ C_1G_4) = d$

Once the mathematical model is set up, several additional steps are required to evaluate whether the causal model is consistent with the data. The methodology of modern path analysis based on maximum likelihood estimation as described by Shipley (2016) involves:

- Deriving the best predicted variance and covariance between each pair of variables in the model;

Decomposition of the total association between each pair of variables in the model into direct effects and indirect effects

Variable Pair	Direct	Indirect	Common Causal Ancestor	Unresolved Causal Relationship
C_1G_2, C_1G_3	None	None	None	None
C_1G_2, C_1G_4	None	None	None	None
C_1G_2, C_2G_2	$C_1G_2 \rightarrow C_2G_2$	None	None	None
C_1G_3, C_1G_4	None	None	None	$C_1G_3 \leftrightarrow C_1G_4$
C_1G_3, C_2G_2	$C_1G_3 \rightarrow C_2G_2$	None	None	None
C_1G_4, C_2G_2	$C_1G_4 \rightarrow C_2G_2$	None	None	None

- Estimating the free parameters by minimising the difference between observed and predicted variances and covariances (a, b, c in the hypothetical causal model reproduced above);
- Calculating the probability of having observed the measured minimum difference, assuming that the observed and predicted covariances are identical for random sampling selection;
- If the calculated probability is large enough (e.g. larger than 0.05), then the causal model and the data are consistent. Conversely, if the probability is low (e.g. less than 0.05), then an alternative causal model might be considered.

Direct versus indirect effects of variable interactions

In addition to validating a hypothetical causal model, path diagrams are also useful to decompose variable interactions into different types of causal relationships: direct, indirect, common ancestor, unresolved relationships. As shown in the table above, the hypothetical causal model of occupancy in terms of physical structure can be decomposed into three direct relationships and no indirect ones. Variables do not have common causal ancestors. It is of course a very simplistic model for the sake of illustration. More complex path diagrams should be explored.

To generalise the application of path models to commercial real estate risk analysis, one could envision that archetypical path diagrams of real estate total returns be designed for the four property types (office, retail, industrial, hotel) given various sets of lease structure genes. Furthermore, path analysis could also be used for studies of comparable assets, for instance, office buildings in international financial centres, along the lines of twin studies conducted in genetic epidemiology (i.e. comparable buildings in different environments to gauge environmental impact on similar genotypes).

Food for thought: combining path analysis and hedonic regression models

As a potential application of path analysis in real estate studies, it would be interesting to explore how path analysis and hedonic regression might be applied concomitantly to add a causal dimension to hedonic pricing models. Both methods suppose linearity and additivity of variables. Hedonic variables and their pricing are identified in a classic hedonic regression model. Path analysis could then be applied to the selected utility-contributing variables in order to validate each variable based on the genetics framework while unbundling its pricing in terms of risk factors (i.e. interaction of variables in the genetics-based model). If a hedonic variable passes the test of maximum-likelihood selection in a path diagram customised for the property, then its selection in the hedonic regression model is validated. In the process, causal relationships which involve genes in the genetics-based model and might affect hedonic variables pricing are identified to infer a risk model of a particular property from a multivariate hedonic regression model.

Appendix 1.6

Model of combinative property derivatives (after Lecomte, 2007)

Explanations

Sections 1 to 5 are based on Lecomte and McIntosh (2006). Futures contracts will be either annual or pluri-annual. Choice of factors in section 6 will depend on selected property type. Selections in sections 5, 7, and 8 will determine economic factors in section 9 (choices and pricing). For instance, if a user selects property Type = Office, EBC = Manufacturing and MSA = 1 million, option on economic indicator #1 (e.g., GDP growth rate) will be based on estimated growth rate for the particular location profile. Economic indicators may cover a wide range of macro-variables. The overall setting is domestic but the model could easily adapt to an international investment environment.

① Type of Return

Total ☐

Income ☐

Capital Appreciation ☐

② Type of Hedge

Portfolio ☐

Individual Property ☐

If Portfolio is selected:

Number of Properties ☐

Enter detail of each property individually (Yes/No) ☐

③ Hedge Horizon

Anticipated Expiration Date ☐

④ Number of Contracts

Face Value $1,000,000

⑤ Property Type

Apartment:
- Garden ☐
- High rise ☐

Industrial:
- Warehouse ☐
- R&D ☐
- Flex ☐

Office:
- CBD ☐
- Suburban ☐

Retail:
- Neighbourhood ☐
- Community ☐
- Regional ☐
- Super Regional ☐

Hotel: ☐

Depending on property type selected in 5, customized scroll menu with:

⑥ Additional Information for Portfolio/ Individual Property:

Assessed Market Value (in M$) ☐

Year of Completion ☐

Total Square Feet Area ☐

Micro-variables related to Lease Structure (Individual Property), e.g.:

Number of Tenants ☐

Occupancy Rate (%) ☐

Weighted Average Remaining Lease Maturity (in months) ☐

Add-On Features (e.g., options based on Region and Location factors):

⑦ Select the dominant Economic Base Category (EBC):

Diversified ☐ Finance/Insurance ☐ Manufacturing ☐ Services ☐ Mineral Extraction ☐ Government ☐ Transportation ☐ Military ☐

⑧ Enter MSA Size (in '000)

⑨ Select underlying characteristics (you may choose any number of economic factors). Total number of options depends on total number of futures contracts selected above.

	Economic Indicator #1 (e.g., growth rate)	Economic Indicator #2 (e.g.,unemployment rate)	Economic Indicator #3 (e.g., Consumer Price Index)	Economic Indicator #4	Economic Indicator #5	Economic Indicator #6
Call	☐	☐	☐	☐	☐	☐
Put	☐	☐	☐	☐	☐	☐
Strike in %	☐	☐	☐	☐	☐	☐

For each selected factor, right click to enter your expectation and standard deviation. You will then access a table of real time prices for currently trading options.

Appendix 2.1

Glossary of the main terms used in the analysis of smart space

Concept	Definition
Affordance[2]	Affordance is a term coined by Gibson (1977). It represents a use or purpose that a thing can have, that people notice as part of the way they see or experience it (Cambridge Advanced Learner's Dictionary). In Gibson's own words, "the affordances of the environment are what it offers animals, what it provides or furnishes, either for good or ill".
Cyber-Dasein[1,2]	Cyber-dasein is a model of space user in smart cities modelled after Heidegger's *Dasein* and Mitchell's (2003) M++ *Cyborg-Self*. According to Watts (2011), "the original German term for being is das sein […] derived from the infinitive to be". In Heidegger's philosophy, Dasein embodies a "being characterised by affective relationships with surrounding people and objects". (Oxford Dictionary of Philosophy, 2nd ed.)
Gegend [(1)]	From the German word meaning regions used in Heidegger's philosophy. It refers to the region(s) in smart space within which cyber-dasein carries out his daily activities.
Misaffordance[2]	Evans and McCoy (1998) refer to misaffordance in the context of a building when "we are unable to readily discern the functional properties of a space or incorrectly gauge building or technological function". A misaffordance in smart space distracts from a space's intended use.
Preoccupation[1]	Cyber-dasein's daily concerns (e.g. commute, work, eat, travel). Preoccupations are defined by their intensities at any point in time, which results in rankings (e.g., primary, secondary, tertiary) captured in *preoccupation maps*.
UmWelt[1,2]	The concept of UmWelt plays a central part in Heidegger's philosophy. It can be translated as "environment" or "surrounding world". It represents the everyday world of human activity. Lecomte (2019a) applies the concept to describe space users' highly personalised digital environment in smart real estate. Cyber-dasein's digital environing world unfolds in time as more data are being uploaded each time cyber-dasein interacts in smart space. UmWelt is fluid and mutable.

Sources: [1]Lecomte (2019a), [2]Lecomte (2020).

Appendix 2.2

The legal nature of digital rights in smart buildings

This appendix presents a few important concepts underlying the legal nature of property rights in smart buildings (digital rights), as presented in this book.

The 'riparian doctrine' and its model customarily applied by US law scholars to study water rights attached to land can help shed light on digital rights. Let's introduce this model in non-technical terms and explore how it applies to smart space.

The water rights model: the riparian doctrine of property rights

The water rights model was fashioned at the time of the 18th-century industrial revolution when access to water was paramount to economic activities of the new manufacturing water mills (Rose, 1990).[4] Water rights follow what law scholars call the riparian doctrine. The riparian doctrine provides a useful framework for the analysis of digital rights.

According to Butler (1985), "the basic tenant of [the riparian doctrine] is that a party owning land abutting a watercourse has the right to make reasonable uses of the water in that watercourse for the benefit of his riparian land". These rights are vested property rights: a riparian owner cannot be deprived of his/her water rights "by the state without due process". By the same token, "the rights of a riparian owner are not absolute, for other riparian proprietors along the same watercourse also have an 'equal right' to make reasonable uses of the watercourse".

These are two key principles in the riparian doctrine: (i) "a riparian proprietor can exercise his rights only for the benefits of riparian land", (ii) "a riparian's use must be reasonable". These principles, while favouring low-density uses tend

---

4 Not all law scholars agree with that view. For instance, Trelease (1954) argues that the riparian doctrine spontaneously developed in the mid-19th century at the time of the gold rush in Western USA, rather than as a legacy of early pre-riparian English law during the first industrial revolution.

to disapprove of "unrestrained transfers of use rights". Another important dimension of the riparian doctrine stems from the appurtenance of water rights.[5] According to Haar and Gordon (1958), the appurtenance of rights supposes that:

> The right to use of water whether vested [...] or acquired [...], shall be appurtenant to the gross area of land to which the right relates and shall pass as an appurtenance with the title to such land.

Furthermore, Haar and Gordon (1958) explain that "no such [water] right shall be deemed valid unless the right to construct diversion works or reservoirs upon the land [...] shall have been acquired in a lawful manner [...]".

Applying the riparian doctrine to smart buildings

Interestingly, water and smart space share a striking similarity insofar as they are both intangible. Freyfolgle (1989) notes that:

> Water [...] is not a physical thing. Water is intangible. It is a use-right to make use of a particular water flow- and not a right to control physical object that you can point and seize.

Digital Usage Rights explicitly refer to smart space's use-right for owners and tenants. In the context of smart buildings, applying the riparian doctrine implies that:

- Digital rights on smart space are permanently attached to property rights on physical space. The latter are the principal property rights while the former are incidental rights (see axiom #1 in the economic foundations of digital rights).
- The transferability of digital rights should be restrained. In the proposed regime, Digital Access Rights (DARs) are not transferrable whereas Digital Usage Rights (DURs) are transferrable within set limits. All DARs and DURs should always revert to property rights holders in case of change in ownership or tenancy respectively (see axiom #2 in the economic foundations of digital rights).
- Digital Usage Rights on smart space can only exist if Digital Access Rights are lawful, i.e. the domination of physical space has been carried out in respect of the law.

All the above-mentioned points inferred from the riparian doctrine guide the digital rights regime introduced in this book. The water rights model seems also well-suited for rights pertaining to access and use of smart grid in smart buildings (e.g. prosumer buildings).

---

5 Appurtenance is a legal term denoting "an incidental right (such as a right-of-way) attached to a principal property right and passing in possession with it" (Merriam-Webster English dictionary).

Index

Note: **Bold** page numbers refer to tables, *Italic* page numbers refer to figures and page number followed by "n" refer to end notes.

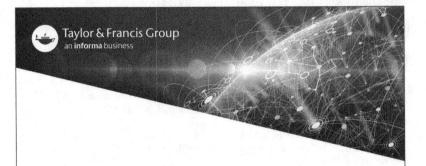

Printed in the United States
by Baker & Taylor Publisher Services